Oscar Browning, Earl Charles Whitworth

England and Napoleon in 1803

being the despatches of Lord Whitworth and others, now first printed from the originals in the Record office, edited for the Royal Historical Society

Oscar Browning, Earl Charles Whitworth

England and Napoleon in 1803

being the despatches of Lord Whitworth and others, now first printed from the originals in the Record office, edited for the Royal Historical Society

ISBN/EAN: 9783337349868

Printed in Europe, USA, Canada, Australia, Japan

Cover: Foto ©ninafisch / pixelio.de

More available books at **www.hansebooks.com**

ENGLAND AND NAPOLEON
IN 1803

By the same Editor.

DESPATCHES OF EARL GOWER
ENGLISH AMBASSADOR AT PARIS
FROM JUNE 1790 TO AUGUST 1792.

CAMBRIDGE UNIVERSITY PRESS.
1885.

ENGLAND AND NAPOLEON IN 1803

BEING THE

DESPATCHES OF LORD WHITWORTH

AND OTHERS

NOW FIRST PRINTED FROM THE ORIGINALS IN THE RECORD OFFICE

EDITED
FOR THE ROYAL HISTORICAL SOCIETY
BY
OSCAR BROWNING, M.A., F.R.Hist.S.
CORRESPONDING MEMBER OF THE SOCIÉTÉ D'HISTOIRE DIPLOMATIQUE

LONDON
LONGMANS, GREEN, AND CO.
AND NEW YORK: 15 EAST 16th STREET
1887

All rights reserved

PRINTED BY
SPOTTISWOODE AND CO., NEW-STREET SQUARE
LONDON

PREFACE.

THE present collection of despatches, which is published by the generosity of the Royal Historical Society, is an important contribution to the history of England and France at a momentous period. The rupture of the peace of Amiens in 1803, although it introduced a state of war which lasted twelve years and which tried the resources of England to the utmost, was not so decisive as the first participation by England in the war against the Revolution in 1793. The peace of Amiens had always been regarded from the side of England as an armed truce: on the side of Napoleon it had a very different character. The first and second coalitions were directed against the French Republic and the Revolution. Napoleon, on his return from Egypt, used his first opportunities as the head of the State in proposing peace to Austria and England, the two belligerents who still remained in arms. These overtures were rejected by both Powers, but the battles of Marengo and Hohenlinden led to the Treaty of Lunéville, and when the Treaty of Amiens had been signed Napoleon had attained his object. The rupture renewed a contest which only ended in his defeat and captivity. It is, therefore, of the utmost importance to the student of Napoleon's life and character to determine whether, as English writers generally assert, he only regarded the peace of Amiens as a breathing space in which he might recover strength to measure himself against England and Europe, or whether, while determining to develop the internal resources of France on the one hand and to be the first power in Europe on the other, he sincerely desired peace and was reluctant to begin a struggle which he knew would be internecine. I do not propose to discuss this question, but the papers included in this volume offer materials for its determination. It may be doubted whether we have yet reached a period in which the views and character of Napoleon can be fairly estimated. Napoleon worship in France has been succeeded by Napoleon hatred. The French press has produced in the last fifteen years many volumes which argue from original documents that Napoleon had few talents and no virtues, and Lanfrey is not more eagerly welcomed on this side of the Channel than Seeley is regarded as an impartial judge on the other. Americans, who are devoted to the study of modern history, and who have no national passions to gratify in the great debate, would appear to be the most trustworthy arbiters, and their verdict is generally favourable to Napoleon. It may, at any rate, be laid down that no account of Napoleon's career can be true which does not credit him with some intelligible motive for his actions. It is impossible to believe that 'the most splendid genius that has appeared on earth,' as Lord Acton, a competent judge, declares him to have been, was the sport alternately of tumultuous passions, of wild and unreasoning ambition, and of a 'vice of nature' which drove him against his better judgment into disastrous courses.

These papers will also contribute to settle the long debated question as to whether England was justified in the rupture of the peace. A careful reader must admit that we were guilty of a breach of faith in not surrendering Malta. The promise of its surrender was the principal article of the treaty; it was the point most hotly disputed between the contracting Powers. The treaty would never have been made at all unless we had agreed to the cession of the island; we could only refuse to carry out our engagement by the plea that Napoleon had failed to keep his side of the bargain, or that the instinct of self-preservation compelled us to break faith even at the risk of war. The reasons alleged in support of our action were (1) the efforts used by Napoleon towards supremacy on the Continent; (2) his designs against Egypt, clearly shown by the report of Sebastiani and (3) his demands for restricting the liberty of the press and the activity of the emigrants in England. It may be urged, in answer, (1) that several of the encroachments complained of were effected before the ratifications of the treaty were exchanged, and the others were known to be in contemplation; (2) that Napoleon always denied that he had designs against Egypt, and asserted that Sebastiani's report was intended for a very different purpose. It would certainly have been easy to keep the report secret, while its publication was rather meant as a diplomatic menace to England than as a serious indication of aggressive action. (3) With reference to the last charge, Napoleon might complain with justice that enemies of his person and government used the laws and liberties of England as a cloak for the most persistent attacks. Their impunity might not be a reason for his declaring war upon us, but his complaints could be no ground for our declaring war against him. To discuss the whole of this question would be to write the history of the time. It is, indeed, doubtful whether the secret history of the third coalition can be accurately known until the Russian archives are more thoroughly explored. But attention may be directed to two points. The royal message of March 8, 1803, for calling out the militia was based on the fact that very considerable military preparations were carrying on in the ports of France and Holland. Lord Whitworth wrote on March 17, 1803: 'In the meantime I think I can say with certainty that no armaments of any consequence are carrying on in the French ports. Orders were given (as I mentioned to your Lordship in a former despatch) a fortnight ago to equip what there was in the different ports; but the total want of naval stores, and the absence of by far the greatest part of the naval force, render such an order almost nugatory.' Indeed, the King's message may be regarded like the publication of Sebastiani's despatch, more as a diplomatic threat than a real measure of precaution. These threats are dangerous weapons, and often produce the war which they are intended to avoid. The message of March 8 caused the famous scene between Napoleon and Lord Whitworth on Sunday, March 13, which is the second point to which I would draw attention. Alison, in the 'History of Europe' (v. 109), gives what may be called the received version of the story which has been copied into all histories. He represents Napoleon as addressing a violent and continuous harangue to Lord Whitworth at a court the date of which he misstates, and adds, in his own words: 'This violent harangue, rendered still more emphatic by the gestures with which it was accompanied, induced the English Ambassador to suppose that the First Consul would so far forget his dignity as to strike him; and he was deliberating what he should do in the event of such an insult being offered to the nation which he represented when Napoleon retired.' There is not the slightest foundation for the last imputation. Indeed, the despatch of Lord Whitworth, now printed for the first time in its integrity, places the matter in an entirely different light. Speaking of the First Consul's temper, he says that on the previous day he was a witness of 'and in some degree a sufferer from' its violence. Napoleon asked him if he had any news from England, and had a short conversation which ended with the words, 'You wish me to fight fifteen years more, and you force me to it.' The next words were addressed not to Whitworth but to Marcoff and Azzara, who were standing at a little distance. Napoleon then went his round, and everyone saw that he was irritated. On returning to Lord Whitworth he resumed the conversation,

Lord Whitworth says, 'by something personally civil to me.' Then followed the last words of the conversation as reported by Alison. Whitworth, after commenting on the 'total want of dignity as well as of decency' of Napoleon, says that he intends to tell M. de Talleyrand that he cannot go to the Tuileries if he is to be attacked thus in that public manner by the First Consul on topics which were made to be discussed in the cabinet. 'I hope, however, he will feel the impropriety of his conduct; and, indeed, I may be satisfied with the impression it has made on the public, by which his conduct is generally disapproved and ridiculed.' A despatch of March 17 gives Talleyrand's explanation of the scene, and adds: 'As the First Consul will have three weeks to reflect I trust I shall find him more temperate the next time we meet in the same place.' This meeting took place on April 4. 'The Corps Diplomatique were assembled yesterday at one o'clock for the purpose of paying their compliments to the First Consul. . . . He received us, and I had every reason to be satisfied with his manner towards me.' We see thus that the 'insult to the British Ambassador,' which so many historians assign as a reason for the war, dwindles into nothing but a *brusquerie* which was certainly unknown to the courtliness of the *ancien régime*, but to which modern diplomatic history would afford some striking parallels.

Another matter on which these despatches will throw light is the possibility of our coming to some terms with Napoleon by a temporary retention of Malta. Wilberforce, who strongly opposed the declaration of war, said in Parliament: 'The language of Bonaparte in the latter stages of the negotiations affords reason to believe that he would have acquiesced in the independence of Malta, if not our retention of it for ten years.' It appears that if we had not insisted upon an ultimatum containing terms which were insulting to Napoleon, and which he could not possibly have accepted, the negotiations, even in the hands of so haughty and unbending an aristocrat as Lord Whitworth, might have ended in a favourable result.

The despatches contained in this volume were in large part published at the time, and are to be found in the Parliamentary History. Only such documents were published as would suit the arguments of the Minister, and the despatches themselves are ingeniously garbled by the omission of words and phrases which give a different colour to the sentences in which they occur. I have not thought it worth while to mark these variations, which any student can do for himself.

In conclusion, I venture to express a hope that the publication of documents such as are contained in this volume will not be left much longer to private enterprise. Of the official calendars published by Government only one series is at present devoted to foreign affairs, and this is still occupied with the affairs of the sixteenth century. It is surely far more important for us at the present day to know the truth about the foreign policy of England in the period of the Revolution and of Napoleon than to be informed of every tergiversation of the tortuous Elizabeth. In that epoch we took a line of our own, and incurred an immense responsibility, the effects of which we are feeling at the present day. If there is any connection between history and politics, it must be of vital importance for us to know the grounds on which our ancestors acted, to be informed of the precise nature of the problem before them and of the manner in which they dealt with it. Not to mention the correspondence of Napoleon I., which, however imperfect, reflects credit on the Government which produced it, the French Government is publishing at this very moment the correspondence of Barthélemy in 1792; Germany is printing public documents of the first decade of this century; Russia is loading our shelves with most precious information about the Empress Catharine and the Emperor Alexander. We not only neglect to place our case before Europe, but we allow it to be stated by foreigners. Le Bon has treated of the intrigues of Windham with the *émigrés*, and the best documents relating to English policy in 1813 and 1814 are to be found in Oncken. Surely some of the money devoted either to the Calendars or to the Rolls series, which is limited to the reign of Henry VII., could be spent upon the publication of documents of the past and present century, interesting in themselves, valuable to the whole of Europe, invaluable to Englishmen. Statesmen advise us to study the policy of William Pitt. The career of no English Prime Minister is better worth our most minute attention, yet the only trustworthy evidence of his actions abroad and at home, in finance, in the treatment of Ireland, in administration, and above all in foreign policy, lies in the masses of paper written in his well-known hand, bound in the volumes at the Record Office, undiscovered, unread, and in many cases signed by the names of others. These priceless documents cannot be properly edited by private enterprise, but if no new funds can be found for such an undertaking, it might at least receive a share of those which are at present devoted to similar but less important objects.

KING'S COLLEGE, CAMBRIDGE:
August 27, 1887.

DESPATCHES.

INSTRUCTIONS TO LORD WHITWORTH.

INSTRUCTIONS for our right trusty and well-beloved councillor Charles, Lord Whitworth, whom we have appointed our Ambassador Extraordinary and Plenipotentiary to the French Republic. Given at our Court at St. James's the tenth day of September, 1802, in the Forty-second year of our reign.

1. We, reposing the highest trust and confidence in your prudence, experience, and abilities, have thought proper to appoint you to be our Ambassador Extraordinary and Plenipotentiary to the French Republic, and to give you the following instructions for your guidance.

2. You are, upon the receipt of these our instructions and letter of credence, to proceed with all convenient speed to Paris, and upon your arrival there you will inform yourself concerning the steps to be taken for presenting our credential letter to the First Consul, and the forms to be observed upon that occasion, on all which you will follow the methods which you shall find to have been adopted by Ministers of other crowned heads of equal rank and character with yourself. Having delivered our credentials to the First Consul, you shall add to the assurances therein given such further declarations as may evince our determination to observe with scrupulous good faith all the engagements at present subsisting between us and the French Government, or which we may hereafter contract, for the reciprocal advantage of both; and our desire to give proof on all occasions of our sincere disposition to cultivate a good understanding between the two countries.

3. You shall carefully observe the motions and intentions of that Government with respect to us and our dominions, and whether they are entering into any, and what, new leagues or engagements with other Powers which may be prejudicial to us, or endanger the tranquillity of Europe.

4. You shall use your utmost endeavour to discover what plans or secret designs the Government of France may have formed, or may be forming, in the East or West Indies: what number of ships of war or land forces may have been sent from the different parts of the French Republic to those quarters; what ships or land forces may be preparing for foreign service; what orders have been sent to the commanders of their forces at their several settlements; and generally what plans they may have in contemplation for the acquisition of new colonies, or for improving or fortifying those of which they are now in possession.

5. You will make it an object of your very particular attention to discover whether any, and what, treaties are either in agitation, or actually entered into between France and any other European state, and in either case you will take every measure in your power to be informed of the nature and extent of such treaty or treaties, and to procure and transmit correct copies thereof.

6. You will likewise endeavour to discover whether any foreign ships of war are actually in any of the ports of the said Republic, to ascertain as far as possible the number, force, and destination of them respectively.

7. You will assist and countenance our subjects trading to any of the dominions of the French Republic, or who may have any suits or pretensions depending there, procuring for them good and speedy justice and all the favour you are able; yet for our honour and your own credit you must not engage yourself in any complaints which may raise clamour without a justifiable cause or legal proofs, but only such as may deserve the interposition of our name for the relief and support of our subjects in their rights.

8. You shall constantly correspond with our several

Ministers employed in foreign Courts during your residence in France, for your mutual information and assistance, but you are on no account to communicate with your private friends on public affairs.

9. You will in general be extremely attentive in making yourself master of the interior state of the government of France, in studying the dispositions and interests of the several persons of both sexes, who are or may be in the confidence of the First Consul; and in making the closest enquiries possible into the views and character of the Ministers of State, not only with regard to their pacific and warlike inclinations, but to their particular connections with one another, their opinions, their abilities, their power, and the degree of influence each has, or may have, with the First Consul.

10. As it is essentially necessary to our service to be as accurately informed as possible of the interior state of France, you will not fail to pay attention to the proceedings of the several constituted authorities throughout the Republic; and you will use your endeavours to obtain an accurate knowledge of the characters and views of the persons who may have had the lead in the respective departments, and of the factions which may prevail therein, and you will regularly transmit to our aforesaid Secretary of State all such accounts upon this subject as may appear to you to be interesting for our information.

11. On your arrival at Paris you will receive from our Minister there the whole of his correspondence, and you are to consider the instructions contained therein, as the rule of your conduct as far as the present circumstances will admit, and you shall also, at the expiration of your mission, either deliver to your successor, or transmit to the office of our aforesaid Secretary of State, the originals of the official papers in your custody and your official correspondence.

12. You will make our interest in commerce an object of your constant attention, and will take an early opportunity to enter into discussion with the French Government upon

such matters arising out of the late definite treaty of peace as may require speedy adjustment, and which may hereafter lead to arrangements of a more extensive nature for the mutual advantage of the two nations.

13. You will use your best endeavours to procure us as exact an account as possible of the countries under the dominion of the Republic, particularly as to the state of their defence, accompanied with accurate descriptions of their fortifications, and also as to the number and condition of the forces by land and sea of the Republic, and the means of augmenting the same upon occasion.

14. You are likewise to inform yourself accurately of the ordinary expenses of the Government, of the particulars, the amount and state of the revenue, and whence it arises; and of the resources which the Republic may have for levying any, and what, extraordinary supplies.

15. You are further to procure an account of the population of the dominions of the Republic, and of the extent and nature of the commerce and manufactures carried on in the different parts of them, and of the situation and treatment of British merchants resident therein.

16. You will from time to time impart to us all such intelligence as you can procure on the several points prescribed to you in these instructions, or on any other, not particularly specified herein, which may relate to our service or to the advantage of our kingdoms. But you will send your accounts of the dominions, forces, revenues, expenses and resources of the Republic, and of the population and commerce of its subjects, in separate letters confined to these things only, and addressed to our principal Secretary of State for Foreign Affairs; and in order that our said instructions may be transmitted to you with great security, and also for the better conduct of your correspondence, as well as with our said Secretary of State as our Ministers residing in foreign parts, with respect to such matters as may require particular caution and secrecy, we have ordered

to be delivered to you proper cyphers and decyphers, which you will keep carefully deposited under secure locks, and use every other precaution to guard against their being discovered, which would be so highly prejudicial to our service.

17. Whereas by an Act passed in the 22nd year of our reign for regulating the payment out of our Civil List Revenue, it is amongst other things enacted that receipts from our Ministers, Commissioners, and Consuls in foreign parts shall be filed in our Exchequer for all sums of money which shall be issued and paid to our principal Secretary or Secretaries of State for foreign secret service, and which shall be sent or given by such Secretary or Secretaries of State to any of our said Ministers, Commissioners, or Consuls respectively, for the said purpose, and in order to discharge or acquit such Ministers, etc., who will thereupon stand charged at our Exchequer with the sums so received by them for that purpose, an oath, according to the form in the said Act prescribed, should be taken by them within one year after their arrival in Great Britain. We, to the intent that the provisions in the said Act in this respect should be strictly observed, have directed an extract thereof to be delivered to you with these instructions; and we do hereby strictly require and command that you punctually conform yourself thereto upon all occasions which may arise during your employment abroad. We have also directed to be delivered to you, herewith, a printed extract of an Act passed in the fifth year of the reign of our Royal Predecessor, King George I., to prevent the inconveniences arising from seducing artificers out of our dominions. It is our will and pleasure that you take proper steps to procure exact information respecting all persons of that description who may be resident in France, and that you use your best endeavours to induce them to return—strictly conforming yourself to the provisions of the said Act for this purpose.

18. At your return we shall expect from you a narrative in writing of whatever may have happened at Paris worthy

our notice, together with such observations on the situation and views of the Republic as your knowledge of it shall enable you to make.

Lord Hawkesbury to Lord Whitworth.
(Most secret and confidential.)

Downing Street, November 14, 1802.

I take the first opportunity of communicating to your Excellency, for the regulation of your conduct, the instructions which his Majesty is pleased to give you on such points as are or may become subjects of discussion between his Majesty and the French Government; and to desire that you will endeavour to conform yourself to them in all your conversations with the French Ministers. You will lose no proper opportunity of expressing his Majesty's earnest solicitude for the preservation of the peace which subsists between the two countries; his disposition to do everything in his power for that purpose which is consistent with the honour of his crown and the interests of his dominions; and his regret at any circumstances which may have arisen to interrupt that harmony and good understanding which are so important to the welfare and happiness of both countries. You will, however, state most distinctly his Majesty's determination never to forego his right of interfering in the affairs of the Continent on every occasion in which the interests of his own dominions or those of Europe in general may appear to him to require it. This right his Majesty possesses in common with every other independent Power; it rests upon general principles, and does not require the confirmation of any particular treaty. It is nevertheless important that you should observe that the circumstances which led to the conclusion of the last peace, and the principles upon which the negotiations were conducted, would give his Majesty a special right to interpose in any case which might lead to the extension of the power or influence of France. In the communications which took place between the two Governments previous to the signature of the preliminary articles, his Majesty proposed as the basis of the negotiation that if the French Government would not relinquish the Continental acquisitions which they had obtained from other Powers in the course of the war, his Majesty would claim the right of keeping part of his conquests as a compensation for the important acquisitions of territory made by France upon the Continent. This principle was formally recognised by the French Government in an official note in the following words: 'Cependant on reconnoit que les grands événemens survenus en Europe, et les changemens arrivés dans les limites des grands Etats du Continent, peuvent autoriser une partie des demandes du Gouvernement Britannique.' The terms of the treaty of peace were negotiated in conformity to this basis, and it appears, therefore, clear that the then existing state of possession and of engagements as respect the Continent were the foundation of the peace itself, and that his Majesty has, therefore, an undoubted right to interpose in consequence of the treaty in every case in which the state of possession may appear to him to have undergone any material alteration, or in which the engagements which were then subsisting had been violated to the prejudice of his Majesty or of the other Powers of Europe. You will proceed to observe, that the annexation of Piedmont to France, since the conclusion of the definitive treaty, makes a most material difference in the state of the fixed and permanent possessions of France. That the renunciation of the Duchy of Parma in favour of France, a circumstance which was concealed at the time of negotiating the peace, and which is become of the greatest importance from its furnishing an additional instance of that system of *secret cession* which is totally inconsistent with any system of security to Europe, makes a most essential difference likewise in the relative circumstances of the two countries. That at the time of concluding the peace, the French Government were bound by the most sacred engagements to respect the independence of the Helvetian and Batavian Republics, and to allow the people of these countries to choose whatever form of government they might think proper. That the violation of this right in the Swiss people and the invasion of their territory, notwithstanding the representation which was made in their favour by his Majesty, makes a most material alteration in the state of engagements contracted since the conclusion of the Definitive Treaty, and adds most considerably to the influence and power of France, to the prejudice of a state which was then acknowledged as independent. That the conduct of the French Government to the Batavian Republic was not less objectionable. That the independence of this Republic was acknowledged both by the Treaty of Lunéville and by the Treaty of the Hague of the year 1795. That by the Treaty of the Hague the French Government were permitted to keep garrisons in that country *only* till the time of general peace. That by a convention signed in August 1801 the French troops were to remain there till the conclusion of the Definitive Treaty of Peace between Great Britain and France. That the French troops have not to this period evacuated the country, and that the First Consul is represented lately to have declared, that in the event of any differences amongst the people of that country, on the subject of their internal government, he would march with his whole army to suppress them. That this is an obvious violation of the independence of the Batavian Republic, and that his Majesty has a peculiar right to interpose on the present occasion, as he consented to make numerous and most important restitutions to the Batavian Government in the treaty of peace, on the consideration of that Government being independent and not being subject to any foreign control. It is necessary for me to recommend to your Excellency to make these representations with moderation and temper. You will attend very particularly to any explanations which may be given to you respecting them, and you will engage to report such explanations to his Majesty's Government. You will avoid with peculiar caution committing his Majesty's Government as to what may be their ultimate determination upon all or any of these points—viz. whether under any circumstances an unsatisfactory explanation respecting them might lead to war on the part of his Majesty, whether it might induce his Majesty to claim some additional acquisition to counterbalance the acquisitions of France, or whether it might be thought most prudent for the present to acquiesce. His Majesty's conduct in this respect must be determined by a variety of considerations, and particularly by the information which he may receive of the sentiments and intentions of other European Powers. It is natural to suppose that the French Ministers will take an early opportunity of bringing forward, at least in conversation, any grievances which they may choose to allege against his Majesty's Government, and I have no doubt the most prominent will be the complaints which they have so often advanced already respecting the liberty of the press in this country, and the conduct of the French emigrants who are resident here. Upon these subjects it is unnecessary for me to do more than to refer you to my despatch to Mr. Merry, No. 20, and to desire that you would strictly conform yourself to the instructions therein contained. In the event, however, of any conversation on this subject, it is material that you should remark on the paragraphs which have lately appeared in the 'Moniteur' calumniating his Majesty's Government, and that you should dwell particularly on the distinction existing between paragraphs of this nature appearing in a paper avowedly official and the paragraphs in our English publications over which the Government of this country have no previous control, and which have been repeatedly and explicitly disavowed by his Majesty's Government. If the French Government should enter into any conversation with you on the subject of the Island of Malta, it is of great importance that you should avoid committing his Majesty as to what may be eventually his intentions with respect to that island. It is evident that the arrangement stipulated in the 10th Article of the Definitive Treaty cannot as yet be carried into effect; that neither the Government of St. Petersburg nor of Berlin has given any decisive answer to the application that has been made to them to become guaranteeing Powers of the arrangement; that according to the article the Grand Master must be chosen before there can be any person properly authorised to receive possession of the island, that Prince Ruspoli has declined the situation of Grand Master, and that it will be necessary therefore for the Pope to make some other selection. I recommend you, however, to avoid saying anything which may engage his Majesty to restore the island even if these arrangements could be completed according to the true intent and spirit of the 10th Article of the Treaty of Amiens. His Majesty would certainly be justified in claiming the possession of Malta, as some counterpoise to the acquisition of France, since the conclusion of the Definitive Treaty; but it is not necessary to decide in the present moment whether his Majesty will be disposed to avail himself of his pretensions in this respect. It would be better, therefore, that you should not bring the subject of Malta forward at present, unless it should be first mentioned by the French Ministers. You will then conform yourself to the instructions above stated, and you will be very particular in representing to me everything which may pass on this important subject. I shall not fail to inform your Excellency from time to time of the substance of the conversations which may take place between General Andréossy and myself; as it is of the utmost importance that your language to the French Minister for Foreign Affairs should correspond as much as possible with mine to the French Ambassador.

Lord Whitworth to Lord Hawkesbury.

Calais, November 10, 1802.

I trouble your Lordship with a very few lines, merely to say that we arrived here this day at three o'clock, after a pleasant passage of four hours and a half. We were received on our landing by an immense concourse of people, and with much huzzaing. The guns were fired, and flags displayed on the church steeples, etc. When we arrived at our inn, where I found a captain's guard mounted, I was complimented by the constituted authorities, consisting of the Mayor, the Commissary-General Margaud, the Juge de Paix, etc. After them came General Barbasaude at the head of the officers of the garrison, and after them the *poissardes* with a present of fish—in short, nothing was wanting. After dinner we were formally invited to assist at the theatre, in order, as it was said by the Mayor, that the public might have an opportunity of seeing what had been so long and ardently desired, an English Ambassador in France. We could not resist an invitation on such grounds, and we were received with great enthusiasm. 'God save the King' was struck up, and played for a quarter of an hour, but almost drowned by the applause of the whole house, who followed our example of standing up while it was playing, in the good old English fashion. We are just returned, and I write this in great haste to be ready for the mail which is just setting out with Mr. Merry's despatch. He sent it to me under a flying seal.

P.S.—I hear that the First Consul returned from Havre to Paris last night.[1]

Paris, November 16, 1802.

I have the honour to acquaint your Lordship that I arrived here the day before yesterday. We were longer on the journey than I expected, in consequence of the indifferent state of part of the road, and of a number of horses being taken from each post for the service of the First Consul, who was returning to Paris at the same time from Rouen by the way of Beauvais. I saw Mr. Merry immediately on my arrival, and received from him every satisfaction which I could require. Your Lordship will not, however, at this moment expect from me any opinion on what I may have heard; Mr. Merry, whom I should wish to retain here for a fortnight or three weeks, will continue to keep your Lordship informed of everything necessary, until I am better

---

[1] He was really at Dieppe.

enabled than I now am to speak from my own observation or judgment. The country through Picardy appeared in a high state of cultivation, and the road, but for the rains which had fallen, would have been better than I remember it some years ago; but the same and indeed a much greater degree of misery and poverty seems to press upon the peasantry. We were escorted as far as Boulogne by a detachment of dragoons, and received there with a discharge of artillery from the ramparts, and by the officers of the garrison in a body; we passed quietly through the other towns on the way, until we came to St. Denis, where the *poissardes* of Paris did not fail to meet us, and receive us according to the old custom. Yesterday Mr. Merry announced my arrival to Monsieur Talleyrand, and he appointed to receive me at two o'clock this day. I am just come from him, and were it permitted to judge of his disposition by the manner in which he received me, and by the terms in which he answered the assurances I gave him of the conciliatory tendency of my instructions, I might look forward to some degree of satisfaction in my intercourse with him. We did not enter into any kind of conversation on the present state of affairs; I communicated to him a copy of my credentials, and upon my requesting that he would take the First Consul's orders on the subject of my presentation, he told me that he did not apprehend that there would be any opportunity until the regular day of presentation, which is in something less than three weeks. Mr. Merry will have acquainted your Lordship with the motive assigned for the extraordinary levée which was held yesterday, and with the hasty and summary manner in which the Corps Diplomatique were summoned to St. Cloud; at all events, I could not possibly have been in time for it. M. de Marcoff called upon me yesterday morning, and made many professions of cordiality. He has not, however, the talent of inspiring confidence, and, indeed, his conduct here is such as to render any confidential intercourse with him extremely dangerous.

Paris, November 20, 1802.

My Lord,—In the expectation of those instructions with which your Lordship may be able to furnish me long before I have an opportunity of presenting my credentials, I have not sought the occasion of engaging in any political discussion whatever with the Minister for Foreign Affairs. I have seen M. Talleyrand but once since I have been here, when I found him civil and even cordial; and he seemed to mark an extraordinary degree of *empressement* by returning the visit the same evening. I feel, however, not the slightest temptation to depart in any degree from that mode of conduct I have prescribed to myself, and which has been so strongly recommended to me by your Lordship, of drawing as strong a line as possible between my conduct towards that Minister and that of some of my colleagues, who it must be acknowledged appear rather to seek their own personal gratification than the dignity of their sovereigns; and I hope and trust that by so doing I shall bring no disparagement on his Majesty's affairs. Mr. Merry will have informed your Lordship in detail of that which seems at present to occupy principally the First Consul's attention: I mean the state of things at St. Domingo, where the French army is nearly annihilated, and the negroes are again in a state of successful insurrection. It becomes, therefore, of the utmost moment to see what may be the measures of the First Consul under these circumstances. Will he persevere in his project of re-establishing a colonial system, or will he turn the whole of his attention to the extension of his dominions and influence on the Continent, and thus, as it is modestly called here, endeavour to keep peace with Great Britain in her acquisition of wealth and power in the East and West Indies? I profess myself too ignorant of the secret springs of this Government to be able to form any but very hazardous notions; but if we may now, as on former occasions, calculate on the personal character of the First Consul, we may expect to see him become more desperate and headstrong by opposition, and exert his whole strength and power in the conflict. This certainly is most ardently to be wished. On the other hand, there are, I am told, those who would advise, as far as they dare advise (for in this respect, as in many others, I find frequent occasion to recollect the Emperor Paul), a different line of conduct, and, as I mentioned above, confine their views and efforts to the neighbouring states in Europe. This is what we have to fear; neither is it easy to be prevented until the other great Powers of Europe become more sensible of the danger as it approaches, and awake from the lethargy under which they labour. So situated it must, I fear, be our lot to remain quiet spectators of the course of ambition which this country is pursuing. But even in this we shall find some consolation in reflecting that, however the First Consul may extend his frontier or his influence, he acquires neither friends at home nor abroad, and that, in fact, while he is running after the shadow he loses the substance. I feel that I have occasion for all your Lordship's indulgence for these reflections; they are not new, but they are just. They are such as your Lordship had in contemplation in making the peace, and they are such as may encourage us to preserve it. I mentioned in my last that my presentation to the First Consul, for it cannot be called an audience, was fixed for the first usual day of reception, which happens about the end of the first week in the next month. It was expected by some people, more sanguine I confess than myself, that an earlier day would have been named, but I have reason to think that this is meant as a reciprocity for the etiquette observed toward General Andréossy, who, however, I am glad to find speak of his reception by your Lordship in terms of great satisfaction.

P.S.—I have the honour to acquaint your Lordship that Mr. Talbot arrived this day and delivered to me your Lordship's instructions of the 15th instant. I will not delay the messenger further than to say that they shall be most strictly adhered to, and to express my satisfaction that my ideas should have coincided so perfectly with those of your Lordship.

LORD WHITWORTH TO MR. GEORGE HAMMOND.

Paris, November 20, 1802.

I trouble you with these few words merely to tell you that I shall soon begin to put in motion the two messengers whom I brought with me. One will be despatched from hence on Wednesday next, the 24th instant, the other on the Saturday following, and so on every week without fail. The journey from hence to Calais may be calculated on an average at thirty-six hours, so that they will arrive there every Monday and Friday morning, and return the moment they receive their despatches from the packet. By this means a regular communication will be kept up, and I wish with all my heart I may have satisfactory intelligence to communicate to you. I beg you to send back the box regularly although you should have nothing to send in it.

LORD WHITWORTH TO LORD HAWKESBURY.

Paris, November 22, 1802.

I have this moment received the despatches which accompany this from M. Talleyrand, by whom it is very apparent that they had been opened, and I lose no time in transmitting them to your Lordship by a messenger. Their contents are indeed of a very extraordinary nature, but not more so than might have been expected from the character and system of the First Consul, who seems determined to put our patience and forbearance to the utmost test. It is, however, to be feared that Colonel Sebastiani's mission is much more important and comprehensive than General Stuart seems to apprehend, and a reference to Mr. Merry's despatch of September 25 will ascertain very clearly that the First Consul's views extend to no less than the second conquest of

Egypt. Colonel Sebastiani has sent his report to M. Talleyrand, and I make no doubt that General Andréossy will be immediately furnished with instructions on the subject.

Paris, November 27, 1802.

I beg once more to return your Lordship my very sincere thanks for the clear and ample instructions contained in your Lordship's No. 1, which I received on Saturday morning last by Mr. Talbot. They contain arguments of which I avail myself with great advantage in any discussion which may arise on any of these points on which the two countries are now at issue: but I shall endeavour to avoid every such conversation until I am acquainted with the language your Lordship may think proper to hold with M. Andréossy. It is evident that the acquisition of Egypt is the object which the First Consul has most at heart, and that to which our utmost attention should be directed. Everything which Mr. Merry has had occasion to report to your Lordship, and above all the personal character of the First Consul (galled to the highest degree at having been so disgracefully foiled in his first attempt), would be alone sufficient to render it probable. But the efforts that are made to gain the Court of Russia, whose co-operation will be indispensably necessary to obtain the acquisition of the Porte, the great attention paid to the wants of the Army of Egypt (a name which it has always preserved and certainly not without design), the manner in which the artillery of the Army of Italy has been disposed of, and which Mr. Merry has mentioned to your Lordship, and the language held by the Generals who have already been employed on that service, form altogether such a mass of evidence as place the intention beyond a doubt. Indeed, there is the greatest reason to believe that some immediate operation is at this moment in contemplation, and I should not be surprised to learn that, as soon as our troops have evacuated Alexandria, a part of the Egyptian were again conveyed into that country, with the connivance, or perhaps consent, of the Turks, and professedly for the purpose of re-establishing their authority. It is true that as long as we occupy Malta this enterprise will always be attended with much risk; but they have always been able to elude our vigilance, and therefore it becomes of the utmost importance to keep as strict a watch as possible on Toulon, without exciting too much jealousy, and a naval force in the Mediterranean sufficient to repel any sudden act of aggression in any quarter so dangerous to the interests of his Majesty's dominions. The vigilance, however, of his Majesty's cruisers should not be exclusively confined to the Mediterranean. Our policy in still keeping possession of Malta cannot escape the observation of this Government, and it is possible that in order to defeat it they may have recourse to the Adriatic, where the port of Ancona would furnish them with a convenient place of embarkation, and the coasting trade carried on in that sea a sufficient number of small vessels and marines to answer the purpose of so short a navigation. This may undoubtedly be considered as an object worthy of the greatest attention. Mr. Merry will have reported to your Lordship the indecent and outrageous conduct of the First Consul towards Count Stahremberg;[1] he will have mentioned the motive assigned for this act of violence. I will content myself with observing that I see in it only a nearer resemblance to the character of the late Emperor of Russia, and of course I cannot be surprised that their conduct should be so similar. M. Schimmelpenninck called upon me yesterday; his conversation was such as might be expected from a person of his experience and prudence, and, if he acts up to it, I think your Lordship will find him worthy of your confidence; he is, as every Foreign Minister is, and must be, disgusted with the conduct of this Government.

[1] Austrian Ambassador to England. He had been ordered to quit Paris at short notice.

Paris, December 1, 1802.

I have the honour to acknowledge the receipt of your Lordship's letter of the 25th ult. by Shaw, whom I forwarded immediately to his destination, and in such a manner as to escape all observation. With respect to the hints your Lordship is so good as to give me for my guidance, I can with truth assure your Lordship that I shall have the less difficulty n conforming my language and conduct to them, since they perfectly coincide with the notion which a nearer view of the state of things here has enabled me to form; and I took the liberty of expressing as much to your Lordship in an early despatch from this place. Everything I see and hear does, I confess, considerably diminish the apprehensions which I had imbibed in England, of the immediate danger likely to result from the vast acquisition of territory, and of the influence of this country on the Continent. The conduct of the First Consul is as strongly reprobated by nine people out of ten not immediately connected with Government in this country as it is in England; and out of it, the indignation is not the less lively from being suppressed. Every year of peace, whilst it weakens the Consular Government, unsupported as it stands by confidence or affection, will give strength and courage to those whose object and interest it is to overturn it; and we shall, in fact, by peace maintain a more dangerous, and I trust a more decisive, state of warfare against this Government than by the most direct hostility. It must, however, be admitted that there are cases in which perhaps it might be impracticable to persevere in this mode of policy, and any attempt to gain Egypt may be considered as one. With a view, therefore, to peace, it becomes a most essential duty to watch most scrupulously over the conduct of the First Consul in everything tending to this point. It certainly is not the wish of this Government to come to a rupture with Great Britain, but it will always be prepared to avail itself of our security to carry its projects into effect; and it is with this view that his Majesty's most gracious speech, combining as it does conciliation and watchfulness, is less approved of by the Consul and his confidants than by the public. As long as we have Malta, and with it a pretext for keeping up a sufficient armament in the Mediterranean, we shall be able to counteract his plans; but the case will be different, and I fear desperate, should we be obliged by circumstances to resign it to its fate. We should carry with us in all our calculations that Egypt is the great object of the First Consul's ambition; and unless we are well prepared, we shall soon, I fear, have to determine between this danger and that of renewing the war. No aggression hitherto committed can perhaps be considered as sufficiently dangerous to justify a rupture; although, as your Lordship most justly observes, it will imperceptibly serve as a groundwork of a future system with those Powers which have an equal interest with us in restoring the balance of Europe. My audience is to take place on Monday next; but whether at the Tuileries, or at St. Cloud, I have not yet been able positively to learn. In the meantime I have been invited to dine with M. Talleyrand, with whom, if I may trust to appearances, I may be able to maintain a kind of cordial intercourse. Nothing consistent with what I owe to my situation and to myself shall be wanting to accomplish this end.

Paris, December 5, 1802.

I have the honour to acknowledge your Lordship's despatch No. 1, of November 30, with a separate despatch and enclosure by the messenger Sylvester. My presentation to the First Consul is to take place to-morrow—one day sooner than the usual day of reception. Whether this may be considered as a mark of the First Consul's impatience to see me, or to show that the rule to which the delay has been assigned is not indispensable, but entirely subject to his will and pleasure, I will not attempt to determine. It is certain, however, that there does exist in the heart of the First Consul a very considerable amount of rancour and of irritation, of the effects of which I shall in all probability be frequently made sensible. But I will confess that when I see by what means his good-will is conciliated by some of the greatest Powers in Europe, I cannot help glorying as an Englishman in so honourable a distinction. I do, however, really believe that the mortification at the failure of his efforts to subdue St. Domingo does in some degree feed those hostile feelings, which may perhaps be as much imputed to jealousy as to a spirit of enmity. And it is much to be feared that if he finds himself forced to give up the contest (which, however, there is every reason to believe he will not do until he has exerted every nerve) he will use his utmost efforts to reduce the British colonies to the same deplorable condition. It is the prosperity of his Majesty's dominions both at home and abroad, the affections of his subjects to his Royal Person, and all those blessings which his Majesty enumerates in his speech, that excite the envy and hatred of the First Consul, and those motives of hatred are built on too solid a basis ever to be affected by his malice or machinations. Mr. Merry has reported to your Lordship the disturbance which took place in this capital a few nights ago. Notwithstanding the utmost endeavours of the public prints to pass it over and treat it as a private quarrel amongst some young men, it made, and still makes, a very considerable sensation; and this circumstance serves to prove that the spirit of the people is not so far evaporated but that the smallest spark may set it in a blaze. I think it necessary that your Lordship should know without loss of time that the Commander de Bussy, the person who some time ago went to England to notify to the Bailli de Ruspoli his election to the Grand-Mastership of Malta, and who brought back his refusal, is now returned to him with a letter from the Cardinal Legate Caprara, urging him by the most forcible and personal arguments to accede to the nomination. He is given to understand that unless he does so he must expect to feel the utmost weight of the arrogance of the First Consul. This great solicitude of the French Government is an additional proof of its anxious desire to see us quit the Mediterranean.

Paris, December 7, 1802.

The ceremonial of my presentation to the First Consul having been previously adjusted, by which it was determined, after a negotiation of three days, that the First Consul should send three of his carriages for me—the one with six horses, the two others with four: the first to convey me, accompanied by a prefect of the palace; the second, Mr. Talbot; the third, the other gentlemen attached to the Embassy; and my own carriage to follow empty, drawn by six horses—in this order I set out on Sunday last for the Tuileries, and was conducted to the Audience Chamber, at the upper end of which stood the First Consul, with the Second [1] and Third [2] Consuls on his right and left. The Ministers, Generals, etc., behind him, and the Corps Diplomatique in a circle in front, I was led through the open space thus formed, by M. Talleyrand, Minister for Foreign Affairs, and two prefects of the palace, to the First Consul, and in presenting my credentials made use of the following expressions: 'J'ai l'honneur, Général Premier Consul, de vous présenter la lettre de créance du Roi, mon maître, en qualité de son Ambassadeur Extraordinaire et Plénipotentiaire auprès de la République française. Je vous prie d'ajouter foi aux sentiments qui y sont exprimés. Vous n'y trouverez, Général Premier Consul, que le désir sincère du Roi mon maître de maintenir avec vous les relations de paix et d'amitié.' I concluded as usual with something from myself expressive of my zeal in giving effect to these his Majesty's intentions. After he had received the credentials, and delivered them to M. Talleyrand, he replied: 'Je suis très sensible à ce que vous venez de me dire des sentiments du Roi, et je vous prie d'assurer Sa Majesté que je désire ardemment avec elle, non seulement la paix, mais la meilleure intelligence. J'espère que lorsqu'on me connaîtra mieux, on me rendra la justice d'être persuadé de ma sincérité. Je répète toujours, c'est de la paix entre nos deux grandes nations que dépend le bonheur du monde.' He then asked me a few questions about my

---

[1] Cambacérès.   [2] Lebrun.

journey, and I fell back to my place in the circle, where the English gentlemen who were to be presented were placed. In a few minutes he came round, and, after conversing for a short time on indifferent subjects, I presented, one after the other, six-and-thirty persons. He spoke a few words to each, and when he had done, on my apologising for having given him so much trouble, he addressed himself to the English collectively, and said: 'Messieurs, je suis charmé de vous voir ici; je désire que vous vous y amusiez, et qu'en retournant chez vous, vous emportiez l'assurance de l'estime de cette nation pour la vôtre, et que leur bonne intelligence est nécessaire à la tranquillité du monde.' He then completed the round of Foreign Ministers, and made his bow, upon which we all retired. I should observe that Mr. Talbot was the first person presented by me. We then proceeded to the apartment of Madame Bonaparte, where I was presented by the Prefect, and then presented Mr. Talbot and the other gentlemen attached to the mission who had followed me. She received us very affably, but with a great deal of embarrassment. From thence I was conducted home, where I found an invitation to dine at six o'clock at the First Consul's. I accordingly went there with Mr. Merry. At this dinner were present Madame Bonaparte, the family of the First Consul, and her own, with several ladies attached to her person, the Foreign Ministers and their wives, and about two hundred and fifty others. After this dinner, which did not last above half an hour, the First Consul repeated in conversation the substance of what he had said to me more formally in the morning, and talked a considerable time of indifferent matters, with the greatest ease and affability. I yesterday, in compliance with what was signified to me as the established etiquette, made a visit to the Second and Third Consuls, sending previously to them to fix a time, and then to the individuals of the First Consul's family—to Joseph, Lucien, Louis, his mother, and a sister. I left my name with them, as well as with the Ministers of the country, the Président des Sections du Conseil d'Etat, the Governor of the Palace, the Prefect on duty, the First Inspectors of Artillery,

Engineers, and Gendarmerie, the General commanding the division, and the City, and the General of the Guard, all of whom were pointed out to me as entitled by the etiquette to the first visit. I declared I should make no difficulty provided the same had been practised by my predecessors of equal rank, and would be required of those who came after me. Such, my Lord, was the ceremonial of my presentation to this Government, in which I have been the more particular, as it may from its novelty be thought curious. Mr. Merry presented at the same time his letters of recall, and will return in about a fortnight.

Paris, December 9, 1802.

A mode of proceeding between this Government and the Swiss Republic seems at last to be definitely arranged. Four senators—Barthélemy, Desmeunier, Rœderer, and Fouché —are named commissioners to treat with the Swiss Deputies. They are to hold their meetings at M. Talleyrand's, and are to assemble for the first time in a day or two. The First Consul has given them, I understand, one fortnight to adjust this business, at the end of which time they are to submit their work to his approbation. It is not difficult to foresee what a Constitution will be given to these devoted people, framed under such auspices. Count Marcoff was to have gone to-night to meet Count Woronzow on his passage through Lille, but has delayed his journey in consequence of the latter having met with an accident in breaking his carriage near Frankfort, by which his progress is retarded for a few days. Count Woronzow has been much pressed to come through Paris, but has absolutely refused. There is every reason to believe that he is charged with discretionary power by his Court to engage or still withhold the Emperor's acceptance to the guarantee of Malta. Marcoff has certainly urged every argument most likely to persuade his Court to comply with the First Consul's wishes in this respect; but, convinced as I am that such a measure would serve only to place the island under the immediate control of Bonaparte, who is sensible that his favourite projects depend upon its acquisition, I cannot but hope that Count Woronzow will consider such an engagement on the part of the Emperor in the same light as when your Lordship conversed with him on the subject in London. At all events, he probably will not determine until he has communicated with your Lordship.

The Marquis de Gallo has presented his credentials as his Sicilian Majesty's Minister to the President of the Italian Republic.

Paris, December 13, 1802.

I have to acknowledge the receipt of your Lordship's separate despatches of November 30 and December 3, with the enclosures, as well as that containing the demand on the French Government for stores furnished at Jamaica for the repairs of the French frigate 'La Cocarde.' I have already given this account to M. Talleyrand, and your Lordship may be assured that the claimants whose cases you think proper to recommend shall have every assistance in my power. From the extreme difficulty which has hitherto occurred in all matters of restitution, I cannot allow myself to be very sanguine in my expectations of bringing this Government to such a decision as strict justice and reciprocity would require. I trust, however, that it will at last feel its honour, or what is still dearer to it, its interest, nearly concerned in satisfying them, at least inasmuch as regards his Majesty's subjects, some of whom have pretensions which it is shameful to reject. I am sensible that it would be presuming too much to hope to be able yet to render my correspondence anywise interesting to your Lordship. Having had no direct business to transact with the Ministers of this country, I have conversed with them only on general matters. I can, however, assure your Lordship (and I do so with the utmost satisfaction) that the attitude assumed by his Majesty's Government, uniting moderation with firmness and watchfulness, is likely to be attended with the happiest effect. I have been told by persons in the habits of confidence with the First

Consul—and I will mention the Chevalier Azzara in particular—that it had already effected a pause in the policy he has been hitherto pursuing; and that it would, if strictly persevered in, undoubtedly keep within bounds that restless spirit which marks so strongly the character of this Government. He at the same time added that his Court would see it with satisfaction and thankfulness. The Prussian Minister has within these few days been particularly unreserved, considering his connection with this Government, in his demonstrations towards me. He appears anxious to convince me of the friendly and confidential intercourse now subsisting between his Majesty and the Court of Berlin, and professes on this subject much more than I can give credit to. It is possible that there may be at this moment some particular point on which the Prussian Cabinet and this Government may be at variance, and that, in order to give that dignity and energy to their representations which they cannot derive from themselves, they are desirous of availing themselves of that which a more confidential system with his Majesty would not fail to reflect upon them. The measure, therefore, I shall observe with M. de Lucchesini (whose private as well as public character is long known to me) shall be neither confidential nor repulsive until such time as your Lordship may think proper to acquaint me with the circumstances which give occasion to his present conduct towards me. The Batavian Ambassador, Vos von Steenvich, has been instructed to make a representation, couched in the strongest terms, against the conduct of this Government with regard to the French troops quartered in Holland. Your Lordship well knows how long and how anxiously the Batavian Government has been expecting to be delivered from this burthen. The moment was thought to be arrived when a considerable part of that army was ordered to embark for Louisiana, and the most solemn assurances were given to that effect. They now find, however, that in proportion as the troops embark fresh ones arrive to take their places; and it is furthermore signified that it is thought necessary rather to augment than to diminish the armed force kept up in that country.

It is to be feared that the effect of the remonstrance which is to be presented to-day will be the dismissal of the Secretary of State, Van der Goes, and of all those who are not entirely subservient to this Government.

Paris, December 13, 1802.

The Duchess of Dorset[1] was on Thursday last introduced to the First Consul and Madame Bonaparte at St. Cloud. She was received with every possible mark of civility and attention. The Prefect-in-Waiting (the Master of the Ceremonies of this country) was ready to receive her on stepping from the carriage, and conducted her upstairs into the apartment where the Circle was waiting the arrival of the First Consul. The fauteuil next to Madame Bonaparte was kept vacant for her, and every mark of distinction due to her rank—whether as Ambassadress, or in her own individual capacity—was paid to her. I had a few days previous to this ceremony endeavoured to settle the form in which the Duchess should be received; but it was maintained that as Madame Bonaparte could be considered in no other light than as the wife of the First Consul, and had no particular place or precedency assigned to her by the Constitution, nothing could be formally stipulated relating to her. All that could be said was, that if the Duchess of Dorset did Madame Bonaparte the honour to come to her, she should certainly be received *avec tous les égards qui lui sont dus*. This was the footing on which she went, and it must be acknowledged we have no reason to complain of the reception she met with. I have already begun my round of dinners, having yesterday dined with the Second Consul, Cambacérès. On Tuesday I dine with the Third Consul, Lebrun, and after that comes a long succession of engagements to the Ministers of each department. I think it proper to mention to your Lordship that the Duchess of Dorset has received and returned a visit to M. Talleyrand, and, furthermore, intends to accept the invitation, which she has received conjointly with me, to

[1] Wife of Lord Whitworth.

dine with M. Talleyrand on Wednesday next. This will be a great *diplomatique* dinner, and of course no person admitted but such as the Duchess of Dorset can meet with propriety. The same might not be, perhaps, the case at other times or in other places; but we have thought that the line which we are disposed to draw with regard to society should not extend to the house of the Minister for Foreign Affairs, with whom it is my duty to be chiefly in relation, and the more particularly when the lady who presides in his house bears his name, and is in fact married to him, as far as the sanction of the Romish Church can make such a marriage lawful.

Paris, December 16, 1802.

The Swiss Deputies have held their sittings very regularly at M. Talleyrand's from ten in the morning until four or five in the evening for these last four or five days; but if we may judge by the communication which was yesterday made to them from the First Consul, very little progress has been made towards the completion of their business. The purport of this communication was to announce to them that their Constitution must be completed in eight days; that in order to assist their deliberations he had communicated to them his ideas in writing, from which they would see that his intentions were entirely favourable to their independence; and that the only return he should require for the signal marks of favour and friendship which he had at all times shown them, and particularly at this moment, was that they should consider themselves as bound not to form any alliance or connection whatsoever with any other Power but France. Such are the First Consul's notions of independence; and it must be confessed that it holds out a bright prospect of what the Swiss are doomed to enjoy under the protection of their powerful neighbour. It is, however, at the same time fair to acknowledge that, every circumstance duly considered, their situation is likely to be less grievous than might have been expected; since it undoubtedly would have depended upon him to annex that country, as he has others, to the French dominions. If this is not the case, it must be ascribed solely to the influence which the dignified language of his Majesty and the system on which his Majesty's Government professes to act must necessarily have on the politics of the First Consul. On the other hand, I fear we must consider the transaction which has been proposed to the Court of Spain, by which the First Consul agrees to exchange Parma and Placentia for the two Floridas, as unavoidable. The Spanish Ambassador confessed to me yesterday that he saw no possibility of evading it. These two Duchies are to be annexed to the kingdom of Etruria. Count Cobenzl is to receive this day the First Consul's answer to the representations of the Court of Vienna on the subject of the pretensions of the Grand Duke of Tuscany. The answer, as I understand, will, on the whole, be unfavourable, although something will be added to what was allotted to that prince, by the general plan of indemnities. Not a word has been yet mentioned to me by M. Talleyrand either on the subject of Malta or any other point at issue between the two Governments. I thought I had furnished him yesterday with a fair opportunity when I presented to him General Fox, who is here on his way from Malta to England. Count Marcoff is gone to Lille to meet Count Woronzow; I had desired him to take charge of a letter from me, and he promised it, but he nevertheless went away without letting me know; and I do not think myself justified in writing by a special messenger, much less by the post. I have no doubt that it is hoped to gain him over to the views of the First Consul on the subject of the guarantee of Malta. The Batavian Ambassador believes that the answer of the First Consul to his representations will be more favourable than he expected.

Paris, December 20, 1802.

Amongst the various considerations worthy of our attention, none can be deemed more important than the state of the finances of this country. Upon them must ultimately depend the success of the ambitious projects and widespreading speculations of the First Consul; and there is every reason to believe that the more accurate our information upon this subject may be the less cause we shall find for apprehension. I hope very shortly to be able to lay before your Lordship a statement of this part of the First Consul's administration, such as will afford a most striking contrast to that exhibited lately in the British Parliament, and convince us that amongst all the Powers of Europe no such auxiliary can be found as those we possess in the very heart of this country—the disaffection, I might say the contempt, of the nation for his government, and the total derangement of his finances. Until I can submit to your Lordship the statement I am promised, I will content myself with observing that such is at this moment the penury of the Government, that it does not possess the means of sending out even the necessary reinforcements for St. Domingo, and it has only been within these very few days that those means have been very scantily supplied by extorting different sums from the bankers of Paris. It must not, however, be expected that difficulties like these will deter the First Consul from attempting any favourite project. He is, on the contrary, determined to exert his utmost efforts, not only to subdue that colony, but to strengthen himself in Louisiana and the Floridas; and so pressing are his instances with the Court of Spain for the possession of those two provinces, that they will inevitably be ceded to him in the course of the month of January. I am perfectly aware of the effect which the knowledge of this transaction will have in England, where it will no doubt be considered, and justly so, as a direct attack upon his Majesty's dominions in the West; whilst the possession of Egypt, which he will possibly gain by a compromise with the Porte, will threaten with an equal degree of danger those in the East. That such are his motives and such his projects is not to be doubted; and, as I said before, the ally to whose assistance we are principally to look is the total want (unless recourse be again had to those measures of terror, which he would scarcely venture to attempt) of the means indispensably necessary for their success. It may, however, be added that, supposing war to be inevitable, that which he would by those means carry into this distant part of the world would be of all others the most favourable to us and the most dangerous and disadvantageous to him. The Americans, whom the avowal of such a project would not fail to unite to us in a common cause, might effectually prevent the settlement of such neighbours, whilst our fleets would cut off all intercourse with Europe. These are the difficulties the First Consul would have to encounter; but no difficulties deter the presumptuous and the headstrong, and therefore we must be prepared to meet the attempt. At the same time that the First Consul is meditating such distant enterprises he is not unmindful of his own gratification at home, and there is every reason to believe that the object of a long sitting of his Privy Council a few days ago was to prepare a *Senatus-Consulte*, which is to give him an Imperial or Royal title. The former is supposed to be most to his taste, and the affectation of giving the Emperor of Russia the title of Czar only in his Court Calendar is considered as an indication that he means to be an Emperor himself and think two sufficient.

Paris, December 23, 1802.

I have the honour to acknowledge the receipt of your Lordship's separate letters by Vick, whom I immediately forwarded to his destination. Count Marcoff, since his return from Lille, has been frequently in conference with M. Talleyrand, and, as I have reason to believe, on the affairs of Malta. I yesterday was confirmed in this belief by his acquainting me, with an appearance of much satisfaction, that the Emperor of Russia had at length consented to accede to the guarantee of Malta, under certain restrictions, relating only to the formation of the newly established *Langue de Malte*. He gave me to understand that the Emperor had been induced to this measure solely with a view of giving his Majesty a proof of his sincere desire to acquiesce as far as possible in his Majesty's wishes. He further told me that Count Woronzow would have instructions to discuss this subject with your Lordship. However much his Majesty's wishes may be gratified, those of this Government, or at least of the First Consul, are most undoubtedly so by the prospect of the evacuation of that island and of the Mediterranean by his Majesty's forces; and I should be tempted to believe that this is the object which M. de Marcoff has had principally in view. I contented myself with telling him that I had no instructions relative to that subject, but that I could assure him of the pleasure with which his Majesty would meet any arrangement by means of which the burthen of maintaining so expensive a garrison might be taken from him, and the intent of the stipulations with regard to Malta so far fulfilled as to insure its perfect independence. M. Talleyrand, with whom I dined yesterday, and in whose house I remained till near ten o'clock, made no mention of this, or of any other political subject whatever. I am assured that the First Consul is at this moment recurring to a measure of which your Lordship has already received some intimation: I mean his divorce from his present wife, and his assumption of the title of Emperor of the Gauls. But these points have, as I am credibly informed, been submitted to the Senate, and, it is said, are shortly to be made public. Should the divorce take place, he is to marry the only remaining daughter of the Margrave of Baden, a princess only fourteen years of age, whose brother is now here, and much caressed by the Consul and his courtiers. By means of this marriage he would become brother-in-law to the Emperor of Russia and to the King of Sweden; but I do really believe that he would by the same means so completely ruin the small remains of popularity which he still possesses as to give his enemies the opportunity, which they are anxiously looking for, of openly attacking his person and his Government. Of this he is sometimes aware; but such is his presumption, and so completely is he intoxicated with his situation, that the admonitions of reason are no longer attended to. I shall in the course of a very few days have, in all probability, occasion to mention this subject again more fully and more positively. It has not as yet reached the public, but it is much talked of by those who are well informed of what is passing in the interior of St. Cloud, where Madame Bonaparte, notwithstanding all the honours which have been lately paid her, is in the deepest affliction. The Swiss deputies and their coadjutors have completed their business within the given time, and their work is now before the First Consul. The Swiss are to be called independent. They renounce the right of contracting alliances with any other Power than France, and the First Consul reserves to himself the appointment of their magistrates. Mr. Merry proposes leaving this place on Monday next.

Paris, December 27, 1802.

It is now supposed that, notwithstanding the ardent desire of the First Consul to be invested with a higher title, motives of prudence have prevailed, and he has rejected it. A deputation of the Councils of State waited upon him a few days ago at St. Cloud to offer him that of king, to reason with him, and to overcome those scruples which he affected to entertain against accepting the offer. His apprehensions, however, of the opposition, not only of the public, but of many of those who are nearest his person, have, it is said, prevailed over their arguments, and we may conclude that this measure will be laid aside until a future and more favourable opportunity. The same may in all probability be said of the divorce. If the First Consul finds himself sometimes cramped and thwarted in his gratifications at home, he seems determined to give full scope to the extent of his influence abroad. A project is now on foot, and is expected soon to be carried into effect, of uniting the Ligurian to the Italian Republic, by which he will acquire another port in the Mediterranean, and, what is the great object of his policy, the means of limiting the intercourse between his Majesty's dominions and the Continent. That such at least is an object he has much at heart the experience of every day must convince us; but unfortunately that same experience will prove that, however great his power, it does not extend so far, and that even in France the commercial relations with Great Britain are such as to have brought the exchange to par, which a few months ago was from ten to twelve per centum against us. Amongst the most striking features of the present policy of this Government is its extreme solicitude to conciliate the Court of Russia. The public prints are filled with the grossest flattery, the loyalty and the integrity of the Russian character are perpetual subjects of admiration, and the Russian language is recommended as the most important and interesting study to Frenchmen. The greatest stress is laid upon the advantages which must accrue to both countries from the strictest relations of politics and commerce; in short, every effort is made to gain the Court of St. Petersburg, not only as having the power which would be the best able to second the views of Great Britain in fixing a limit to the ambition of the First Consul, but also as that without the co-operation of which those projects which tend to the destruction of the Turkish power, and by that means open a road to India, must be considered as too visionary to be even attempted. I hope and trust that the Russian Ministers are too enlightened to be gained by such artifices. The present Chancellor, Count Woronzow, who from his experience and the place which he holds must have great weight, is certainly no Frenchman; and though he has always endeavoured to render Russia, in a commercial point of view, less dependent on Great Britain, yet he is perfectly sensible that France can never replace her, and that their natural connection is with us. I am not, therefore, apprehensive of this Government succeeding beyond a certain degree; but still it will be incumbent upon us to use all our endeavours to counteract it at Petersburg, and, without having the appearance of endeavouring to stimulate (which would only alarm and indispose), to inculcate the doctrine of their having a common interest with us in watching carefully over the encroachments of this country. Your Lordship will pardon my troubling you on this subject; it is only inasmuch as it is connected with the policy of this Government that I venture to touch upon it. The Deputies from the Valais were received some days ago at the Court of St. Cloud. The Grand Bailiff, the President, in a speech of considerable length, expressed the gratitude of his fellow-citizens to the First Consul for his having declared their Republic independent, and in concluding this address he presented the decree of the Diet, whereby the First Consul of the French Republic and President of the Italian Republic has been pronounced *Restorer of the Independence of the Republic of Valais.* Great notoriety has been given to this event, but Bonaparte has not thought it expedient to give an equal degree of publicity to the Constitution framed by himself for the remainder of Switzerland and recommended by him to the delegates assembled here, although it professes to declare the country independent of all foreign influence. The latest accounts from Brest confirm the information which I have communicated to your Lordship with respect to Bonaparte's determination to persist in his efforts to accomplish the reduction of St. Domingo, for it appears certain that five sail of the line and a frigate have recently sailed from that port with reinforcements for that island. I have the honour to send enclosed a despatch which I received last night, to be forwarded to your Lordship from Mr. Drake. To the information therein contained I have to add that a convention was signed yesterday evening by Count Cobenzl, Count Marcoff, and Joseph Bonaparte, by virtue of which the territory of Eichstadt, containing a population of seventy thousand souls, and producing a revenue of four hundred thousand florins, together with some ecclesiastical possessions in Bavaria, are to be ceded to the Grand Duke of Tuscany in addition to what was allotted to him by the original plan of indemnities. In consequence of this arrangement Passau is to be restored to the Elector. Mr. Merry, who has been detained some days longer than he expected, proposes to set out to-morrow on his return to England.

He has put me in possession of the cyphers and papers belonging to the mission, and I beg leave to observe that there are amongst them some relating to the negotiation of Amiens, which, I conceive, ought to be deposited in your Lordship's office. I have the honour to enclose herewith a list of passports granted by me up to the present date.

P.S. I omitted to mention that the dignity of Elector is to be added to the above-mentioned terms, obtained by the Court of Vienna in favour of the Grand Duke of Tuscany.

Paris, January 4, 1803.

An opportunity now presents itself of putting to the test the desire of this Government to conciliate the Court of Petersburg. Count Marcoff has since his meeting with Count Woronzow, who brought him some instructions on that head, received the most positive orders to return to the charge, and insist on an indemnity for the King of Sardinia. It is evident that Count Marcoff feels himself considerably embarrassed with this commission, anxious as he is at all times to steer such a course as to preserve his credit with his own Court, without endangering that which he, perhaps too obsequiously, seeks to gain with the First Consul and his Ministers. I have not learnt with precision the progress he has been able to make in this negotiation, but I have reason to believe that he has received a proposal from this Government (and the Siennese is mentioned) so much below what would be likely to satisfy his own Court, that he does not transmit it to Petersburg, and is waiting the result of his further representations. It is not easy to foresee what may be the extent of the concessions of this Government, or where, indeed, the indemnity for such a loss as that which his Sardinian Majesty has sustained is to be found. But when we go to the source from whence this zeal for the service of the unfortunate monarch is derived, we may conclude that his interests will be followed up with more than common importunity. Your Lordship will recollect that Prince Czartorinsky, for some years past the intimate and most confidential friend of the present Emperor of Russia, was about three years ago appointed to reside near the King of Sardinia in quality of Russian Envoy. In the course of this mission, Prince Czartorinsky's feelings, and the natural generosity of his character, to which may be added perhaps some motive of female society, were so interested in the misfortunes of the King, that even in the reign of Paul his representations were sufficient to provoke from him some strong remonstrance on the subject. The King of Sardinia, however, shared the fate of all the Emperor's friends, and his concerns were abandoned as soon as the Emperor discovered that Bonaparte was alone worthy of his friendship and confidence. At his death Prince Czartorinsky was recalled to the Court, and is now second in point of precedency, but perhaps first in point of influence in the Foreign Department. It is the Minister (and it must also be recollected that he is a Pole, and consequently not much interested in preserving the tranquillity of Russia) who instigates the Emperor, and we may, I think, expect that, under such auspices, this affair may be carried on with a degree of perseverance and importunity capable of shaking the good understanding which the First Consul appears so anxious to establish. It is highly possible that the affairs of Switzerland, upon which Count Marcoff was also instructed to make a vigorous representation, may create another obstacle in the way of such a union. The Russian Minister was at first given to hope that his Court would be entirely gratified on this point, and that the Swiss were to remain independent. The manner, however, in which this business has been carried on and concluded must appear to the Court of Petersburg such a mockery of everything conciliatory or decent, as well towards the unfortunate people on whom the First Consul now imposes the yoke, as towards Great Britain and Russia, who have interested themselves in their favour, as to open its eyes and excite the utmost disgust. Had the representations of the Court of Petersburg been combined with those of his Majesty (and I hope and trust that this example will convince the Russian Ministers that separate and unconnected influence can have no effect on this Government), I make no doubt they would have met with that degree of respect and attention which such a concert would not fail to command. The negotiation with regard to the two Floridas begins to be more publicly talked of, and, as far as I have been able to observe, it should seem that the opinion of the public would not coincide with that of the Government. Mr. Livingstone, the American Minister, who did not think that it would be brought forward so precipitately, is in the utmost consternation. In a conversation I had with him two days ago he gave it as his decided opinion that should the measure be attempted it would have the immediate effect of uniting every individual in America, of every party, and none more sincerely than himself, in the cause of Great Britain. Should such be the event, we may, from this gentleman's known political bias, expect to have few enemies remaining in that country. I can perceive that the little intercourse which has arisen between him and myself gives a considerable degree of jealousy to M. Talleyrand. Your Lordship will have observed, and perhaps not without surprise, that I have never permitted myself to remark on the scurrilous and vulgar abuse which occasionally appears in the public prints of this Government. That contained in the 'Moniteur' of January 1,[1] and which was probably intended by the author—whose name may be easily guessed from the style—as a New Year's gift, seems to have been worked up with more than common pains and acrimony. I make no doubt that the same motives which have induced me to be silent will have operated on your Lordship so as completely to defeat the purpose of the author. I am convinced that the best, and certainly the most dignified, revenge we can take is to treat all such indecent virulence with the contempt it deserves, and not to appear even to observe it. The only remark which I have allowed myself to make, when

[1] A leading article abusing those persons in England who desire to stir up war against France.

I was asked whether I had seen it, was that the matter was worthy of the language in which it is expressed, and both so contemptible as to defeat its own purpose. The project of uniting the Ligurian to the Italian Republic is abandoned, but the port of Spezzia is required to be ceded to the latter.

Paris, January 4, 1803.

I reserve for this separate despatch a communication which was made to me yesterday evening by M. Talleyrand in a conference to which I was formally invited by that Minister. He began the conversation by giving me the strongest assurances of the sincere desire of the First Consul to cultivate the best understanding with his Majesty, and went over the old ground of the effect which such a good understanding must have on the rest of Europe. He then told me that he was ordered by the First Consul to mention to me a subject on which his Majesty had the means of conferring a particular and personal obligation upon him, and that on a point which he had much at heart. He said that since the conclusion of the peace different representations had been made to his Majesty's Government on the subject of the princes of the House of Bourbon resident in his Majesty's dominions; that the First Consul had been informed that Monsieur (he called him Count d'Artois) had assisted not long ago at a review in Scotland wearing the insignia of the Order of the St. Esprit; that he could not but consider such a practice as tending to keep alive the spirit of discord, and as holding out a possibility of a change in the Government by which the Order might again be restored; that, considering it as such, he could not pass it over in silence, and therefore he did request, as a proof of his Majesty's desire to conciliate, that he would discourage it by every means in his power. What he should, therefore, expect was that those princes should withdraw to Warsaw, where they might reside in tranquillity without being near enough to give umbrage; or, if that should be thought too harsh (and I took upon myself to assure him before he proceeded further that it never would be complied with), that at least it might be required of them to desist from wearing their orders. I cannot give your Lordship an adequate idea of the earnestness with which M. Talleyrand urged this point, and of the degree of importance which he attached to his Majesty's acquiescence. He told me that he had it in command from the First Consul to assure me that he should feel himself much obliged to his Majesty for a compliance with his wishes in this respect, and that he should be anxious to have an opportunity of proving his sense of it by adopting any arrangement or by setting aside any difficulty which might on his part stand in the way of a perfect cordiality and good understanding between the two Governments. He mentioned this repeatedly, and with a view of giving me to understand that it would in fact be so acceptable to the First Consul that we might propose our own terms. I did not, however, seem to understand it in that light, as it appeared to me to be infinitely more agreeable to his Majesty's dignity, should his Majesty be disposed to comply at all with the request, that it should be done without any appearance of a compromise. I am, however, not the less persuaded that it may tend to what he professes, and facilitate a more cordial intercourse with this Government. I would not take upon myself to give any hope of such an act of complaisance on the part of his Majesty; all I said was that his Majesty never would or could oblige those individuals to quit his dominions as long as they continued to comport themselves with that propriety (and I particularised Count d'Artois) which had invariably marked their conduct since they had been in Great Britain. With regard to the second point I could say nothing, but I would not fail to make my report to your Lordship of the purport of M. Talleyrand's communication. Your Lordship will naturally wonder that any act of complaisance should be expected at the same moment that the official prints of this Government are filled with the most virulent invective. Such inconsistencies are, however, natural to the character of the man; and I make no doubt that the more we are acquainted with it the less reason we shall have to be surprised.

Paris, January 7, 1803.

Although the subject has not been mentioned to me by M. Talleyrand, I nevertheless have reason to believe that the delay which has occurred in regard to the evacuation of Malta excites a considerable degree of anxiety at this moment. The person who suggested this to me may have been commissioned to sound me, and therefore I was not sorry to have an opportunity of saying to him what I should consider it as my duty to say to M. Talleyrand should he think proper to introduce the subject. I told him, therefore, that the sole object which his Majesty's Government had in view in framing the articles of the Treaty of Amiens which related to Malta was to render that island as independent as it was possible to make it under the existing circumstances; that had those stipulations been fulfilled by the accession of those Powers which were invited to guarantee, and by the election of a Grand Master, the Treaty would undoubtedly, with regard to Malta, as in every other point, have been carried into effect without the smallest hesitation. It so happened, however, that none of these stipulations were complied with; Russia had not yet accepted the guarantee, and the person elected to the Grand-Mastership had declined it. Under these circumstances there could be no question of giving up Malta. Such, I told the Spanish Ambassador (for it was with him that the conversation took place), had been the intention of my Court. But how far events which had taken place, and others—very important ones indeed both to his Court and mine, which were at this moment near their accomplishment—might operate on the counsels of his Majesty, I could not undertake to foretell. I professed to speak entirely from myself, being without instructions on the subject; but I said I would make no scruple to give him my private opinion, which was that Malta could not with any degree of prudence be given up whilst this country was making and meditating such acquisitions as could not but excite the utmost jealousy and justify the utmost precautions on the part of the other Powers of Europe. The Chevalier Azzara professed to be perfectly of my opinion, and I am the more inclined to believe him, as I know he is at this moment under the extreme displeasure of his Court, or more properly of the Prince de la Paix, for not having quite kept part with him in his subserviency to the French Government in his project relating to the Floridas. The business was first mentioned to him by the First Consul some months ago. He endeavoured, as he has repeatedly assured me, to dissuade him from it by every argument; and, upon finding him determined to persist, he begged that the negotiation might not be entrusted to him, but committed to the sole management of Beurnonville, who has arranged the whole business with the Prince of Peace. Mr. Frere will probably have reported to your Lordship, by the messenger who went through Paris on Tuesday last, the precise state of this negotiation. According to my intelligence, it may be considered as concluded, and the Convention is expected to arrive here toward the end of this month. It is probably with a view to this that General Bernadotte is appointed to the American mission instead of M. Otto, who, it is presumed, will go to Berlin.

Paris, January 7, 1803.

I have the honour to acknowledge your Lordship's separate despatches of December 30, 1802, with their enclosures, and shall lose no time in endeavouring to give effect to your Lordship's instructions. Wednesday last being the usual day of audience, the First Consul received at the Tuileries. I had, as usual, a considerable number of gentlemen to present, for a list of whom I beg leave to refer your Lordship to the 'Moniteur.' The Duchess of Dorset and myself had the honour of dining the same evening with the First Consul, with about two hundred and fifty other guests. The enclosed French papers will explain to your Lordship all that is yet made public of the project for giving a greater degree of influence and *éclat* to the Senate. It is understood that this is not to be carried into effect until one year has elapsed.

Paris, January 11, 1803.

The arrangement of the Swiss Constitution does not seem to be so near its conclusion as I had reason to suppose. It now appears that the First Consul has changed his opinion as to the form of government most suitable to that country, and instead of a federative system he proposes that the totality of the Cantons shall be parcelled out into separate States, each consisting of two or three Cantons at most, and that each shall be subject to the same form of Consular government as that now subsisting in France. Such is the project which he has now submitted to the Commissioners. It has, however, met with more opposition than might have been expected, and Rœderer in particular has combated with great boldness the opinion of the First Consul. Hitherto the Commission has been allowed to discuss the question without molestation; but it cannot be expected that any opposition should be effectual, and indeed it should seem that the system now recommended is too favourable to the future views of this Government to be abandoned without stronger arguments than those now urged. It is worthy of remark that the same doctrine is preached, as your Lordship will see by Mr. Drummond's despatch, which accompanies this, by Colonel Sebastiani to the States to which he has been deputed, and doubtless with the same intention. Count Marcoff seems to think that this Court will resist the introduction of such a system in a country so immediately under the protection of the Emperor, and he is accordingly preparing a representation upon the subject. The effect can scarcely be expected to be such as the dignity of the

Emperor might demand; but one effect of the general conduct of this Government most assuredly will have that of drawing together those by whose consent and co-operation Europe may yet be saved. The project which I mentioned in my last, of giving a greater degree of importance to the Senate, and which is now more detailed in the 'Moniteur,' creates much conversation in the public. It is considered as an indication of an intention in the First Consul to create a power, or rather the shadow of a power, which is to be like the House of Peers in England. Its real intention, however, is to divert the attention of the public from other matters and to increase his own patronage.

Paris, January 11, 1803.

The news of the death of General Leclerc was received some days ago, and announced in the public prints the day before yesterday in the manner formerly observed with regard to sovereigns only. It seems that he fell a victim to the yellow fever. His loss is very little regretted. It is said that he contributed to the prolongation of the troubles in St. Domingo by his avarice and vexations of all kinds. As a general or statesman, his reputation is below mediocrity. On the occasion of this event another step has been taken by the First Consul towards putting himself on a footing of royalty. An extraordinary audience of the Corps Diplomatique was yesterday morning announced for the same day at one o'clock, and half an hour after came a letter from M. Talleyrand to announce a mourning of ten days in consequence of the death of the First Consul's brother-in-law. As I understood that the other Ambassadors and Ministers meant to put on mourning, I did the same; but we have agreed to consider it as a compliment to the First Consul on making him our compliments of condolence, and not to wear it in society. I shall, I hope, soon have it in my power to furnish your Lordship with a correct statement of what is going on at Brest and the other considerable French ports. But I can in the meantime set your Lordship's mind perfectly at ease with regard to any effectual steps towards a regeneration of the Navy. The magazines are completely empty, nor is it possible to find either money or credit to fill them. The utmost efforts have been made to equip the few vessels that sailed a week ago from Brest (and which are gone from thence to Toulon to take in troops, in consequence of the disaffection of those in Brittany for the service), which were, I am assured, in such a state as to render the voyage an object of the utmost danger. It is, however, the determination of the First Consul to persist at all events in his efforts to reduce the colonies to obedience, and this occupation will be of itself sufficient to tranquillise us with regard to his other speculations.

Paris, January 14, 1803.

That which seems now to occupy the attention of this Government, to the exclusion of almost every other object, is the providing reinforcements for St. Domingo. It is certain that, what with the climate and the vigorous attacks of the blacks (for war is now become entirely offensive on their part), the number of the French troops is so much reduced as to afford scarcely a hope of their being able to hold out until those succours can arrive. Every effort is making for that purpose, and I am assured that the First Consul is determined to make another effort to reduce the colony, by sending out as expeditiously as possible a body at least of thirty thousand men; and orders are already gone to Brest, to Rochefort, and to Toulon to fit out everything which can serve to convey troops, and to hire transports for the same service. From this your Lordship will judge of the importance which the First Consul attaches to the reduction of the colonies; but I think we shall not deceive ourselves if we place this perseverance rather to the account of vanity and offended pride than to any principle of true policy. Whatever may be his motive, I have, whenever an occasion has offered of expressing an opinion on this subject, been particularly careful to express no great degree of anxiety for the measures which he is preparing to adopt, in the idea that, should he be once led to imagine that we consider him as playing our game by this diversion of his force, he might perhaps sacrifice his own feelings to the desire of depriving us of such a gratification. It was with a view to this that when the First Consul introduced the subject in the little conversation I had with him on Monday last at the audience, it was my object rather to dwell on the difficulties of the enterprise than to give him the least reason to believe we wished to commit him, by affecting to diminish the danger. He concluded the conversation by saying, 'Tout cela est vrai; c'est à ce prix que nous achetons le sûr, mais malgré cela il nous en faut.' I have had occasion to make the acquaintance of the General who is going out to take the command at Pondicherry; his name is Decaen. He is a young man, and bears a very fair character in private life, but possesses no very shining talents either as a general or a statesman. We may therefore conclude that, as far as he is concerned, it is intended rather to improve what possessions they already have in India than to extend them by conquest or intrigue. The Swiss Deputies are still making the best defence they can against the government prescribed for them by the First Consul. They have been allowed the appearance of a reference to their principals, which will have the effect of prolonging their stay at Paris, but certainly will produce no change in their favour.

Paris, January 17, 1803.

The final adjustment of the affairs of Germany is still the subject of some difficulty. The Elector of Bavaria remonstrates, with a warmth which begins to displease the First Consul, accustomed as he is to the submissive tone of the German princes, against the infraction of the guarantee of his possessions by the French Government, and the Court of

Prussia, in now depriving him of the bishopric of Eichstadt in favour of the Grand Duke of Tuscany. His Electoral Highness instructs his Ministers here to declare that he will not relinquish that possession until he is compelled by force so to do. He quotes the example of the King of Prussia, who, it must be allowed, supported his pretensions with a vigour and independence which perhaps might not succeed equally with another. It seems to be a maxim of this Government to consolidate by every means the force of Prussia; but the Elector of Bavaria has not the same claims to favour, and consequently he will gain nothing by resistance. Count Marcoff has received the most satisfactory assurances that no steps shall be taken to subvert the order of things (which, however, it must be confessed, is now become a disorder) originally agreed upon for the government of the seven isles. The instructions, therefore, of Colonel Sebastiani, as far as they relate to this object, are to be annulled. The same Minister is endeavouring to carry into effect his instructions in favour of the King of Sardinia. He tells me that he is not without hope of obtaining Piombino in addition to the Siennese, and perhaps even the Isle of Elba--a point on which he assures me he will make a most obstinate stand. It is reported that the First Consul will make a journey ere long into the Low Countries; but this will probably not take place until the troops from the quarter are embarked for St. Domingo, where, it is said, they are to proceed instead of Louisiana. In the meantime the First Consul is living retired in the country, without the enjoyment of any of the smallest degrees of domestic comfort: occupied the whole day with the most trivial details of internal arrangement, and such as suit the natural turn of his mind, prone to all the extremes of suspicion. He passes three or four hours each day in reading over himself the letters of individuals, which are sent to him for that purpose from the post at Paris, and from which he collects pretexts for tormenting frequently those who are nearest to him, as well as those who think themselves the safest by the distance from him. Three or four different polices equally desirous to manifest their zeal are established in this city, and from their inquisition no class of society is secure. In short, he is a scourge to himself and to the nation, which for its punishment he has subdued to his will. But I must repeat to your Lordship that the nearer he is viewed the less formidable he appears to those not immediately under his grasp. I am sorry to mention that the Duc de Choiseul has again incurred the displeasure of the First Consul, who has banished him to the distance of forty leagues from Paris. This is said to be in consequence of his having inconsiderately applauded a passage in a play, in the presence of the First Consul, which bore an allusion to the restoration of the Royal Family.

Lord Hawkesbury to Lord Whitworth.

Downing Street, January 14, 1803.

Having received an application from several of his Majesty's subjects interested in the French funds, and having learnt that they propose addressing themselves to your Excellency, I think it right to apprise you of their intention. As I am informed that the sequestration imposed by the French Government during the war on British property in France still continues, I have to signify to your Excellency his Majesty's pleasure (in the event of this information being correct) that, as all restraints of this nature have been removed in this country, you require from the French Government that the sequestration of British property in France should be taken off without delay. You will, however, be careful, in any discussions which your Excellency may have upon this subject with the French Ministers, to confine your representations to property actually existing, without reference to such as may have been confiscated either wholly or in part by the authority of the Government during the war. With regard to property of which description, you will content yourself with requiring that his

Majesty's subjects may be placed on the same footing in this respect as other foreigners who may be in similar circumstances.

Lord Whitworth to Lord Hawkesbury.

Paris, January 20, 1803.

I have the honour to acknowledge the receipt of your Lordship's despatch No. 1 of the 14th inst., and the separate despatch and enclosures which accompanied it. Your Lordship will do me the justice to believe that I have not waited for such a repetition of your Lordship's instructions to attend to the claims which his Majesty's subjects may have on this Government. If I have not followed up my representations with that perseverance which some of the claimants may have wished, it is that I conceive his Majesty's dignity would be committed were I to place myself in the situation of a solicitor to this Government. The strongest appeals to its justice (for we claim on no other ground) have been made on this subject by Mr. Merry, and have been repeated by me. Hitherto, I am sorry to say, they have been fruitless, and they have been so because they have been made on a principle which does not exist. It shall, however, be my business, as it is my duty, to give the French Ministers to understand that whilst they show themselves so backward in fulfilling one positive stipulation of the treaty, to which they constantly refer, they can have no right to complain of any delay which has arisen, or may yet occur, on the part of his Majesty's Government in giving effect to another. I do propose, however, renewing my application in behalf of the British claimants, at whose impatience I am not at all surprised, in the course of a few days; and I shall not fail to attend to the just distinction which your Lordship points out. As an instance of the difficulty of bringing the French Ministers to any decision, I enclose the answer I have this moment received to an application which has been twice made in favour of an English vessel detained in the port of Flushing, and on the subject of which Mr. Merry had presented some memorials before I came into the country. There has fallen another victim to the suspicions of the First Consul in the person of the Duc de Laval. He was ordered three days ago to leave Paris, and on going to the Grand Judge to enquire into the cause of his exile he was told it was because he was in the pay of England. He cleared himself of this charge by producing his papers, which proved that he had had no money concerns whatever with the British Government since he had resigned his regiment seven years ago. He was still accused of receiving remittances from England, and at last it occurred to him that it might be the interest of a sum of money which he had placed in the English funds, and from whence he derives his only subsistence, the whole of his immense property having been confiscated in this country. He endeavoured to explain this transaction, but it was still considered as suspicious, and availed him nothing. He was obliged, therefore, to leave Paris yesterday, and is gone to Bordeaux. The day before the Duc de Choiseul left Paris he had occasion to see M. Chaptal, the Minister of the Interior, who, as soon as he learnt his name, avowed to him that he was in possession of Chanteloup, the seat in Touraine of the late Minister, and that he had bought it for six thousand pounds. He enlarged much on the improvements he projected, adding that if ever the Duc de Choiseul should chance to come that way he should be glad to show them to him. This will give your Lordship some idea of the morality of those amongst whom this M. Chaptal bears a fair and respectable character.

Paris, January 24, 1803.

There is every reason to believe that there is in the contemplation of the First Consul a step relative to a change in the government or in the political existence of Holland. Such a rumour has reached me from different quarters, and indeed seems to have excited very serious apprehensions in the

Batavian Mission here. Your Lordship has been too long prepared for such an event, by the conduct which this Government has invariably pursued, to be much surprised should it take place. I cannot, however, I confess, easily persuade myself that anything serious is intended. The opposition which was made to his measures in Switzerland by his Majesty and the Emperor of Russia, the only sovereigns in Europe who dare to assert their dignity, will, although not sufficient to save that country, convince the First Consul that a similar attempt upon Holland would be attended with difficulties proportioned to the greater importance of the object. And although I believe that he feels that the state of tranquillity in which he has placed this country, contrary perhaps to his inclination, is not that which is best calculated to promote his own individual interest, yet I do not think that he will by any violent act of aggression incur the risk of uniting against him the two Powers, from whom he has everything to fear, without any of those advantages to expect which might serve to stimulate this country and reconcile it by success to a renewal of hostilities. I am therefore inclined to consider this report rather in the light of a demonstration with a view to induce us to abandon Malta and Alexandria (the evacuation of the latter, which is not known here, though anxiously expected), or as a means of forcing the Dutch to purchase his forbearance by money. It is the want of this which has nearly determined the First Consul to give up the attempt to reduce St. Domingo to his obedience. I am assured that he has twice within this fortnight resolved to leave it to its fate, and to send back Toussaint, towards whom more lenient measures have been adopted. The shame of being defeated in his purpose, although the most dangerous—for he has to contend with the climate—has got the better of every other consideration, and the greatest exertions are accordingly continued for the speedy reinforcement of General Rochambeau, who is appointed to succeed General Leclerc. Such is the want of money, or of good faith, or of both, that the bills of exchange drawn by Leclerc for the common necessaries of the expedition are protested, and several individuals have fallen victims to their confidence in Government. What, however, is more astonishing is that others are found who, not deterred by their example, present themselves with a moral certainty of experiencing the same fate. At the moment Count Marcoff was induced to believe that he should gain his point in regard to obtaining the Island of Elba for his Sardinian Majesty, he saw by the 'Moniteur' that it was considered as a department of the Republic, and an administration prepared for it by this indefatigable legislator. He feels much mortified, and is persuaded that his Court will be highly offended. I am sorry to have to announce an act of rigour on the part of the First Consul against the person of one of his Majesty's subjects. A Mr. Edgeworth, who had been resident at Paris about four months, and whose pursuits have been entirely literary, received the day before yesterday an order from the police to quit Paris in twenty-four hours, and the French territory in a fortnight. He came immediately to me, and, in consequence of his declaring himself unconscious of any offence against this Government, I wrote to M. Talleyrand desiring to know the motive of this rigour. In the meantime Mr. Edgeworth discovered that the crime of which he was accused was that of being brother to the Abbé Edgeworth, that respectable ecclesiastic who attended Louis XVI. in his last moments. He complied with the order and retired to Passy, just without the Barrière, leaving his family here. From thence he remonstrated against the injustice he has suffered, declaring that he is not the brother of the Abbé Edgeworth, whom he never saw in all his life, and only a distant relation. He was then required to give a petition to the First Consul stating this fact, which he has declined doing, but is ready to sign a declaration to the same effect; and this, I have no doubt, will be sufficient to procure his return, since they must be ashamed of so unprovoked an act of violence. I am assured that an *arrêté* will shortly appear, by which it is enacted that no emigrant can possess within the French Republic more than 100,000 livres, whether it be in land or money. The residue of their claims in any property, notwithstanding the sequestration may have been taken off, is to be considered as national property. Count Cobenzl has received the ratification of the Convention of December 26. The First Consul with his family removed to-day from St. Cloud to the Tuileries.

Paris, January 27, 1803.

I have to report to your Lordship the purport of a conversation I had on Tuesday last by appointment with M. Talleyrand. He had invited me some days ago for this purpose, but a bad cold had prevented my meeting him till that day. The communication he had to make to me related to two points, both equally important, as he said, to the maintenance of good harmony between the two Governments; with this difference, however, that the one originated with himself and was dictated by his anxiety to do away with everything which might feed the mutual irritation of the two countries, and the other by the express order of the First Consul. That which came from himself related to the English newspapers, against which he pronounced the most bitter philippic, assuring me that the First Consul was extremely hurt to find that his endeavours to conciliate had hitherto produced no other effect than to increase the abuse with which the papers of both sides of the question in England continually loaded him. He expatiated much upon this topic, and endeavoured to establish a fact, which I assured him a reference to any one of the newspapers in Paris would instantly refute, that during four months not a word of provocation had appeared in any French journal which could justify a retort from those published in England. For the rest he advanced nothing but what has been said on more than one occasion to Mr. Merry, and reported by him to your Lordship. I was, however, given to understand that the First Consul was in fact highly incensed, and the more so, he was pleased to say, as it came from a country of whose good opinion he was so very ambitious. In my reply I could but go over the old ground, and endeavoured to make M. Talleyrand understand, first, that whatever was said in the English papers might be considered as a natural retaliation for what was published in the French papers; secondly, that what was *officially* published here was by no means so in England; and, thirdly, that although the Government possessed a control over the press in France, the English Government neither had, nor could have, unless they purchased it at the same price, any whatever in England. Upon this he endeavoured to prove to me that there were papers in England attached to different parties, and went over their names and supposed connections with great precision, and that consequently his Majesty's Ministers might so far control those at least which depended upon them as to prevent their inserting that abuse which must be considered as having their sanction. I endeavoured to explain to him what the influence was which he supposed Ministers to possess in England; that it amounted to nothing more than a preference which your Lordship, for instance, might give to one paper rather than to another, by sending to it any articles of news which it might be wished to make public; but that your Lordship's influence went no further, and that if the editor of such paper conceived it more for his interest to continue to write after his own fancy and uncontrolled than to be the publisher of such occasional articles, in that case all influence was at an end. I told him that if he had remarked any abusive article in any paper of such a description it was natural and fair to conclude that it did not depend upon Government to prevent it. He persisted in his opinion that his Majesty's Ministers might keep certain papers in order, as I did in assuring him that until the First Consul could so far master his feelings as to be as indifferent to the scurrility of the English prints as the English Government was to that which daily appeared in the French, this state of irritation was irremediable. I told him, however, that I would report the substance of this communication to your Lordship, although I could assure him that your Lordship could add nothing to the explanation which had been given, and in such detail, by Mr. Merry from your Lordship. The second point related to

Malta, and M. Talleyrand, with great solemnity, required of me to inform him, and this by the express order of the First Consul, what were his Majesty's intentions with regard to the evacuation of that island. He again on this occasion made great professions of his sincere desire to set aside everything which could interrupt the good understanding between the two Governments; adding that it was absolutely necessary that the French Government should know what it was meant to do when the clause in the Treaty of Amiens which stipulates the cession of Malta should be fully accomplished. He said that another Grand Master would now very soon be elected; that all the Powers of Europe invited so to do, with the exception of Russia, whose difficulties it was easy to remove, and without whom the guarantee would be equally complete (as indeed I fear it would be), were ready to come forward; and that consequently the term would very soon arrive when Great Britain could have no pretext for keeping long possession. In answer to M. Talleyrand I professed to be without instructions; that therefore I could not say what were his Majesty's intentions or what his Majesty's opinion might be of the changes which had taken place in the relative state of Europe since the conclusion of the Treaty of Amiens; but that I would report to your Lordship, and would have the honour of communicating to him your Lordship's answer as soon as I should receive it. Such was the nature of M. Talleyrand's communication, and I must do him the justice to acknowledge that there was nothing in his manner which could give the smallest offence.

Paris, January 27, 1803.

Colonel Sebastiani returned unexpectedly two days ago, and came from Genoa with a degree of expedition which might give reason to believe that his business was very urgent. He confirms the account of the total defeat of the Turks in Egypt, which he represents as so complete as to give the whole country to the Mamelukes, without any hope on the part of the Turks of recovering their influence. Under such circumstances the First Consul will not fail to renew his offers of assistance to the Porte, and under colour of such a concert endeavour to regain a footing in Egypt. There can, I think, be no doubt that the policy of the First Consul leans strongly this way, and it certainly will be incumbent upon us to watch his motions with the utmost attention. I cannot suppose that the appearance at Genoa of the four sail of the line and two frigates which sailed some time since from Brest, and were supposed to have gone round to Toulon to take in troops for St. Domingo, can be connected with the views of this Government on Egypt. It is, however, worthy of observation that at the same moment great complaints are made of the conduct of the Dey of Algiers, and vengeance denounced against him for a pretended insult offered to the French commercial agent. At all events, we have, and I trust shall continue to have, in the Mediterranean wherewithal to observe the motions, and to counteract them if necessary. The French army stationed in the Italian Republic has hitherto been maintained by that Government at the monthly expense of nearly two millions of livres. The President has now ordered that that sum shall henceforward be paid into the Treasury at Paris, but the charge of maintaining the army will in all probability, although the contrary is pretended, rest with the Italian Republic. The same measure may soon be expected in Holland, so that these States, and all those under similar circumstances, will now become strictly tributary, and in the aggregate will make a considerable increase in the revenue of this country.

P.S.—M. de Lima's successor, the Chevalier de Souza-Coutinho, proposes setting out on his way to England on Monday next. He has desired me to inform your Lordship that he has delayed his journey so long in the hope of seeing a favourable issue to the misunderstanding between the First Consul and the Court of Lisbon. All hope of a friendly compromise is now at an end. The Court of Lisbon has absolutely refused to discharge the Chevalier d'Almeida, and the First Consul has determined to send General Lannes back to Lisbon to resume his diplomatic functions.

Paris, January 31, 1803.

There is every reason to believe that the project which we have long attributed to the First Consul, of attacking the Barbary States, with the double view of seizing their treasures and of facilitating his views upon Egypt, is now near its execution. A pretext for a quarrel with the Dey of Algiers has been found in the importunity with which his agent here demanded the accomplishment of that clause in the treaty lately concluded which stipulated the immediate discharge of the debt due by the French Government to the Dey and to different individuals. This demand was reduced to four million piastres, and was due in part for naval stores furnished by Algerine merchants, and in part for the usual presents, which it was then agreed should be continued. The Dey has strictly complied with all the terms of this treaty, but when he required reciprocity on the part of the Government he was given to understand that he must be content with receiving 25 per cent. in paper, which when negotiated would produce about 10 per cent.; and that even for that he must wait the conveniency of the First Consul. After much altercation the agent has positively refused such a compromise, and when he demanded a passport to return it was refused him. Under these circumstances the Chargé d'Affaires of the Porte has called upon me requesting that I would report to your Lordship the above facts, and at the same time to assure your Lordship that, according to the latest intelligence he has received from the Porte, the Turkish Government is determined to support its vassals, and to oppose by every means in its power every step which tends to the re-occupation of Egypt by the First Consul, whether it be under the character of friend or foe. I assured him that I would lose no time in representing to your Lordship the purport of his communication, adding that I had no instructions upon the subject, but that, as far as my own private opinion went, I could not doubt that the same motives of friendship towards the Porte, to which might also be added those of self-security, would operate with equal effect, on any future occasion, upon his Majesty's councils, and call forth those good offices which such important interests might justly demand. In addition to this intelligence from the Turkish Chargé d'Affaires, I have the authority of the Danish and Swedish Ministers, to both of whom M. Talleyrand has given it to be understood that the First Consul was determined to crush the Dey of Algiers, and required the assistance of their Courts for that purpose. The Danish Minister, as he told me himself, expressed in warm terms the obligations his Court would feel for such a benefit; but the Swede was more reserved. I endeavoured to convince them of the little cause they had to be thankful, since their interests entered but very little indeed into the calculations of the First Consul. We may, however, soon expect to hear this project announced to the several Courts of Europe, dressed up in all the tinsel of French philanthropy and French public spirit. An appeal will in all probability be made to Great Britain, and his Majesty be invited to lend his aid, or at least to give his sanction, to such measures as, under the cloak of the most generous feelings, are directed against his dearest interests. In case your Lordship should not have received the 'Moniteur' of yesterday, I enclose it. Your Lordship will there see such a detail of the expedition of Colonel Sebastiani as evidently proves the projects of the First Consul. His observations on an English general officer of the highest merit are highly indecent in an official paper, and would be much more disgusting were not abuse from such a quarter rather flattering than offensive. Count Cobenzl has not yet dared to communicate to me a copy of the Convention of December 26, and it is from Vienna that I now receive it. The accomplishment is still subject to much litigation. The point now in dispute relates to a small strip of territory lying immediately contiguous to the suburbs of Passau, and which Count Cobenzl consented to cede, although he wished it might not be inserted in the treaty. He now hesitates to fulfil this agreement, but must give way. This is indeed but too much the case on every occasion. I have no doubt that such language as Mr. Paget mentions in his despatch, which accompanies this, has on many occasions been held to Count Cobenzl. The treatment he experiences is humiliating in the extreme, and nothing would be able to reconcile the most indifferent observer, were it not that his own conduct is so marked by meanness as to entitle him to no respect whatsoever. As a proof of that in which his own Court is held, I have frequently heard it calculated by generals who are supposed to be in the confidence of the First Consul that the total destruction of the House of Austria would be the business of one very short campaign; and I am almost afraid to think that their calculation is just. I mentioned in my last despatch that General Lannes was shortly to return to Lisbon; this is now announced in the official prints, accompanied by a public acknowledgment from the First Consul of his eminent services there, and recommending to him on his return to his post to continue to protect the French trade, as he had already begun to do in the first year of his mission. Such a justification of the most ungentlemanly conduct on the part of General Lannes requires no comment. Since writing this despatch I have deciphered Lord Elgin's despatches. Had I seen them before the conversation with M. Talleyrand which made the subject of my last despatch, I doubt whether I should not have been tempted to assert that, after such an unequivocal avowal on the part of France of its intention to interfere in the affairs of Egypt, his Majesty would not be justified in evacuating Malta. By a late *arrêté* of this Government a diminution of two-thirds of the former duty is allowed on the importation of sal-ammoniac from Egypt.

Paris, February 3, 1803.

I cannot think it an unfavourable symptom for the repose of Europe when the capital affords nothing sufficiently interesting to justify my giving your Lordship much trouble. My despatch, therefore, by this message will be short. We have many reports respecting the forlorn situation of the remains of the French army in St. Domingo, as well as of a resolution on the part of the First Consul to abandon the undertaking altogether. This is so contrary to the known character of the man, and so subversive of his hopes of regenerating his navy, which he well knows can be done only by means of his colonies, that I cannot bring myself to believe that he hesitates about it. It is, however, certain that the service is so unpopular as to have rendered the reinforcing that army not only a matter of difficulty but of danger, and it becomes extremely interesting to see how far the First Consul, who has hitherto carried all before him, will now submit to control, and from such a quarter. If, however, the project is abandoned, it must be imputed to this cause, notwithstanding the different motives which may be assigned. It would be difficult to account for Count Marcoff's continuing to flatter himself that he shall still be able to procure Piombino, and even the Island of Elba, for the King of Sardinia, in addition to the part of the Siennese and the Presidi of Tuscany which is offered him; but he assures me that the case is not hopeless. Certainly the refusal of his Sardinian Majesty to accede to any formal act of renunciation of his original possessions, or to admit on any terms the word compensation, will not facilitate the negotiation. Such, however, M. Marcoff tells me, is the case. I yesterday had an opportunity of seeing Colonel Sebastiani at M. Talleyrand's at dinner; when, without any observation on my part which could lead to such a conduct, he recanted everything he had said in his report disrespectful to General Stuart, and mentioned him in terms of great esteem.

Paris, February 7, 1803.

I have the honour to acknowledge the receipt of your Lordship's separate despatch of January 28, enclosing a letter and its enclosures from Mr. King to Mr. Hammond. The change in the conduct of the American Minister towards me is too obvious not to be remarked, and tends, perhaps, to confirm your Lordship's observation of the natural understanding and concert between all those countries exposed to the policy of France, which the conduct of that Government cannot fail to produce. Whatever may be the cause, I have certainly of late found Mr. Livingstone more than usually cordial, and although not very confidential yet professing that his instructions strictly enjoined him to be so. Should this be really the effect of a system, your Lordship will have perceived symptoms of it from other quarters. It is, however, natural to suppose that the American policy, like that of every other country not immediately under the rod of France, will be to play off such an appearance of cordiality and concert with Great Britain, as a demonstration against the Government, and for the attainment of any particular object. Mr. Livingstone is inclined to think that the acquisition of the Floridas will not be attempted at this moment; but I think it not unreasonable to suppose that, should the difficulties of subduing St. Domingo be such as to induce the First Consul to renounce the enterprise, he will turn all the means which were destined for that object to the accomplishment of his views on Louisiana and the Floridas, as affording some compensation to his vanity, and a means, although remote, of annoying the British colonies and trade. Whatever may be the resolution of the First Consul, we may be sure that his views on Egypt will not be abandoned. All his feelings are engaged in the object; and although the subject is avoided, M. Talleyrand having never touched upon it since the conversation which I reported to your Lordship in my despatch No. 8, yet I have every reason to be convinced that it is uppermost in the First Consul's thoughts. In a very short time we must expect to be summoned again to evacuate

Malta. The nomination of a Grand Master is expected daily. I cannot take upon myself to premise what may be his Majesty's determination, but I do not hesitate to declare to your Lordship my perfect conviction that from the moment that Malta is under the influence of France—which it must be from the moment that his Majesty's troops are withdrawn—we can no longer depend on the preservation of peace on any terms with this country, supposing that the occupation of Egypt by France is to be resisted. As long as the two important points of Malta and Alexandria are ours, their views on Egypt must be suspended; but our retreat will be the signal for their advancing. These reflections and many others will have occurred to your Lordship, and they will certainly go far to justify an assertion, however paradoxical it may appear, that the continuance of peace does not depend upon our fulfilling, under the present circumstances, the Treaty of Amiens, but on keeping in our hands those possessions, the immediate reoccupation of which by the French would force us into a war under every disadvantage, and for the doing of which we have such sufficient justification in the conduct of the First Consul from the moment of the treaty to this very day. It is said that a considerable body of troops in Corsica—as many as eight thousand—is preparing for embarkation. The French ships which sailed some time ago from Brest are still at Genoa, as well as those under the command of Admiral de Winter. It is possible this force may be destined, as was originally given out, either for St. Domingo or the continent of America; it is also possible that it may be employed in the Mediterranean. Such is the impetuosity of the First Consul, and his impatience of control, that we should be prepared to meet the most daring attempt.

Paris, February 7, 1803.

Since writing the preceding despatch I have had a conversation by appointment with M. Talleyrand, in which it was evidently his object to endeavour to do away every suspicion to which the publication of Colonel Sebastiani's report might have given rise. He assured me that the object of that officer's mission was solely commercial and for the purpose of ascertaining how far it might be practicable to resume the former habits of trade between France and the countries which he had visited; that it was true he had been instructed to ascertain the fact of the British army remaining in Alexandria, and, if there, to inquire with what intention and for what length of time; that if he had gone beyond the line of his instructions and had entered into any military detail or speculation, it must be imputed solely to the zeal and ardour of a young officer, too hastily presuming that from the circumstance of so important a clause in the Treaty of Amiens being so long unaccomplished the British Government looked to a renewal of hostilities. He then read to me a letter which he had, by the express orders of the First Consul, written to General Andréossy (which letter was sent last night by a messenger), enjoining that ambassador, and in rather peremptory language, to demand on what motives his Majesty's troops continued in Egypt, and when they, as well as the garrison of Malta, would be withdrawn in compliance with the tenth article of the Treaty of Amiens. As the communication was made to me in order that I might be convinced of the justice of the demand, I thought myself at liberty to enter into some kind of explanation on the subject, and I will confess to your Lordship that I was not sorry to have an opportunity, professedly without instructions from your Lordship, of preparing this Government for those difficulties in the accomplishment of their wishes which, I hope and trust, they will yet experience. I expressed myself, therefore, extremely glad to learn from M. Talleyrand the real motives of Colonel Sebastiani's mission, and the more so as I conceived it to be of the very utmost importance that every cause of jealousy or of suspicion on so interesting an object should be removed. I took upon myself to assure him that could the stipulation in the Treaty of Amiens which related to Malta have been carried into effect in any reasonable time after its conclusion, that island would in course have been evacuated by the British troops; that his Majesty had been induced to keep possession of it, at a very considerable expense, because that clause had not been fulfilled; but I could not undertake to say that no other motive had since occurred. Various had been the reports respecting the views of the First Consul. Many of them must have reached his Majesty's Ministers, and they would all be now in a great measure confirmed by the plain and candid avowal of the agent deputed by the First Consul ostensibly with a view to prepare the way for the reoccupation of Egypt. This publication of intentions so hostile to the interests of Great Britain would naturally have an effect on the public in England, as well as on his Majesty's Ministers. I represented, therefore, to him how highly important it was that such causes of suspicion should be entirely done away, lest the object of the present reclamation might be still subject to further delay and difficulty. He immediately felt the drift of my argument and interrupted me, denying any the smallest intention of the First Consul's again interfering in the affairs of Egypt; that he was heartily tired of Egypt; that he positively had no other views than those which he had already told me, and which were purely commercial. And he even went so far as to give me his *word of honour* that we might implicitly depend upon this assertion of the First Consul. Your Lordship may be assured that I felt the full weight of such an assurance, but I desired him nevertheless to consider how necessary it was that every suspicion should be removed in order that there should remain no pretence for still further delay, and I gave him fairly to understand that until perfect confidence was restored the First Consul must be prepared for every measure of precaution on the part of his Majesty's Government which an object so nearly connected with the dearest interests of Great Britain must demand. M. Talleyrand had, I suppose, nothing more convincing to offer than what he had already advanced on the strength of his own veracity. I maintained the same language, and thus I think I have prepared him to receive without any degree of surprise whatever may be his Majesty's resolution on this important point. Such, therefore, is the ground on which we now stand; and I trust your Lordship will think with me that, every circumstance considered, it is not unfavourable. The First Consul will now be prepared, if M. Talleyrand makes a faithful report, to consider as an object of negotiation that which the natural ardour of his imagination, and his impatience perhaps to accomplish his ends, had brought him to believe was already within his grasp. This conversation, although touching upon points of great irritation, was carried on without any appearance of ill-humour, and concluded with great cordiality by my engaging him to dine with me two days after. The enclosed paper, containing a report of some pretended design on some individual here, was at the same time given to me by M. Talleyrand. I must do him the justice to say that he did it with reluctance, and apologised for troubling me with such a business. I told him that if the First Consul gave himself the trouble to attend to such idle stories I could not do less than take upon myself that of transmitting them to your Lordship. I should think, however, that the matter requires no further notice, unless your Lordship should think proper to mention it to General Andréossy.

Croyez-vous qu'on s'occupe encore d'un projet d'enterrement semblable à celui de Clément de Ris? que cet enterrement doit tomber, si l'on peut, sur un fonctionnaire supérieur? que, pour se mettre à l'abri des poursuites de la police, on transportera le prisonnier *en lieu sûr*? qu'alors on redemandera la liberté de Bourmont et des autres chefs de Chouans, qu'on dit arrêtés par une violation manifeste des traités faits avec eux, et qu'on ne rendra qu'après leur délivrance l'ôtage qui aurait été enterré? Ce complot a été tramé chez Georges, qui réside à cinq milles de Londres, afin d'être moins observé, et chez qui se tiennent souvent des conciliabules nombreux. Celui qui a, dit-on, donné cette idée, et à qui les principaux moyens d'exécution seront confiés, est un aventurier qui se fait appeler Marquis de la Chapelle, et qui demeure près de

Portman Square. Les auteurs du complot ont dans l'île de Jersey quelques points où ils croeint pouvoir descendre en sûreté et cacher leur prisonnier sans que le gouvernement de l'île en soit instruit, ni que la police de Paris puisse en avoir la moindre connaissance. On assure que c'est là le *lieu sûr* où ils retiendraient l'ôtage qu'ils se préparent à enterrer. On avait cru jusqu'à présent qu'il n'y avait qu'un comité distributeur des secours aux malheureux émigrés : il y en a un second, absolument distinct et n'ayant aucune communication avec le premier, pour les Vendéens. Georges est le chef suprême de celui-ci, accordant des pensions à qui il lui plaît et les fixant à sa volonté. La Chapelle reçoit deux guinées par jour, indépendamment de huit shellings pour sa femme et de trois pour ses enfants. Le séjour des Princes à Edimbourg fait l'orgueil de la noblesse. Tous s'intéressent à leur sort, et il n'y a personne qui ne déclame contre le Gouvernement français. On voit cependant de mauvais œil que le Prince n'appelle pas auprès de lui son épouse, et qu'il a logé sa maîtresse dans une petite maison isolée qui n'est qu'à dix pas de son palais.

Lord Hawkesbury to Lord Whitworth.

Downing Street, February 9, 1803.

Your Excellency's despatches to No. 10 inclusive have been received and laid before the King. In answer to your Excellency's despatch No. —, relative to the inquiry made of you by the French Government on the subject of Malta, I can have no difficulty in assuring you that his Majesty has entertained a most sincere desire that the Treaty of Amiens might be executed in a full and complete manner; but it has not been possible for him to consider this treaty as having been founded on principles different from those which have been invariably applied to every other antecedent treaty or convention, namely, that they were negotiated with reference to the actual state of possession of the different parties, and of the treaties or public engagements by which they were bound at the time of its conclusion; and that if that state of possession and of engagements was so materially altered by the act of either of the parties as to affect the nature of the compact itself, the other party has a right, according to the law of nations, to interfere for the purpose of obtaining satisfaction or compensation for any essential difference which such acts may have subsequently made in their relative situation; that if there ever was a case to which this principle might be applied with peculiar propriety it was that of the late Treaty of Peace, for the negotiation was conducted on a basis not merely proposed by his Majesty, but specially agreed to in an official note by the French Government, viz. that his Majesty should keep a compensation out of his conquests for the important acquisitions of territory made by France upon the Continent. This is a sufficient proof that the compact was understood to have been concluded with reference to the then existing state of things; for the measure of his Majesty's compensation was to be calculated with reference to the acquisitions of France at that time; and if the interference of the French Government in the general affairs of Europe since that period; if their interposition with respect to Switzerland and Holland, whose independence was guaranteed by them at the time of the conclusion of the Treaty of Peace; if the annexations which have been made to France in various quarters, but particularly those in Italy, have extended the territory and increased the power of the French Government, his Majesty would be warranted, consistently with the spirit of the Treaty of Peace, in claiming equivalents for these acquisitions, as some counterpoise to the augmentation of the power of France. His Majesty, however, anxious to prevent all ground of misunderstanding, and desirous of consolidating the general peace of Europe as far as might be in his power, was willing to have waived the pretensions he might have a right to advance of this nature; and as the other articles of the Definitive Treaty have been in a course of execution, which, according to its terms, has been rendered impracticable by circumstances which it was not in his Majesty's power to controul, a communication to your Lordship had accordingly been prepared conformably to this disposition when the attention of his Majesty's Government was attracted by the very extraordinary publication of the report of Colonel Sebastiani to the First Consul. It is impossible for his Majesty to view this report in any other light than an official publication; for, without referring particularly to explanations which have been repeatedly given upon the subject of publications in the 'Moniteur,' the publication in question, as it purports to be the report to the First Consul of an accredited agent, as it appears to have been signed by Colonel Sebastiani himself, and as it is published in the official paper, with an official title affixed to it, must be considered as authorised by the French Government. This report contains the most unjustifiable insinuations and charges against his Majesty's Government, against the officer who commanded his forces in Egypt, and against the British army in the quarter—insinuations and charges wholly destitute of foundation, and such as would warrant his Majesty in demanding that satisfaction which, on occasions of this nature, independent Powers in a state of amity have a right to expect from each other; that it discloses, moreover, views in the highest degree injurious to the interests of his Majesty's dominions and directly repugnant to and utterly inconsistent with the spirit and letter of the Treaty of Peace concluded between his Majesty and the French Government; and that his Majesty would feel that he was wanting in a proper regard to the honour of his crown and to the interests of his dominions if he could see with indifference such a system developed and avowed. His Majesty cannot, therefore, regard the conduct of the French Government on various occasions since the conclusion of the Definitive Treaty, the insinuations and charges contained in the report of Colonel Sebastiani, and the views which the report discloses, without feeling it necessary for him distinctly to declare that it will be impossible for him to enter into any further discussion relative to Malta unless he receives a satisfactory explanation on the subject of this communication. Your Excellency is desired to take an early opportunity of fully explaining his Majesty's sentiments as above stated to the French Government; but you will refrain from making any written communication on the subject without further orders from his Majesty.

Lord Whitworth to Lord Hawkesbury.

Paris, February 11, 1803.

I did not mean to have troubled your Lordship at all by this messenger, and I do so now merely to communicate to your Lordship the copy of a letter which I received late last night from M. de Talleyrand, with the answer which I wrote to him. I beg leave to refer your Lordship to the 'Morning Post' of February 1 for the article which has given such disgust. And it must be confessed that the editor has upon this occasion left his colleagues far behind him. It certainly would contribute not only to silence the abuse which daily appears in the French prints, but also essentially to allay the extreme irritation in the First Consul, could some satisfaction be given on this occasion.

Lord Whitworth to M. de Talleyrand.

Paris, le 11 Février 1803.

Monsieur,—Je reçois comme une marque de votre confiance la communication que vous venez de me faire, et je vous prie de croire que je suis aussi dégoûté de la lecture que vous m'avez proposée, que vous avez pu l'être vous-même. Ce n'est plus la liberté mais l'anarchie de la presse qui tolère de pareilles indécences, et je désire de toute mon âme qu'il existe dans le Gouvernement le pouvoir d'en punir l'auteur. Si son jugement était soumis à un juré qui pensât comme moi, il sentirait toute la rigueur de la loi, et il me semble véritablement que celui dont il est question dans ce moment s'y est exposé. Au reste je ne manquerai pas d'en faire un rapport fidèle à ma cour, et je réitère mes vœux pour qu'il soit aussi facile au Gouvernement anglois de réprimer de pareils abus qu'il le seroit au Gouvernement françois. Je me permettrai même d'ajouter que les occasions d'exercer ce pouvoir de la part du dernier ne se présentent que trop fréquemment, à mon très grand regret. Je saisis cette occasion pour renouveler à Votre Excellence l'assurance de ma haute considération.

(Signed) WHITWORTH.

M. DE TALLEYRAND TO LORD WHITWORTH.

Paris, le 22 Pluviose (February 11), 1803.

My Lord,—Dans la conversation que j'eus l'honneur d'avoir avec vous il y a quelques jours, et dans laquelle je trouvai vos sentimens si bien d'accord avec les miens sur les rapports de nos deux pays, je m'engageai avec plaisir à vous communiquer immédiatement tout sujet de plainte que mon Gouvernement pourroit avoir contre le vôtre, persuadé que vous seriez empressé d'en prévenir les effets. Je vous adresse donc aujourd'hui un numéro du 'Morning Post' dont je vous invite à supporter la dégoûtante lecture. Je m'abstiens de toute réflexion et je laisse à votre excellent esprit le soin de juger s'il est possible qu'en Europe, en France, on s'imagine que le Gouvernement britannique n'a pas le moyen d'empêcher ou de punir de pareilles horreurs, et si leur publication tolérée ne doit pas nuire essentiellement aux relations des deux Etats.

Agréez, My Lord, l'assurance de ma haute considération.

(Signé) M. TALLEYRAND.

Lord Whitworth to Lord Hawkesbury.

Paris, February 14, 1803.

I have the honour to acknowledge the receipt of your Lordship's despatch of January 9, with its several enclosures, by Basilico. He arrived here the night before last at eleven o'clock, and I forwarded him the next day at twelve. I beg leave to assure your Lordship that I shall have very particular pleasure in executing the instructions with which I am furnished by this occasion. Your Lordship will perceive by my despatch No. 12 that I had in some degree anticipated them by preparing this Government for such a determination, and I flatter myself the communication I have now to make will be received without any extraordinary surprise or marks of displeasure. I am particularly gratified with the intelligence your Lordship gives me from Petersburg, as it justifies the opinion I have ever entertained. I should have been cruelly disappointed if the Emperor had thrown himself so decidedly into the arms of France as some had imagined. A system of observation on the part of Great Britain and Russia will, I should hope, be sufficient to check the ambitious career of the First Consul; and such a system, I am happy to see, is now almost brought to bear. The arrival of a Russian officer, an aide-de-camp of the Emperor, has in the meantime excited great curiosity amongst my colleagues, as well as mine. He came about ten days ago, and was kept very close till he had been presented to the First Consul; he had a private audience three days after his arrival, and delivered a letter from the Emperor his master. He appeared on the last public day at the Tuileries, and although he had never been presented in public he was invited to the dinner, contrary to the established etiquette. I have not, however, been able to learn with any degree of certainty whether he has been charged with any important mission. Count Marcoff assures me not, and seems to laugh at the alarm which is excited amongst the politicians. He tells me that the letter from the Emperor was merely complimentary, and that the distinction with which General Hittorff has been treated must be attributed solely to the desire of the First Consul to gain the Emperor by every act of attention and flattery. He says the object of this officer's journey and stay here is to see a little into the discipline in the army, and to collect anything worthy of imitation in the interior economy of the Government considered in a military point of view. This may be true; but my confidence in Count Marcoff is not blind, and I shall not give him entire credit till the statement is confirmed from other quarters. Some people here imagine that the partition of Turkey is not decidedly opposed, and that the Emperor of Russia begins to yield to the temptation. It is certain that when I first mentioned the subject of General Hittorff's arrival to Count Marcoff he immediately said: 'Je parie qu'on dit qu'il est de nouveau question du partage de la Turquie.' This, then, was certainly uppermost in his mind, and the point on which he was most anxious to satisfy me. He appeared, however, at the same time so convinced of the little advantage which Russia would reap from such a measure, and of the danger to Russia as well as the rest of Europe of lending a hand to the increase of the already so enormous power of France, that one can scarcely believe any man capable of acting so directly in contradiction to such sentiments, founded as they are upon truth and good policy. There is, however, a strange coincidence in the movements we see in Italy and in the Mediterranean. The rendezvous of so many ships of war at Genoa; the report which was so industriously spread, and which now appears at least doubtful, that they were to take in troops for St. Domingo; the assembling of a large body of troops in Corsica, evidently placed there not for the purpose of keeping that country in subjection, but with some view to the Mediterranean; the journey of Louis Bonaparte which was to have taken place about a month ago, and which now, without any plausible reason, is deferred; the supposed concert with Russia, and the extreme and more than usual irritation of the First Consul against England: all these circumstances, and many others which might be added, certainly do create a belief that some great operation was intended to be carried into effect at this time, and it has been prevented or delayed by some unforeseen event, to the great disappointment and mortification of the First Consul. In my own opinion, the event which has had so salutary an effect is no other than the delay which has taken place in the evacuation of Alexandria and Malta. It was calculated that by this time the Treaty of Amiens would have been fulfilled in all points, and the movements we see are the effects of this calculation. This, if not founded—and no one wishes more than myself that it may not be so—is at least fair ground for conjecture, and such as must command every measure of vigilance and precaution on our part. There are those who imagine that all this preparation is destined against Algiers. But this is perhaps doing the Dey too much honour; at least, if such is the intention of the First Consul, it must be considered as the forerunner only of more important attempts. It appears by recent accounts that the three French sail of the line at Genoa under the command of Rear-Admiral Bidon have taken on board two thousand men of the Polish demi-brigade, and have steered to the eastward. They were joined by another French ship from Leghorn, likewise with troops on board. It is said that they were destined for St. Domingo. Sir Richard Bickerton will long ere this have been able to ascertain the truth of this report. There is at this moment a considerable movement of the troops in the Belgick. They are drawing towards Havre and Dunkirk, where all the transports which can be collected are appointed to assemble and take them on board. Two thousand men from Brussels are ordered to march to Lisle, where they are to receive their further orders; and volunteers from the different departments are collecting in the same quarter. It is given out—and I am not inclined to doubt it—that they are destined for St. Domingo. But we are too well acquainted with the character of this Government and the great object of all its policy not to follow all their movements with the most suspicious vigilance. There is nothing hostile or perfidious that we may not expect if we lay ourselves open to an attack.

Paris, February 17, 1803.

I have the honour to acquaint your Lordship that I saw M. Talleyrand on Tuesday last for the purpose of carrying into effect your Lordship's instructions of the 9th instant. It was my wish to give no extraordinary degree of solemnity to the communication I had to make to him, but rather to have it considered as a matter of course, and one on which we did not expect to be much at issue with this Government. I did not, therefore, write to him to desire a conference, but called upon him in the morning, when I knew he would be at leisure. I began by telling him that I had nothing new to communicate to him, but merely to confirm officially that which I had already from myself promised. I did not, however, pass over with the same indifference the arguments with which your Lordship has furnished me—I recapitulated them all: the principle on which the Treaty of Amiens was founded, and the right which naturally arose from that principle of interference on our part for the purpose of obtaining satisfaction or compensation for any essential difficulties which may have arisen in the relative situation of the two countries. I instanced the cases, beginning with Italy and concluding with Switzerland, in which the territory or influence of France had been extended subsequent to the Treaty of Amiens. I represented to him that this principle of compensation had been fully and formally admitted by the French Government in the course of the negotiation at Amiens. I then told him that, notwithstanding the indisputable right which his Majesty might have derived of claiming some counterpoise for such acquisitions, instructions were actually preparing for me, by which I should have been empowered to declare his Majesty's readiness to carry into effect the full intent of the tenth article of the treaty, when the attention of his Majesty's Government was roused by the official publication of Colonel Sebastiani's report to the First Consul. It was useless to recapitulate the particulars of this very extraordinary report, but I appealed to him whether it was not of a nature, exclusive of the personal allusions it contained, to excite the utmost jealousy in the minds of his Majesty's Ministers and to demand on their part every measure of precaution. I concluded with the distinct declaration that it was impossible for his Majesty to enter into any further discussion relative to Malta unless he received satisfactory explanations on the subject of the First Consul's views. M. de Talleyrand in his reply did not attempt to dispute the drift of my argument. He admitted, in an affected tone of candour, that the jealousy we felt on the score of Egypt, with a view to our possession in India, was natural. But he could not admit that anything had appeared in the conduct of the French Government in justification of the alarm we expressed. After repeating what he had said to me in a former conversation on the subject of Sebastiani's mission, which he asserted to be strictly commercial, he expatiated at great length on the sincere desire of the First Consul to maintain inviolable the peace which had been so lately concluded; adding that the situation of the French finances was such, that, were not this desire of peace in the First Consul an effect of system, it would be most imperiously dictated to him by the total impossibility in which this country found itself of carrying on that extensive state of warfare which even a partial rupture would naturally lead to. This was the argument on which he laid the greatest stress; and so anxious was he to convince me, that he would, if that had been possible, have exaggerated the reduced state of their resources. He expressed great surprise, therefore, that any suspicion should attach when the means of disturbing the public tranquillity were, as must be well known in England, so completely wanting, and desired to know what was the nature and degree of satisfaction which his Majesty would require. On this I told him that I had no instructions; that I could not pretend to say by what means those apprehensions which the conduct of this Government had raised in England were to be allayed; but I could assure him that in the discussion of them we should be animated solely by a sincere desire to be convinced of the truth of his assertions, since on that depended the peace and happiness of Europe. I took this opportunity of assuring him that although, according to his statement of the situation of France, we might possess in a greater degree the means of supporting the expense of a war, since those means arose from sources which even a state of warfare did not dry up, yet such was his Majesty's sincere desire of maintaining peace, that nothing but absolute and unavoidable necessity would ever induce him to deprive his subjects of the blessings which they begin to enjoy. Such was the purport of my conference with M. de Talleyrand, and I trust that I have succeeded at least in enabling them without any extraordinary degree of irritation to view only as an object of negotiation that which was considered as one of certainty; and such a transition, in a mind like that of the First Consul, and in pursuit of so favourite an object, is not without its share of danger. It remains now to be seen what is the kind of satisfaction which they can give or we receive. On this point we may be as difficult as we please, and we cannot be too much so. But at the same time we negotiated with that in hand which will, I am persuaded, more effectually insure the continuance of peace than any concession whatsoever. I have had occasion to converse with the Spanish Ambassador on the discussion which has arisen with his Court on the subject of Honduras, and he seems fully persuaded that the proposal of reverting to the Convention of 1786 will be accepted without much hesitation. He assures me that the difficulties which have arisen have not been suggested by this Government.

Paris, February 17, 1803.

The termination of the German indemnifications is retarded by the difficulty in finding for the Elector of Bavaria an equivalent for the cession which he has been obliged to make of the Bishopric of Eichstadt to the House of Austria, and likewise by the difficulty in finding a source from whence to draw the three hundred and fifty thousand florins wanted to complete the revenue of the Elector Archchancellor, who estimated that the territories granted to him will not produce above six hundred and fifty thousand florins annually instead of a million which has been assigned to him; and such is the condescension towards him that there is a disposition to admit this calculation, although it is well known that those territories are fully equal to produce the sum required. In order to satisfy this demand, together with some claims, it has been proposed to establish moderate tolls upon the navigation of the Rhine. The ancient tolls, which were indeed exacted with much vexation on the part of petty princes along that river, amounted to two millions and a half of florins. It has been determined to restrict them to eight hundred thousand florins annually, but the King of Prussia, who has not abolished those belonging to him, has acted in this respect in the same manner as with regard to the *Biens Médiats* expressly reserved by the original plan of the mediating Power, and he still maintains them after a hard struggle. Bonaparte, at present extremely complaisant towards the Court of Berlin, has yielded or is on the point of yielding in this particular, as he has already done on the question of the *Biens Médiats*, and has not turned his thoughts to another plan sent from Ratisbon, which consists in withdrawing a portion of the revenues granted to the Teutonic Order and to the Order of Malta. It must be acknowledged that these bodies have been treated with some degree of liberality, and it appears that after deducting a fourth part from the Teutonic Order its revenue will amount to near eight hundred thousand florins. Thus the matter rests for the present.

Paris, February 17, 1803.

The interior of the Consular family is at this moment in a state of discord. Lucien is at daggers drawn with the First Consul. This last was heard to say to him in a fit of rage that he only repented he had not had him executed on the Place de Grêve like a brigand as he was, and the other replied, 'What! Are you such a fool as to imagine I am to be treated like a Frenchman?' In the meantime a perfect reconciliation has taken place between the First Consul and General Lannes. He lately took an opportunity of declaring in public that General Lannes was a very estimable character, and that he had only committed some few *légèretés*, which were very excusable. It is, however, remarked that since the conversation which General Lannes has had with the First Consul the Consular guard has mounted with loaded arms and their pouches filled with cartridges, and that their pay has been augmented to thirty sols a day, which makes an annual expense of 1,200,000 livres. It is inferred from all this that Lannes, who had been much sought after by Moreau and the discontented generals, has betrayed to the First Consul what he has been able to draw from them, and this will naturally have been considered by the First Consul, uneasy and suspicious as he is, as a most important service. The discussion which has arisen at Stockholm on a point of etiquette between Mr. Arbuthnot and the French Minister, but which appears to be nothing more than a very natural civility to the former, and always customary when a Prince of any particular Minister is on a visit to the Court, has drawn down upon the Swedish Minister here such a reprisal as might be expected from the irritability of the First Consul. He addressed him on Sunday last at the Tuileries loud enough to be heard by all who were around him, and said: 'Je suis fâché, Monsieur, d'apprendre ce que le ministre de la République me mande de Stockholm. Il est étonnant que le roi de Suède ait oublié la reconnaissance qu'il doit à la France; mais je suis encore plus étonné que pendant que les plus grandes Puissances s'empressent à se témoigner réciproquement toutes sortes d'égards, un prince qui peut à peine prétendre à être compté parmi les Puissances du troisième ordre puisse se permettre une pareille licence. Je pourrai user de représailles envers vous, mais je ne le ferai pas.' He then turned upon his heel and walked away. He afterwards addressed himself to me and to many others with great good humour, and talked on indifferent subjects, as if his temper had not been at all ruffled. I confess I did not suspect him of being so completely master of his feelings.

Paris, February 21, 1803.

It is to be feared that his Majesty's determination with regard to Malta will not be adopted by this Government without a struggle. My last despatch, in which I gave your Lordship an account of my conference with M. de Talleyrand, was scarcely gone when I received a note from him informing me that the First Consul wished to converse with me, and desired that I would come to him at the Tuileries at nine o'clock. He received me in his cabinet with tolerable cordiality, and after talking on different subjects for a few minutes he desired me to sit down, as he himself did on the other side of the table, upon which he placed his elbows, and began. He told me that he felt it necessary, after what had passed between me and M. de Talleyrand, that he should in the most clear and authentic manner make known his sentiments to me in order to their being communicated to his Majesty; and he conceived this would be more effectually done by himself than through any medium whatever. He said that it was a matter of infinite disappointment to him that the Treaty of Amiens, instead of being followed by conciliation and friendship, the natural effects of peace, had been productive only of continual and increasing jealousy and mistrust, and that this mistrust was avowed in such a manner as must bring the point to an issue. He now enumerated the several provocations which he pretended to have received from England. He placed in the first line our not evacuating Malta and Alexandria as we were bound to do by the treaty.

In this he said that no consideration on earth should make him acquiesce; and of the two he had rather see us in possession of the Faubourg St. Antoine than Malta. He then adverted to the abuse thrown out against him in the English public prints, but this he said he did not so much regard as that which appeared in the French papers published in London, and particularised one, which he said was paid by Lord Pelham; this he considered as much more mischievous, since it was meant to excite this country against him and his Government. He complained of the protection given to Georges and others of his description, who, instead of being sent to Canada, as had been repeatedly promised, were permitted to remain in England, handsomely pensioned, and constantly committing all sorts of crimes on the coasts of France, as well as in the interior. In confirmation of this he told me that two men had within these few days been apprehended in Normandy, and were now on their way to Paris, who were hired assassins, and employed by the Bishop of Arras, by the Baron de Rolle, by Georges, and by Duteille, as would be fully proved in a court of justice and made known to the world. He acknowledged that the irritation he felt against England increased daily, because every wind (I make use as much as I can of his own ideas and expressions) which blew from England brought nothing but enmity and hatred against him. He now went back to Egypt, and told me that if he had felt the smallest inclination to take possession of it by force he might have done it a month ago (as I am firmly persuaded he would have done but for the precautions we had taken) by sending twenty-five thousand men to Aboukir, who would have possessed themselves of the whole country in defiance of the four thousand British in Alexandria; that instead of that garrison being a means of protecting Egypt it was only furnishing him with a pretence for invading it. This he should not do, whatever might be his desire to have it as a colony, because he did not think it worth the risk of a war, in which he might perhaps be considered as the aggressor, and by which he should lose more than he could gain, since sooner or later Egypt would belong to France, either by the falling to pieces of the Turkish Empire, or by some arrangement with the Porte. As a proof of his desire to maintain peace, he wished to know what he had to gain by going to war with England. A descent was the only means of offence he had, and that he was determined to attempt, by putting himself at the head of the expedition. But how could it be supposed that after having gained the height on which he stood, that after having raised himself from little more than a common soldier to the head of the most powerful country on the Continent, he would risk his life and reputation in such a hazardous attempt, unless forced to it by necessity, when the chances were that he and the greatest part of the expedition would go to the bottom of the sea? He talked much on this subject, but never attempted to diminish the danger. He acknowledged that there were one hundred chances to one against him; but still he was determined to attempt it if war should be the consequence of the present discussion; and that such was the disposition of the troops (he then had perhaps in his mind the five or six generals who were loitering in his antechamber) that army after army would be found for the enterprise. He then expatiated much on the natural force of the two countries: France with an army of four hundred and eighty thousand men—for to this amount it is, he said, to be immediately completed, all ready for the most desperate enterprises; and England with a fleet that made her mistress of the seas, and which he (modestly) did not think he should be able to equal in less than ten years. Two such countries by a proper understanding might govern the world, but by their strifes might overturn it. He said that if he had not felt the enmity of the British Government on every occasion since the Treaty of Amiens, there would have been nothing that he would not have done to prove his desire to conciliate—participation in indemnities, as well as in influence on the Continent, treaties of commerce, in short anything that could have given satisfaction and have testified his friendship. Nothing, however, had been able to conquer the hatred of the British Government, and therefore it was now come to the point whether we should have peace or war. To preserve peace the Treaty of Amiens must be fulfilled; the abuse in the public prints, if not totally suppressed, at least kept within bounds, and confined to the English papers; and the protection so openly given to his bitterest enemies (alluding to Georges and suchlike) must be withdrawn. If war, it was necessary only to say so, and to refuse to fulfil the treaty. He now made the tour of Europe to prove to me that in its present state there was no Power with which we could coalesce for the purpose of making war against France; consequently it was our interest to gain time and, if we had any point to gain, renew the war when circumstances were more favourable. He said it was not doing him justice to suppose that he conceived himself above the opinion of his country or of Europe. He would not risk uniting Europe against him by any violent act of aggression; neither was he so powerful in France as to persuade the nation to go to war, unless on good grounds. He said that he had not chastised the Algerians from his unwillingness to excite the jealousy of other Powers, but he hoped that England, Russia, and France would one day feel that it was their interest to destroy such a nest of thieves and force them to live rather by cultivating their land than by plunder. In the little I said to him—for he gave me in the course of two hours but very few opportunities of saying a word—I confined myself strictly to the tenor of your Lordship's instructions. I urged them in the same manner as I had done to M. de Talleyrand, and dwelt as strongly as I could on the sensation which the publication of Sebastiani's report had created in England, where the views of France towards Egypt must always command the utmost vigilance and jealousy. He maintained that what ought to convince us of his desire of peace was on the one hand the little he had to gain by renewing the war, and on the other the facility with which he might have taken possession of Egypt with the very ships and troops which were now going from the Mediterranean to St. Domingo, and that with the approbation of all Europe, and more particularly of the Turks, who had repeatedly invited him to join with them for the purpose of forcing us to evacuate their territory. I do not pretend to follow the arguments of the First Consul in detail; this would be impossible from the vast variety of matter, and from his constantly flying from one subject to another, so as to render what he said so completely incoherent and sometimes unintelligible. His purpose was evidently to convince me that on Malta must depend peace or war, and at the same time to impress upon my mind a strong idea of the means he possessed of annoying us at home and abroad. With regard to the mistrust and jealousy which he said constantly prevailed since the conclusion of the Treaty of Amiens, I observed that after a war of such long duration, so full of rancour, and carried on in a manner of which history has no example, it was but natural that a considerable degree of agitation should prevail, but this, like the swell after a storm, would gradually subside if not kept up by the policy of either party; that I would not pretend to pronounce which had been the aggressor in the paper war of which he complained, and which was still kept up, though with this difference, that in England it was independent of Government, and in France its very act and deed. To this I added that it must be admitted that we had such motives of mistrust against France as could not be alleged against us, and I was going to instance the accession of territory and influence gained by France since the treaty, when he interrupted me by saying, 'I suppose you mean Piedmont and Switzerland; ce sont des bagatelles' (the expression he made use of was too trivial and vulgar to find a place in a despatch, or anywhere but in the mouth of a hackney coachman), and it must have been foreseen while the negotiation was pending; 'vous n'avez pas le droit d'en parler à cette heure.' I should have followed my argument, but saw he was losing his temper, and I thought it needless to press it further; I continued, therefore, with alleging as a cause of mistrust and of jealousy the impossibility of obtaining justice or any kind of redress for any of his Majesty's subjects. He asked me in what respect, and I told him that since the signing of the treaty not one British claimant had been satisfied, although every Frenchman of that description had been so within one month after that period; and that since I had been here, and I could say as much of my predecessors, not one satisfactory answer had been obtained to the innumerable representations which we had been under the necessity of making in favour of British subjects, and property detained in the several ports of France and elsewhere without even a shadow of justice. Such an order of things, I said, was not made to inspire confidence, but, on the contrary, must create mistrust. This, he said, must be attributed to the natural difficulties attending such suits, when both parties thought themselves right; but he denied that such delays could proceed from any disinclination to do what was just and right. With regard to the pensions which were granted to French or Swiss individuals, I observed that they were given as a reward for past services during the war, and most certainly not for present ones, and still less for such as had been insinuated, of a nature repugnant to the feelings of every individual in England and to the universally acknowledged loyalty and honour of the British Government; that as for any participation of indemnities or other accessions which his Majesty might have obtained, I could take upon myself to assure him that his Majesty's ambition led him rather to preserve than to acquire; and that with regard to the most propitious moment of renewing hostilities, his Majesty, whose sincere desire it was to continue the blessings of peace to his subjects, would always consider such a measure as the greatest calamity; but that if his Majesty was so desirous of peace it must not be imputed to the difficulty of obtaining allies, for perhaps inadequate services would all be concentrated in England and give a proportionate increase of energy to our exertions. At this part of the conversation he rose from his chair and told me that he should give orders to General Andréossi (with whom, I think, I could perceive he was not well satisfied) to enter on the discussion of this business with your Lordship; but he wished that I should at the same time be made acquainted with his motives and convinced of his sincerity rather from himself than from his Ministers. He then, after a conversation of two hours, during the greatest part of which he talked incessantly, conversed for a few moments on indifferent subjects, in apparent good humour, and retired. Such was as nearly as I can recollect the purport of this conference. The impression I brought away with me, taken rather collectively than from any particular topic of discourse, was evidently that the object of the First Consul was, if he could not persuade us into those measures which must facilitate the accomplishment of his plans, to frighten and to bully. I need not observe that this conduct in private life would be a strong presumption of weakness. I believe the same will hold good in politics; at least I strongly suspect it to be the case in the present instance. It must, however, be observed that he did not, as M. de Talleyrand had done, affect to attribute Sebastiani's mission to commercial motives only, but as one rendered necessary in a military point of view by the infraction by us of the Treaty of Amiens.

P.S.—This conversation took place on Friday last, and this morning I saw M. de Talleyrand. He had been with the First Consul after I left him, and he assured me that he had been very well satisfied with the frankness with which I had made my observations on what fell from him. I told him that, without entering into any further detail, what I had said to the First Consul amounted to an assurance of what I trusted there could be no doubt—of the readiness of his Majesty's Ministers to remove all subjects of discussion where that could be done without violating the laws of the country, and to fulfil strictly the engagements which they had contracted in as much as that could be reconciled with the safety of the State. As this applied to Malta and Egypt, he gave me to understand that a project was in contemplation by which the integrity of the Turkish Empire would be so effectually secured as to do away with every cause of doubt or uneasiness, either with regard to Egypt or any part of the Turkish dominions. He could not then, he said, explain himself further. Under these circumstances no one can expect that we should relinquish that assurance which we have in hand till something equally satisfactory is proposed and adopted.

Paris, February 28, 1803.

I have had no opportunity since my last of ascertaining from my own observation the effect of the conversation which made the subject of that despatch to your Lordship. If we are to judge from the message of the First Consul to the Legislative Body, which I lately transmitted to your Lordship, we might suppose him determined to consider our refusal to give effect to his requisition on the subject of Malta as a sufficient pretext for commencing hostilities; and indeed such is the language of those who are nearest his person, though perhaps not most in his confidence. On the other hand, there are those who are inclined to believe that the First Consul, like other impetuous characters, is not so insensible to personal danger as to hurry him beyond the bounds of moderation, and particularly when he meets with that cool but firm resistance which gives time to reflect and tends rather to dispassionate discussion than to those desperate measures in the prosecution of which he stands committed to expose his person and his fortune to the utmost hazard. Such reflections will, I am persuaded, have their due influence, and the more they are considered the deeper will they strike. In the meantime the language which is held by the Court of Petersburg is admirably calculated to have an effect on the determination of the First Consul, and if it had been actually concerted with his Majesty it could not have come at a better moment or be better adapted to the purpose. A note was given in by Count Marcoff a few days ago in answer to one from this Government, in which the Emperor expresses his surprise that he should have been considered so bigoted to his pacific system as to become indifferent to the general welfare of Europe. He desires it to be understood that his love of peace arises from a convic- on that he can better promote the happiness of his people by attending to the improvement of his present possessions than by running after new ones; and he earnestly recommends the same moderation to those whose practice differs from his principles. He then proceeds to declare that he considers it as a duty imposed upon him by the situation he holds to watch with a jealous eye the conduct of any Government which may have an influence on the general tranquillity. He disclaims with great frankness and energy not only the most distant intention of lending a hand to the dismemberment of the Turkish Empire, but his determination to maintain its integrity by every means in his power. He takes a view of the geographical position of Russia, inaccessible, from its climate, on the north, excepting by sea, and on the south a neighbour from whom he can have nothing to fear; that, setting every other consideration aside, that of self-security requires that no change should be made in such a disposition; and that he shall therefore always consider any attempt to effect it as hostile against Russia. It is the *perfect* integrity of the Turkish Empire which he maintains to be essentially necessary to the maintenance of peace, and he adds that as long as the French Government manifests an intention (and such an intention was fully avowed by the First Consul in his conversation with me) of possessing itself of Egypt no peace can be permanent with England, and therefore it is the perfect integrity of the Turkish Empire which must be maintained in order to insure the general tranquillity. In short, the whole tenor of this communication is of a nature to convince the First Consul, first, that he must not depend implicitly on the pacific disposition of the Emperor of Russia; secondly, that no concert can be established with him for the partition of the Turkish Empire, but, on the contrary, that he will oppose it; and, thirdly, that he considers the alarm which the First Consul has created on the subject of Malta as sufficient to excite the utmost jealousy of Great Britain and to threaten Europe with a renewal of war. This despatch is dated January 31 (N.S.), and was communicated *in toto* to M. de Talleyrand two days after my conversation with the First Consul. We cannot, however, expect that the acquiescence of the First Consul will be obtained without a violent manifestation of humour, and perhaps an explosion; and indeed, when we consider the disappointments to which he has lately been exposed, we must acknowledge that a more even temper than that which he possesses might have been ruffled. Amongst the first, and perhaps the most severe, we may rank the state of the English finances as exposed by Mr. Addington in the late budget. This was a dreadful blow, and all their rancour and all their ingenuity have been since exerted to do away the impression it has made. In the next place, the conduct of America, from whose President everything subservient was expected, and by whom it is now foreseen that every opposition will be made to the projects of the French Government in that part of the world, and that, so far from being able to gain quiet possession of the Floridas, the settlement even of Louisiana may be considered as doubtful. Then comes the disappointment in his hopes of subduing St. Domingo, and of regenerating his navy, which, I believe, he begins to understand cannot be effected but by the prosperity of his colonies, and last, though not least, the grand disappointment of Malta, which he had calculated would, as well as Egypt, have been at this moment in his possession. These, with many other minor subjects of mortification, may be allowed to discompose the temper of a great man ambitious of universal empire and to convince the world that everything must bend to his will. Were I to give credit to public rumours, I might be led to suppose that all this weight of vexation is to fall upon his Majesty's dominions. Plans of invasion are said to be revising; armies are to be conveyed up the Thames; General Masséna, who was destined to command that which was lately devoted to the same dangerous attempt, is again called to assist in council; and he will encourage the projects as far as he is able. But there are other generals, and a very considerable part of the public indeed, who, notwithstanding the pains which are taken to animate them in the cause, would consider a rupture with England as the greatest calamity which can befall this country, and as one which might eventually involve them in all the misery from which they are but just recovering. These considerations must have weight; but whether they will be sufficient to counterbalance the irascible and impetuous disposition of the First Consul, time alone can bring to light.

Copie d'une Dépêche du Chancelier de l'Empire au Comte de Marcoff.

St. Pétersbourg, le 19 Janvier 1803.

Nous avons vu avec étonnement, Monsieur le Comte, que le Premier Consul a paru trouver à redire au ton d'un des rescrits qui vous a été adressé par S. M. I., et qu'il en a inféré un changement de système dans notre politique. Personne n'a plus à cœur que l'Empereur de conserver les égards que se doivent mutuellement les Gouvernemens, et tout ce que S. M. désire, c'est de rencontrer partout une parfaite réciprocité. L'Empereur croit que la meilleure manière de s'énoncer est celle de la vérité et de la franchise, et il n'a jamais eu l'intention d'en prendre une autre. Une supériorité souvent très marquée n'est pas même une raison pour que S. M. veuille employer avec les Gouvernmens un autre ton que celui qui doit subsister entre des états indépendans dont l'Empereur respecte la souveraineté, tout autant dans leur foiblesse que dans leur force ; et certainement S. M. I. ne peut que d'autant plus tenir à ces convenances envers une puissance amie et aussi respectable que la France. Quant au changement de système, l'Empereur dès son avénement au trône n'en a suivi qu'un seul et ne pense pas de s'en départir. S. M. I. est pénétrée du principe que chaque gouvernement doit faire son possible pour préserver la paix à l'extérieur, afin de pouvoir porter tous ses efforts à rendre de plus en plus heureux les peuples qui sont confiés à ses soins ; et nous croyons que ce principe doit être surtout celui de tout état considérable qui est fort de ses propres moyens, et qui peut chercher sa sûreté principale dans leur propre développement, et non dans des vues ou des espérances au dehors. Tel est tout le système présent de la cour de Russie, auquel l'Empereur est attaché par son caractère, et que la position même de son empire lui a fait choisir. La Russie, appuyée en quelque façon à l'un des coins de la terre, n'est attaquable que d'un côté, n'a aucune raison de désirer la guerre, et elle en a encore moins de la craindre. Elle ne veut ni commander ni que personne lui commande. Travailler à sa prospérité intérieure, et pour cela préserver sa tranquillité et celle de l'Europe, est le plus vif désir de l'Empereur. Cependant l'expérience nous démontre malheureusement que pour rester pacifique, il ne suffit pas de l'être soi-même ; il faut que les autres le soient aussi, et que leur conduite permette de conserver la paix. Les derniers tems nous ont nouvellement convaincus qu'on ne peut venir la troubler de loin, et la campagne des Russes en Italie, celle des François en Egypte prouvent assez que les distances donnent à présent une bien foible certitude de repos. Il pourroit donc survenir des circonstances où S. M. I. se verroit obligée de sortir de l'état de tranquillité dans lequel elle se trouve actuellement, et cela arriveroit si l'honneur ou la sûreté de son empire pouvoient être compromis même par contre-coup, ou si la cause de la justice, le maintien de l'ordre et du bien général des nations l'exigeaient impérieusement. Il faut compter parmi ces cas possibles à prévoir celui où il y auroit des Puissances qui voudroient travailler à la destruction de l'Empire ottoman pour en faire leur profit : S. M. ne pourroit sans doute alors qu'intervenir activement pour secourir son voisin et prendre les déterminations qu'elle croiroit nécessaires à l'intérêt de la Russie. Nous avons remarqué que dans les conversations que vous avez eues avec le Premier Consul, il s'est arrêté souvent sur cet objet, en faisant mention de l'état de décadence de l'Empire ottoman et disant que sa ruine lui sembloit prochaine. L'on doit supposer que de semblables discours seront aussi parvenus à d'autres cours ; car l'idée de la dissolution peu éloignée du Gouvernement turc et des événemens qui doivent la précéder et s'ensuivre est généralement répandue en Europe, et c'est à cela qu'il faut attribuer en grande partie que l'Angleterre ne désarme pas encore. S. M. l'Empereur, persuadé qu'au fond les intentions du Gouvernement françois ne sont pas hostiles à la Turquie, et croyant que dans tous les cas la première qualité de la politique et le devoir le plus essentiel de l'amitié est de parler vrai et d'agir avec sincérité et loyauté, vous charge, Monsieur le Comte, d'entrer dans une explication franche sur ce sujet important avec le Ministère de la République. Vous direz que S. M., satisfaite du lot que la Providence lui a assigné, ne veut pas l'agrandir pas plus du côté de la Turquie qu'autre part, et que conséquemment elle ne sauroit non plus voir avec indifférence que personne autre s'aggrandisse aux dépens de la Porte ottomane. C'est le meilleur voisin que puisse avoir la Russie, et S. M. ne désire pas d'en changer. En exposant les motifs qui ne peuvent que fortifier notre cour dans ces sentimens, V. E. y ajoutera que l'Empereur est convaincu que dans ce moment il seroit extrêmement convenable de calmer autant que possible la crainte universelle qui agite tous les cabinets de ce que des événemens nouveaux vont bientôt troubler derechef le monde politique. Si le Premier Consul par quelque déclaration, ou comme il le jugera à propos, détruisoit ces craintes, qui se portent principalement sur le sort futur de la Turquie, et qu'il assurât ne point avoir de vues sur cet empire, il ôteroit par là tout prétexte aux jalousies des autres cabinets, et mettroit fin au germe de dissension et d'inquiétude qui fermente toujours en Europe, et qui empêche que la tranquillité qui vient de lui être rendue ne produise les effets salutaires qu'on devoit s'en promettre. L'Angleterre délivrée de ses appréhensions n'en donneroit plus à son tour au Gouvernement françois, pour lequel il ne peut y avoir rien de plus honorable ni de plus utile que d'inspirer partout de la confiance et du calme, afin que l'on commence à croire à la paix, et que chacun pense chez soi aux améliorations de l'intérieur et laisse en faire autant aux autres. Tous les Gouvernemens ont besoin de tourner leurs vues vers ce but et d'en être le moins distraits que possible, afin de s'occuper sans relâche à perfectionner et consolider chez eux l'ordre et le bonheur social. S. M. I. désire, Monsieur le Comte, que vous vous expliquiez dans ce sens avec le Gouvernement françois, et que vous l'assuriez qu'elle s'est décidée à lui faire ces ouvertures uniquement par son désir sincère de rendre plus intimes les rapports de bonne intelligence qui existent si heureusement entre les deux pays, et d'éloigner toutes les causes qui pourroient les troubler, comme aussi par l'amitié et la considération personnelles qu'elle porte au Premier Consul, qui recevra, nous nous flattons, avec des sentimens analogues ces communications dictées par la seule franchise et la droiture des intentions de votre auguste souverain.—J'ai l'honneur d'être, etc.

Paris, February 28, 1803.

I cannot but consider the dismissal of the editor of the 'Argus' as a strong symptom of a pacific disposition, as far at least as relates to the paper war which has been carrying on for some time past with such bitterness on both sides. It was announced to me a few days ago, and I was given to understand that he had merited his disgrace by the coarse and illiberal abuse which he had dealt about without discrimination or mercy. Your Lordship will perceive that this paper has got into better hands, and I cannot help expressing a sincere hope that they may find no reason in our public prints to renew the war. I almost fear, however, that whilst I utter this wish provocation may already have been given. I yesterday received by the *petite post*, a copy of the 'Courrier de Londres' of the 18th inst., containing a most virulent paragraph against the First Consul and his family, and the following words were written in a disguised hand (I have reason to believe that it was that of the First Consul) on the margin of the paper: 'Il faut qu'un ministère ait bien peu d'honneur et de bonne politique pour payer de pareilles infamies; et lorsqu'en même tems on envoie un ambassadeur à Paris, c'est une lâcheté.' In my conversation with him the other day he certainly did make use of expressions nearly similar, and it was in vain that I told him then, or should repeat to him now, that the *ministère* has nothing to do with it, and that the laws only can punish it, as in the case of Peltier. This they cannot, or more properly will not, comprehend; but in the meantime it most certainly would be much to be lamented if offended vanity should urge him to those extremities which otherwise might be avoided. If war is to be the result of the discussion, I shall impute it much rather to the intemperance of the newspapers than to the politics of the moment.

Lord Hawkesbury to Lord Whitworth.

Downing St., February 28, 1803.

Your Excellency's despatch No. 16 has been received and laid before the King. I have great satisfaction in communicating to you his Majesty's entire approbation of the able and judicious manner in which you appear to have executed the instructions which I gave you in my despatch No. 1 on the 9th instant. The account you have given of your interview with the First Consul is in every respect important. It is unnecessary for me to remark on the tone and temper in which the sentiments of the First Consul appear to have been expressed, or to offer any observations in addition to those so properly made by your Excellency at the time upon several of the topics which were brought forward by the First Consul in the course of your conversation. I shall therefore content myself with referring your Excellency to my despatch to Mr. Merry of ——, in which the subject of the complaints of the French Government respecting the freedom of the press, the emigrants, &c., are particularly discussed. I cannot, however, avoid noticing that nothing approaching to explanation or satisfaction is stated to have been thrown out by the First Consul in answer to the just representations and complaints of his

Majesty, in consequence of the unwarrantable insinuations and charges contained in Colonel Sebastiani's report against his Majesty's Government, the officer commanding his forces in Egypt, and his army in that quarter; but, on the other hand, the language of the First Consul has tended to strengthen and confirm the suspicions which that publication was peculiarly calculated to excite. I shall now proceed to give you some further instructions on the language which it may be proper for you to hold respecting the charge which has been advanced against his Majesty's Government of their unwillingness to fulfil the Treaty of Amiens. The Treaty of Amiens has been in course of execution on the part of his Majesty in every article in which, according to the spirit of that treaty, it has been found capable of execution. There cannot be the least doubt that Egypt is at this time completely evacuated. The delay which has arisen in the evacuation of Alexandria was owing to accidental circumstances, the particulars of which were explained to you in my despatch of November 30 last, and I had every reason to believe, from the communication I had with General Andréossy on the subject, that the French Government were perfectly satisfied with the explanation which he was authorised at the time to give them respecting it.

With regard to that article of the treaty which relates to Malta, the stipulations contained in it (owing to circumstances which it was not in the power of his Majesty to control) have not been capable of execution. The refusal of Russia to accede to the arrangement except on condition that the Maltese Langue should be abolished, the silence of the Court of Berlin with respect to the invitation that has been made to it, in consequence of the treaty, to become a guaranteeing Power, the abolition of the Spanish Priories, in defiance of the treaty to which the King of Spain was a party, the declaration of the Portuguese Government of their intention to sequestrate the property of the Portuguese Priory, as forming a part of the Spanish Langue, unless the property of the Spanish Priories is restored to them, and the non-election of a Grand Master: these circumstances would have been sufficient, without any other special grounds, to have warranted his Majesty in suspending the evacuation of the island until some new arrangement could be adjusted for its security and independence. But when it is considered how greatly the dominions, power, and influence of France have of late been extended, his Majesty must feel that he has an incontestable right, conformably to the principles on which the Treaty of Peace was negotiated and concluded, to demand additional securities in any new arrangement which it might be necessary to make with a view of effecting the real objects of that treaty. And these considerations, sufficient as they might be in themselves to justify the line of conduct which his Majesty had determined to adopt, have received additional force from the views which have been recently and unreservedly manifested by the French Government respecting the Turkish dominions and the islands in the Adriatic (and which have been in a great degree admitted by the First Consul in his interview with your Excellency)—views which are directly repugnant not only to the spirit but to the letter of the Treaty of Amiens. From the postscript to your Excellency's letter it appears that a project was in contemplation by which, according to the declaration of M. Talleyrand, the integrity of the Turkish territory would be secured so as to do away every cause of doubt or uneasiness either with regard to Egypt or to any other part of the Turkish dominions. His Majesty will consider the communication of such a project as indicating a disposition on the part of the French Government to afford him explanation and satisfaction respecting some of the points which have been the subject of his representations. But, after all that has passed, his Majesty cannot consent that his troops should evacuate the island of Malta until substantial security has been provided for these objects, which, under the present circumstances, might be materially endangered by their removal.

Lord Whitworth to Lord Hawkesbury.

Paris, March 3, 1803.

I have nothing very interesting to trouble your Lordship with by this messenger. M. de Talleyrand told me the day before yesterday that he had received an answer from General Andréossy to the despatch in which he gave that Ambassador an account of my conversation with the First Consul. He at the same time appeared very anxious that I should soon hear from your Lordship on the same subject; but I could not give him much hope that I should very soon satisfy his impatience. I am sorry to be again under the necessity of lamenting the bad effects of the scurrility of the newspapers published in London. Another was enclosed to me yesterday, which appears to be the 'Courrier de Londres' of the 22nd ult., containing a paragraph highly offensive to the First Consul, and particularly mischievous in the present moment. I enclose it to your Lordship, that your Lordship may see the observation which was made upon it by the person who sent it to me, and who, I have reason to believe, was the First Consul himself. I am sure your Lordship joins with me in the fervent wish that it were possible to curb the licentiousness of public prints. It surely could never have been intended that the liberty of the press should be so uncontrolled as to put it in the power of any the most obscure writer, who perhaps composes his paragraph in a garret, with no other view than to earn wherewith to procure him a dinner, to involve in war countries which otherwise might be disposed to conciliate, and to meet with temper any discussion which may arise. Such, I have reason to believe, is the case in the present instance; and I am persuaded that if the First Consul has recourse to the desperate alternative of war it must be attributed more to the irritation constantly kept alive by the public prints than to the nature of the questions at issue, however delicate they may be. The conviction of Peltier has doubtless produced a good effect, and will have convinced people here that it is far from the intention of his Majesty's Ministers to screen such offenders from justice. And although I know how much an English lawyer is above the consideration of compliment in the exercise of his duty, yet I cannot forbear from mentioning that the conduct of his Majesty's Attorney-General has been spoken of in terms of great applause. It were, however, to be wished that his Majesty's Ministers had fewer opportunities of manifesting their impartiality in this respect; and I cannot but think that much good might result from the exertion of every power of control, at least for the moment, over the French journalists in London, and in particular the editor of the 'Courrier de Londres.' I am fully aware of the motives and inducements which they, or at least their employers, have in venting their spleen; but certainly they cannot be justified in so doing when they endanger the peace of the country which affords them an asylum. I have no doubt in my own mind that this irritation is kept alive by the agents of the Royalist party, and perhaps by the Jacobins, in the hope of forcing the two countries into a war, by which they could lose nothing, but by which they might eventually be considerable gainers. This is a consideration worthy of attention; and I should think that it would be no violation of the Alien Bill were it applied to those who strive to disturb the peace of the country by such means, as well as by any other. As I am on this subject, I will mention to your Lordship that Goldsmidt, the editor of the 'Argus,' is dismissed, and a person of the name of Badini, who is undoubtedly known to your Lordship by report, is now the conductor of that paper. His instructions are to refrain from personalities, and to be in general conciliatory. The numbers of that paper which have lately been published have, it must be confessed, been inoffensive.

Paris, March 3, 1803.

I have the honour to enclose to your Lordship the copy of a letter which I received this morning from M. de Talleyrand, in which your Lordship will perceive some disposition to justice, though faint, on the part of this Government. After a total silence on the subject of the British claimants to every representation which I have made since I have been in this country, M. de Talleyrand has at length required from me an account of the several claims of his Majesty's subjects on the French Government. I am consequently preparing a list of claimants, with a statement of the nature of their claims, which I shall give him as soon as it is made out. I cannot, however, consider this step as an indication of any real disposition in this Government to give satisfaction to the claimants. It is, I should suppose, rather to weaken any argument which we may wish to derive from the hesitation of the First Consul to fulfil the Treaty of Amiens in this respect, although the clause to that effect is to all intents and purposes as formal as that which stipulates the evacuation of Malta or any other. We may, however, expect that, although the giving immediate effect to that article would be but a just reciprocity for the conduct of Great Britain towards the subjects of France, its execution will be made to depend on the evacuation of Malta. I shall therefore in my discussions on this subject be particularly careful to draw strictly the line between the two cases.

P.S.—Since writing the above your Lordship's despatch No. 2, of the 28th ult., by the messenger Elsworth, and the minute which accompanies it, have been received. I shall not fail to see M. de Talleyrand to-morrow morning for the purpose of executing your Lordship's instructions.

M. DE TALLEYRAND TO LORD WHITWORTH.

Paris, le 11 Ventose, an XI.

Le Ministre des Relations Extérieures au Lord Whitworth, Ambassadeur de S. M. Britannique près la République.

Monsieur l'Ambassadeur,—Le navire anglois 'La Nancy,' réclamé d'abord par M. Merry et depuis par Votre Excellence, a été relâché avec les marchandises non prohibées qu'il avoit à bord. Un autre bâtiment anglois, appartenant à M. Middleton et saisi pareillement à Flessingue, a été relâché de la même manière. Quant aux marchandises prohibées qui se sont trouvées sur ces deux bâtimens, le ministre des Finances n'en a point pressé la condamnation. Il s'est contenté de les faire déposer dans un magasin à Flessingue, laissant ainsi aux propriétaires l'espérance de les recouvrer si l'examen ultérieur, qui sera fait avec une scrupuleuse impartialité, démontre ce que beaucoup d'indices ont fait probable jusqu'à présent, que les dits propriétaires étoient dans un de ces cas où la bonne foi fait excuser l'erreur. Je m'empresse de communiquer ces détails à Votre Excellence en la priant d'agréer les assurances de ma très-haute considération.

(Signé) Ch. Mau. Talleyrand.

Lord Whitworth to Lord Hawkesbury.

Paris, March 3, 1803.

I saw M. de Talleyrand yesterday, and acquitted myself of your Lordship's instructions. I recapitulated the several arguments therein contained, dwelling particularly on the open avowal of the First Consul's views in Egypt, and concluding with the resolution of his Majesty not to withdraw his troops from Malta until some security should be given that by so doing his Majesty should not expose the safety of his own dominions. He heard me with great patience, and in answer endeavoured as before to convince me that there was no reason whatever for the apprehensions which we entertained; that it was true the acquisition of Egypt had been, and perhaps still was, a favourite object of the First Consul's, but that it was not so much as to allow him to go to war for its attainment; that he was sensible that any attempt on his part to gain possession of it must immediately involve him in hostilities with Great Britain; but at the same time he must observe, on the other hand, that the keeping possession of Malta in defiance of treaty must also have the same effect, since he was bound in honour to maintain its observance at all events. M. de Talleyrand dwelt a considerable time on these arguments. His object was to convince me that the First Consul would go to war on what he conceived to be a point of honour, but not in order to obtain the possession of Egypt, or for any other view of aggrandisement. I then told him that what had in a particular manner excited the attention of your Lordship in my last report was the assurance he had given me of some project being in contemplation whereby the integrity of the Turkish Empire would be so insured in all its parts as to remove every doubt or apprehension. I begged him therefore to explain himself on this subject, which I conceived to be of the utmost importance, since it was only by such means that both parties could be satisfied. He then gave me to understand that what he had termed a project was nothing more than what had been expressed in the First Consul's message to the Legislative Body when he says that there is a French Ambassador at Constantinople who is charged to give every assurance of the disposition of France to strengthen instead of to weaken that Government. I expressed a doubt whether this or any other parole security would be considered as sufficient in such a transaction. Hereupon he repeated the question which he has so often asked—' What then is the security which you require, and which the First Consul can give?' This, I told him, must be the subject of the negotiation upon which we were willing to enter, and I trusted that the French Government would bring into it the same temper and the same real desire to conciliate which was manifested by his Majesty's Ministers. M. de Talleyrand now informed me (in order, I suppose, to avoid the trouble of reasoning further on the subject) that the First Consul had five or six days ago ordered instructions to be sent to General Andréossy, by which he was to require an immediate and categorical answer to the plain question whether his Majesty would or would not cause Malta to be evacuated by the British troops; that he concluded that this communication was already made; and that he expected to learn the result of it in a very few days, adding that all the First Consul wanted was to know precisely on what he had to depend. I could not help lamenting this precipitate measure (and I really believe M. de Talleyrand does so himself), since it could answer no good purpose, and would only tend to introduce into the discussion ill-humour and offended dignity in the place of dispassionate reasoning. I begged him, however, to be prepared, and to prepare the First Consul, to meet with more opposition to his will than he had been accustomed to on similar occasions. I told him that his Majesty was willing to discuss the point in dispute with fairness and candour, but certainly never would be intimidated into acquiescence; and I repeatedly urged that if he wished well to the peace of the two countries he should prepare the First Consul for the consequences which might naturally be expected from this step, and thus prevent the effect of any sudden gust of ill-humour. He was unwilling to admit that there could be any chance of satisfying the First Consul short of a compliance with his wishes, founded, as they pretend, on good faith; neither would he allow that self-security could justify a deviation from the strict observance of treaties. Our conversation ended here, and I wait the result of General Andréossy's communication with the utmost impatience. It is impossible to form any decided opinion on the event of this discussion. We all know the temper of the First Consul. We are not now to learn that pride, petulance, and a rooted jealousy and hatred of England are amongst the principal ingredients in his character. All these will urge him to support what he terms his honour at the risk of everything. On the other hand, we know his total want of means to engage in a maritime war; the dispersed situation of what remains of his fleet; his projects in the West Indies and America unaccomplished; the wretched state of his finances; and, above all, the apprehension he feels—and this strongly impressed on him by every individual of his family, particularly by his brothers Joseph and Lucien—that, should he now involve the country in war, his fate would be decided by assassination. These, it must be confessed, are all strong and weighty motives. Some persons with whom I converse are inclined to think they will make a salutary impression, and I am myself disposed to be of that opinion. It is, however, in no case safe to pronounce with confidence, and in none less so than in the present. I should have observed to your Lordship that in my conversation with the First Consul, and again yesterday with M. de Talleyrand, great stress was laid on the promptitude with which the First Consul had caused Tarentum to be evacuated by the French troops, though it is unanimously acknowledged to be the point from which any hostile design against Egypt could be attempted with the greatest chance of success. I could only reply to this that Tarentum could be reoccupied, were it necessary to the First Consul's views, with the same promptitude with which it was abandoned. In the present state of affairs, your Lordship will naturally have turned your mind to the different modes by which such a security as we must require can be obtained. A formal guarantee of the integrity of the Turkish Empire by Great Britain, Russia, and this country will probably have suggested itself as the most likely to answer the purpose. Should this be the case, and should this Government give us time to make such an arrangement, it would, perhaps, be more advisable to make direct overtures to the Court of Petersburg than by the means of Count Marcoff. I should depend more upon his executing with precision the orders he might receive from his Court than on the manner in which he would represent such a proposition to the Russian Cabinet. And should it be made appear to the Emperor as the only means of avoiding perhaps a general war, I think he might be induced to concur in the measure.

P.S.—In the interval between the writing and the transcribing the above despatch, I have taken another opportunity of seeing M. de Talleyrand, and I am glad to find that (for what purpose I know not) he represented the instructions to General Andréossy as much more absolute and offensive than they really are. I found him to-day entirely disposed to give me another opinion, and to convince me that the

First Consul, far from wishing to carry matters to extremity, was desirous to discuss fairly and without passion a point which he admitted was of importance to both countries: to Great Britain, as affecting eventually its interest in the East; to France, as affecting her honour. He repeatedly assured me (without, however, persuading me) that, much as the First Consul might have the acquisition of Egypt at heart, he would sacrifice his own feelings to the preservation of peace, and henceforth seek to augment his glory by improving and consolidating the internal situation of the country rather than by adding to its possessions. I am far indeed from pledging myself for the sincerity of those professions, but I cannot but consider it as a material point gained if we can bring the question of Malta to a temperate and fair discussion. This M. de Talleyrand now declares to be the desire of the First Consul, and I will allow myself to hope that, by means of the Court of Petersburg, some arrangement may be made by which both parties may be satisfied. An officer has been sent in a frigate to Algiers with a message from the First Consul likely to put an end to the dispute between this Government and the Dey. I cannot help suspecting that we shall some day hear that an expedition is gone to that port. Should that take place, nothing will be able to save the Algerines from the rapacity of their invaders.

Paris, March 5, 1803.

I have entered so fully on the subject of my conversations with M. de Talleyrand that I have little or nothing to add. I have only to give your Lordship my opinion on the evident change in his manner and language in the course of yesterday and to-day; and I can attribute the tone he chose to assume yesterday to nothing more than a trick, in the hope of intimidating me, and of drawing from me wherewithal to give confidence to the First Consul in the pursuit of his object. I flatter myself I have withstood the trial without flinching, and I consider the favourable change of to-day as a proof of the victory of honesty and plain dealing over duplicity and low cunning. I most earnestly recommend it to your Lordship to endeavour by every means to engage the Court of Russia to come forward on this occasion, unless it should be determined to keep possession of Malta at all events; and that, I fear, cannot be done without a war. Short of that, the best security would certainly be a joint guarantee. I have no reason to suppose that this Government would come willingly into such a measure; but if it was strongly suggested by Russia it would not be refused. Count Woronzow would, I think, enforce it, and his brother might, if he pleased, induce the Emperor to adopt it. We must be prepared for some definite point of negotiation, and this is perhaps the most eligible. I should apologise to your Lordship for these reflections, which will, I am persuaded, have occurred to your Lordship.

Paris, March 7, 1803.

The audience yesterday produced nothing particularly worthy of observation. The First Consul was civil, as usual, but avoided touching upon any point which could lead to the subject in dispute. He affected rather to be entirely occupied with arrangements for the revival of industry in the great manufacturing towns, and was evidently at great pains to convince me, as well by what he said to me as to those who were near me, that his thoughts and time were wholly devoted to such objects. He repeatedly observed that France was sufficiently extensive, and that it was much better policy to endeavour to augment her means by increasing her industry and improving her cultivation than by extending her frontiers. Your Lordship will perceive the drift of this language, but you will, I am persuaded, give no more credit to it than I do. We shall see what will become of all this moderation and forbearance when he finds that if he does not attain his real object it is because we know him too well to give him credit for either. I neglected to mention to your Lordship (and M. de Souza was not inclined to boast of it) a conversation which the First Consul had with him on the subject of the dispute with General Lannes. In this conversation the First Consul was so violent as to exceed all bounds. He treated M. de Souza with the utmost indignity, and more than once gave him almost reason to fear that he would not confine himself to words. The conclusion was that General Lannes should convince the Portuguese that they were dependent on him, and him alone, for their existence; and that if the Prince Regent gave him any further cause of complaint he would exterminate him and his whole country; then they might see what their English friends could do for them. It is really painful to relate such indecencies, but such is the man who boasts of his moderation and forbearance. One of General Beurnonville's secretaries is returned from Madrid, the object of whose journey is to palliate certain transactions wherein the conduct of Beurnonville has been similar to that of General Lannes in Portugal. It appears that the system of smuggling has been carried to such a height by this Ambassador in Spain as to become intolerable. The first notice which was taken of it by the Spanish Government produced only the most violent reproaches. The Chevalier Azzara is now endeavouring to conciliate, and Beurnonville will probably remain in Spain a privileged smuggler. Such is the position of the German Courts with regard to this Government that it is almost useless to take up your Lordship's time with their concerns. It has, however, been said, and with confidence, that that of Vienna has not shown itself so disinterested as that of St. Petersburg, and that the proposal of dismembering Turkey has not been absolutely rejected. If such a project has been entertained, I should suppose that its execution depends on the evacuation of Malta; for as long as his Majesty's fleet is in the Mediterranean every attempt of such a nature, whether against Egypt or the Morea, must be precarious, if not impracticable. It should, however, be understood that this security can only be for the present; for when the First Consul in time of peace doubles his military force, as he is now doing when he has an army at his command of near five hundred thousand men, every country which is assailable by land, and more particularly Turkey, will be exposed to his invasion. Sure of the acquiescence of Austria and Prussia, he will have on the Continent Russia alone to oppose him. Such an opposition would, however, if well enforced, be effectual for the support of the Turkish Empire, and more particularly when combined with the maritime exertions of Great Britain. The more we reflect upon it the more we must be convinced that this is the only counterpoise to the ambition of the First Consul. I have the honour to enclose to your Lordship a copy of the note which I have received from the Cardinal Legate notifying the election of a Grand Master of the Order of Malta, together with my answer to that communication. In the present state of the discussion, this event has not been mentioned to me by the French Minister. He must feel that a very trifling obstacle indeed is removed by such an election.

A.

D'après le refus' que Lord Whitworth connoît avoir été donné par le bailli Ruspoli de la Grande Maîtrise de Malte, à laquelle Sa Sainteté, suivant le convenu des Puissances, l'avoit nommé, le pape est venu dans la détermination de nommer grand maître de l'ordre de Malte le bailli Tommasi de Cortone. Le cardinal Caprara a l'honneur de faire part de cette nomination à Lord Whitworth, ambassadeur de Sa Majesté Britannique, qu'il prie de la faire connoître au cabinet de St. James, et d'agréer l'assurance de sa haute considération.

(Signé)   J. B. CARDINAL CAPRARA.

Paris, le 4 Mars 1803.

B.

Lord Whitworth, ambassadeur extraordinaire et plénipotentiaire de S. M. B. près la République françoise, a l'honneur de remercier Son Eminence le cardinal Caprara, légat du

St. Siège, de la communication qu'elle a bien voulu lui faire de l'élection du bailli Tommasi de Cortone à la Grande Maîtrise de Malthe, et ne manquera pas de la transmettre à sa cour.

Il prie Son E. d'agréer l'assurance de sa haute considération.

Paris, le 4 Mars 1803.

Lord Hawkesbury to Lord Whitworth.

Downing St., March 9, 1803.

I think it important to lose no time in forwarding to your Excellency the Address of the two Houses of Parliament in consequence of his Majesty's most gracious message. It has been carried unanimously in both Houses, without a single improper question being put to his Majesty's Ministers, or any expression irritating or offensive being made use of with respect to the First Consul of the French Republic. I entertain hopes that the result of this discussion will prove most beneficial, and that it will particularly assist your Excellency in your communication with the French Government. Sure am I that in the event of war there will exist but one voice throughout the country in the support of his Majesty; and the knowledge of this disposition in the people of Great Britain will, it is to be hoped, bring the French Government to sentiments of moderation and justice. The House immediately after agreeing to the Address voted ten thousand additional seamen, and ordered the militia to be embodied immediately.

Lord Whitworth to Lord Hawkesbury.

Paris, March 10, 1803.

Whatever may be the immediate result of the present discussion, I should but ill discharge my duty were I to endeavour to encourage your Lordship in the belief that it can be carried through without coming to extremities. It may perhaps be deferred, but it cannot, I fear, be avoided;

and even this respite can be attributed only to the want of means and to give full effect to the First Consul's revenge and hatred. I had two days ago a very interesting conversation with Joseph Bonaparte, in which he deplored in very strong terms, and such as convinced me that he was not wholly indifferent to personal considerations, the calamities which the question of Malta was likely to draw down upon this country, and eventually on Europe. He gave me clearly to understand—and I am persuaded he did it with a better motive than the First Consul had done—that a war must be the inevitable consequence of our refusal to execute this part of the Treaty of Amiens; that the determination of the First Consul was fixed, and that all the reasoning and arguments of his more dispassionate friends were unavailing. He was clearly of opinion that the First Consul would not attempt to carry his views on Egypt into effect at this moment, even supposing we were not in the way, but he would not undertake to say that the hope of acquiring that country would be ever abandoned. He was candid enough to admit the force of our arguments, and was very much disposed to throw the whole blame on the temper of the First Consul, which, he said, was so irritable on this point that none of his family dared to mention it. In short, the amount of what I could collect from him was that the First Consul was determined to go to war for Malta, in spite of everything which could be urged by his family and by some of his Ministers, or of the unpopularity which such a measure would draw upon him. At the same time, I have it from good authority that an officer has been despatched into Italy with orders to General Murat to demand of the King of Naples a free passage into Sicily for a French army, as a preparatory step to the expulsion of the English forces from Malta. Although no attack is to be apprehended from that or any other quarter, yet the occupation of Sicily by the French will be a very serious misfortune, whether it be considered as depriving eventually the King of Naples of so great a part of his dominions, or as cutting off the supplies which Malta receives from that island. Orders have been also sent to the different French ports to equip as expeditiously as possible, without exciting alarm; and a frigate is despatched to the West Indies to put the fleet and army at St. Domingo, as well as the other colonies, on their guard. The First Consul has also since my last despatch made an attempt on Count Marcoff similar to that which he made upon me. He invited him two days ago to a conference, in which he went over the same arguments he had employed with me, all tending to convince him that he was determined to go to war rather than suffer the English to remain in possession of Malta, and concluding with the hope that the Emperor of Russia would approve his resolution, founded on a sense of dignity and of justice. Count Marcoff assured me that he combated his reasoning with freedom, though without any apparent success. He is persuaded, however, that none of the arguments used by the First Consul will have the smallest weight with the Emperor. In the meantime the First Consul proposes despatching immediately one of his aides-de-camp to Petersburg to make the attempt. I think it right to inform your Lordship that in conversing last night with Count Marcoff on the present situation of affairs, and more particularly on the nature of the security which could be resorted to, supposing we should ever be inclined to evacuate Malta, I was induced to throw out the idea of a triple guarantee of Great Britain, Russia, and France as the most likely means of obtaining the end we proposed. He doubted as well as myself whether even this would be sufficient to restrain the ambition of the First Consul, but admitted that were he, in defiance of such an engagement, to acquire by a sudden invasion either Egypt or any other portion of the Turkish Empire, he must be inevitably expulsed by the united efforts of the Russians and Turks on one side, and those of the British fleet and army on the other. He at the same time declared that such a plan would be so perfectly congenial to the Emperor of Russia's sincere desire to preserve the Turkish Empire, that he should feel himself fully authorised to sign such an act, were it presented to him, without any fresh instructions from his Court. Although this was merely conversation, I think it my duty to state it to your Lordship. I have, however, great doubt whether the First Consul would accede to such a plan, or, indeed, whether under any circumstances his Majesty could consent to relinquish this important point, since it is almost certain that, were we to do so tomorrow in the hope of avoiding a war, we should be very soon drawn into hostilities, but under much more disadvantagoues circumstances, for the defence or recovery of Egypt.

Paris, March 10, 1803.

I have the honour to acknowledge the receipt of your Lordship's three separate despatches, with their enclosures, of the 4th inst. With respect to the facilitating the return of the English seamen who are now in this country, I confess I am at a loss how to proceed. The paper which Mr. Croker presented to Sir Evan Nepean points out the number of such seamen and the expense attending their departure; but it omits the most material point, which is the method by which I am to ascertain their wish of quitting this country and to offer them any assistance should they be so disposed. Any attempt at a communication with them on my part would immediately excite the attention of this Government, and indeed any person I might send would be exposed to great personal danger. In my own opinion, the best method would be for Mr. Croker, who probably has been in the habit of communicating with these people, to come over and take charge of the business himself. It must be done in a secret manner: such is the jealousy of a public mission, that any step I might take would be inevitably defeated, and in all probability occasion the immediate removal of them to the West Indies, or anywhere else more out of our reach. Any formal application on my part to the French Government would probably be answered by the assertion that they had no desire to return, and means would be taken to prevent my ascertaining the truth of that assertion.

Paris, March 10, 1803.

Your Lordship may depend upon my not neglecting the hint you gave me in your letter of the 4th inst., and I wish I could at present see any prospect of giving it effect. I fear there is no compromise to be made with the pride and hatred of the First Consul. Both these will urge him to extremities as soon as he conceives himself in a situation to throw off the mask. We may be able to spin out the negotiation for some months, and then we must expect the effect of his rancour, unless in the interim something should arise in this country more likely to restrain him within the bounds of prudence and moderation than any arguments used. Although the chapter of accidents is not to be depended upon in the common course of politics, yet in the present instance surely some dependence may be placed upon it, and at all events we shall at the end of a few months be better prepared to meet his attack than he to make it. I think, however, I should mislead your Lordship were I to give any hope that we shall be able to retain Malta without fighting for it, even on the terms suggested in your last private letter. I make no doubt that your Lordship will have communicated with Count Woronzow on this subject; he may be of the greatest use in keeping the Emperor right, and, if I may judge from the court Count Marcoff pays to him, his credit is considerable at Petersburg. A Mr. Alsop has written to me to beg I will mention him to your Lordship as a person who is known to me. I made his acquaintance when I was at Copenhagen two years ago, and found him intelligent, uncommonly active, and useful.

Paris, March 12, 1803.

The messenger Mason arrived yesterday morning early with your Lordship's private letter of the 7th informing me that in consequence of the preparations in the ports of France and Holland, which, though avowedly intended for colonial service, might in the event of a rupture be turned against some part of the British dominions, his Majesty had judged it expedient to send a message to both Houses of Parliament recommending in terms void of offence the adoption of such measures as may be consistent with the honour of his crown and the security of his dominions, and at the same time such as will manifest his Majesty's disposition for the preservation of peace. I beg leave to return your Lordship my thanks for having apprised me of this circumstance by a special messenger; I found, however, on going to M. de Talleyrand at two o'clock, that he was already informed of it. He was just setting out to communicate it to the First Consul, and appeared under considerable agitation. He returned with me to his cabinet, and though he told me he was pressed for time, he suffered me to relate the circumstance without interruption. I endeavoured to make him sensible that this measure was merely precautionary, and not in the least degree intended as a menace, which would be equally unworthy of both parties. I explained to him the difference in the forms of such proceedings in the two countries: that in this the Government might adopt and carry into effect any measure it thought proper with a view to offence or defence without any communication whatever; but that in England the case was different, and, however urgent the necessity might be, his Majesty could not depart from the established forms of communicating his intentions by message to both Houses of Parliament; that a degree of publicity was thus given in England which was not necessary here; and it was to that necessity, and not to any idea of menace, that the publicity was to be attributed. I concluded my observations by repeating that it was merely a measure of self-security founded on the armaments which were carrying on in the ports of France and Holland, remarking at the same time that had not even these armaments been as notorious as they were, the very circumstance of the First Consul's determination to augment so considerably his army in time of peace would have been a full and sufficient pretext for such a measure of precaution. M. de Talleyrand now informed me that he was already acquainted with the business; that a messenger had that morning arrived who had brought him a copy of the message, which he communicated to me. I could draw from him no reply whatever to my observations. He confined himself strictly to the assurance which he has so repeatedly made—that there was no foundation whatever for the alarm which was felt by his Majesty's Ministers; that the First Consul was pacific; that he had no thoughts whatever of attacking his Majesty's dominions unless forced to do so by a commencement of hostilities on our part; that he should always consider the refusal to evacuate Malta as such a commencement of hostilities; and that, as we had hitherto hesitated to do so, he was justified in adopting the measures which might eventually be necessary. He disclaimed every idea of the armaments fitting out in the Dutch ports having any other destination than to the colonies, and concluded that for his part he could not comprehend the motives which had necessitated a resort to such a measure on the part of his Majesty's Government. He then desired leave to go to the First Consul, promising that he would let me know the result when we met at dinner at the Prussian Minister's. He did not come there till near seven o'clock, and when we rose from table he took me aside and informed me that, although the First Consul had been highly irritated at the unjust suspicion which his Majesty's Government entertained, yet he would not allow himself to be so far mastered by his feelings as to lose sight of the calamities which the present discussion might entail upon humanity. He dwelt much on this topic, and explained the measures to which he should be obliged to resort. He said that if England wished to discuss fairly he wished the same; that if England prepared for war he would do the same; and that if England should finally determine on hostilities he trusted to the support of the French nation in the cause of honour and justice. It was in vain that I repeated that England did not wish for war, that peace was as necessary to us as it could be to France, that all we desired and all that we were contending for was security, that everything proved to us that that security was threatened by the First Consul's views on

Egypt, and that consequently our refusal to evacuate Malta was become as much a necessary precaution as the defence of any part of his Majesty's dominions. To this kind of reasoning M. de Talleyrand opposed the moderation of the First Consul, his great self-denial, and his determination to sacrifice even the most favourite points to his sincere desire to avoid a rupture. In the common course of this conversation I should mention to your Lordship that I threw out a hint of what your Lordship suggested to me in your private letter of the 4th inst.; but M. de Talleyrand paid but little attention to it, and assured me that the First Consul would neither now nor at any other time, unless forced to do so by the event of a disastrous war, admit any compromise whatever on the subject of Malta. M. de Talleyrand now told me that in order to facilitate my communication to the First Consul's sentiments he would communicate to me a paper which he had that morning drawn up with him; that it was not to be considered as a written communication, or as anything absolutely official; that it was a memorandum to assist me, but such as I might, if I chose, transmit to your Lordship. I enclose it, and will only observe that it appears to mark strongly the state of the First Consul's mind at the moment. Notwithstanding my endeavour to represent the measure which his Majesty has adopted as not intended as a menace, he evidently considers it as such, and the answer is meant as a retaliation. I think, however, there is this difference to be observed. The message of his Majesty is calm and dignified, whilst the First Consul's observations are strongly marked with passion and petulance, and carry with them an appearance of gasconade more descriptive of weakness than of magnanimity. This, indeed, is the picture of the character with which we have to deal. It must, however, be recollected that pride forms also a principal ingredient; and I fear I should mislead your Lordship were I to give any hope of our succeeding in setting aside the clause of the Treaty of Amiens which stipulates the evacuation of Malta, unless it be effected by force of arms. The recurrence to hostilities may be protracted till both parties are better prepared, but

I

cannot, I fear, be ultimately avoided. I yesterday evening received by Courvoisier the Address of the two Houses of Parliament, which your Lordship was so good as to send me. I sincerely congratulate your Lordship on the highly proper manner in which it passed both Houses, and I have no doubt that this circumstance will assist my communication with the French Government. I have thought it better, however, that it should reach them by any other means than mine, in order to obviate every appearance of exultation or menace; but it will, I am persuaded, have its full effect.

---

1. Si Sa Majesté Britannique entend parler dans son message de l'expédition de Helvoet, tout le monde sait qu'elle était destinée pour l'Amérique et qu'elle allait partir pour sa destination; mais d'après le message de Sa Majesté l'embarquement et le départ vont être contremandés.

2. Si nous n'avons pas des explications satisfaisantes sur ces armements de l'Angleterre, et qu'ils ont effectivement lieu, il est naturel que le Premier Consul fasse entrer vingt mille hommes en Hollande, puisque la Hollande est nommée dans le message.

3. Ces troupes une fois entrées, il est naturel que l'on forme un camp sur les frontières du pays d'Hanovre et qu'on remette d'ailleurs de nouveaux corps de troupes à ceux qui étaient déjà embarqués pour l'Amérique, afin de préparer d'autres embarquements et de se tenir dans une position défensive et offensive.

4. Il est naturel que le Premier Consul ordonne la formation de plusieurs camps à Calais et sur les divers points de la côte.

5. Il est aussi dans la nature des choses que le Premier Consul, qui était sur le point de faire évacuer la Suisse, se trouve forcé d'y maintenir une armée française.

6. C'est encore une conséquence naturelle de tout ceci que le Premier Consul fasse passer une nouvelle force en

Italie pour occuper, si cela devient nécessaire, la position de Tarente.

7. L'Angleterre armant, et armant avec tant d'éclat, la France sera obligée de mettre son armée sur le pied de guerre —mouvement tellement considérable qu'il sera un objet d'agitation pour *toute* l'Europe.

Le résultat de tous ces mouvements sera d'aigrir davantage les deux nations. La France aura été obligée de prendre toutes ces précautions en conséquence des armements de l'Angleterre, et cependant on ne manquera pas d'exciter la nation anglaise en disant que la France la veut envahir. La population britannique sera obligée de se mettre sous les armes pour sa défense, et son commerce d'exportation se trouvera, même avant la guerre, paralysé sur toute l'étendue des pays qu'occupe l'armée française. L'expérience des nations et la marche des événements prouvent que d'un tel état de choses à des hostilités réelles il n'y a malheureusement pas loin.

Quant aux différends dont il est parlé dans le message de S. M. Britannique, nous ne nous en connaissons aucun avec l'Angleterre ; car il ne paraît pas imaginable qu'on ait prétendu sérieusement en Angleterre se soustraire à l'exécution du traité d'Amiens sous la protection d'un armement militaire. L'Europe sait bien que l'on peut tenter de déchirer la France, mais non pas de l'intimider.

Paris, March 14, 1803.

The messenger Mason went on Saturday with my despatches of that date; and until yesterday, Sunday, I saw no one likely to give me any information, such as I could depend upon, as to the effect which his Majesty's message had had on the temper (for it is by that alone that he is influenced) of the First Consul. I was, however, on that day a witness of, and in some degree a sufferer by, its violence. At the Court which was held at the Tuileries, and the which I attended for the purpose of introducing some English gentlemen and ladies to Madame Bonaparte, he accosted me evidently under very considerable agitation. He began by asking me if I had any news from England. I told him that I had received letters from your Lordship two days ago. He immediately said, 'So you are determined to go to war.' 'No, Premier Consul,' I replied; 'we are too sensible of the advantage of peace.' 'Nous avons,' said he, 'déjà fait la guerre pendant quinze ans.' As he seemed to wait for an answer, I observed only, 'C'en est déjà trop.' 'Mais,' said he, 'vous voulez la faire encore quinze années, et vous m'y forcez.' I told him that was very far from his Majesty's intentions. He then proceeded to Count Marcoff and the Chevalier Azzara, who were standing together at a little distance from me, and said to them, 'Les Anglais veulent la guerre, mais s'ils sont les premiers à tirer l'épée, je serai le dernier à la remettre. Ils ne respectent pas les traités. Il faut dorénavant les couvrir de crêpe noir.' I suppose he meant the treaties. He then went his round, and was thought by all those to whom he addressed himself to betray great signs of irritation. In a few minutes he came back to me, to my great annoyance, and resumed the conversation, if such it can be called, by something personally civil to me. He then began again: 'Pourquoi des armements? contre qui des mesures de précaution? Je n'ai pas un seul vaisseau de ligne dans les ports de France, mais si vous voulez armer, j'armerai aussi; si vous voulez vous battre, je me battrai aussi. Vous pourrez peut-être tuer la France, mais jamais l'intimider.' 'On ne voudroit,' said I, 'ni l'un ni l'autre. On voudroit vivre en bonne intelligence avec elle.' 'Il faut donc respecter les traités,' replied he; 'malheur à ceux qui ne respectent pas les traités! Ils en seront responsables à toute l'Europe.' He was too agitated to make it advisable to prolong the conversation; I therefore made no answer, and he retired to his apartment repeating the last phrase. It is to be remarked that all this passed loud enough to be overheard by two hundred people who were present. I was fortunate enough not to be betrayed into anything imprudent, or which could be misconstrued; I am persuaded that there was not a single person who did not feel the extreme impropriety of his conduct, and the total want of dignity as well as of decency on the occasion. I propose taking the first opportunity of telling M. de Talleyrand that I go to the Tuileries to pay my respects to the First Consul and to Madame Bonaparte, but if I am to be attacked there in that public manner by the First Consul, on topics which are made to be discussed in the cabinet, I must refrain from presenting myself there until I have assurances that the same thing will not happen to me again. I hope, however, he will feel the impropriety of his conduct; and, indeed, I may be satisfied with the impression it has made on the public, by which his conduct is generally disapproved and ridiculed. I think your Lordship will agree with me that in this there are no traces of a great mind. If he accuses us of wishing to intimidate, his own conduct and language justify us in retorting the charge. M. de Colbert, one of the First Consul's aides-de-camp, has been despatched to Petersburg, and Count Marcoff, who did not choose to write by him, despatches a messenger to-morrow. I trust the Emperor will on this occasion show himself as becomes his dignity and the station he holds. I have written to Sir John Warren by this occasion, and I enclose a copy of my letter. General Duroc is also gone suddenly to Berlin, and it is supposed to persuade that Court to make a demonstration against Hanover. We must be prepared for everything which malice and offended pride can imagine.

Lord Whitworth to Sir John Warren.

Paris, March 14, 1803.

I am indebted to you for two letters, and I assure you this debt has for some time past weighed heavily upon my conscience. You will naturally suppose that under present circumstances a free communication with you would be of all things the most desirable; but such is the danger of the post here, and so circuitous and subject to delay the way of England, that I have depended solely on the promises of Count Marcoff, which have not been fulfilled until this moment. He now sends a messenger to his Court to give an account of the state of the discussion between us and the First Consul, and if he acts up to what he has always professed to me, and more particularly upon this very occasion, he will represent it in such a manner as cannot but convince the Emperor of the rectitude of our intentions, and counteract the effect of Monsieur de Colbert's mission. Both England and France (or I should say the First Consul) look to Russia for support: the former for the protection of what remains of Europe, and the latter for its subversion. I know but little of the Emperor's character, or that of Count Woronzow and Prince Adam. If they will long hesitate on which side to throw the influence of Russia, it will be on the side of justice, honour, and self-security, on the which, perhaps, depends the safety of Europe, and not on that of ambition never satisfied and the most insatiable thirst of plunder. You are not now to learn that it is on the subject of the evacuation of Malta that the two Governments are at issue. I have been instructed a fortnight ago to declare, that until means are found to dissipate those alarms for the safety of Egypt which the conduct of the First Consul has excited, his Majesty does not think himself justified in giving up a point on which the safety of that country, and eventually that of his own possessions, so materially depends. In answer to this assurances have been given that the First Consul has no present views on Egypt; that he has delayed his projects on that country, not because he does not wish for it, but because he is certain it must one day belong to him, either by a private agreement with the Porte, or by the dissolution of the Turkish Empire. This the First Consul told me himself. We have, however, reasons without end; and, had we no other, the mission of Colonel Sebastiani would be sufficient to convince us that the First Consul would not wait for so distant an event, and, I hope, so uncertain an one, but that he would, on the contrary, the moment his Majesty's fleet should be withdrawn from the Mediterranean, and particularly from that point which may be called the Watch Tower of Egypt, carry his views into effect by immediately invading and taking possession of that country. Such is the state of the question; and you will not be surprised at the anxiety of the First Consul to gain the acquiescence of the Emperor, and to induce him to see the question in the light in which he thinks proper to put it,—that is, himself, frank, candid, open-hearted, void of ambition, occupied solely with the improvement of this country, and entertaining none of those projects which are attributed to him by his enemies; and England, false, perfidious, renouncing all pretensions to good faith and the observance of treaties, and endeavouring to keep possession of Malta, not for the purpose of securing Egypt, but in order to crush the trade of France in the Mediterranean and keep the monopoly in our own hands. Such reasoning will, however, have no effect on the Emperor. It would, indeed, be humiliating if our good faith were to be placed in any comparison with that of the First Consul. Our motives speak for themselves, and are, I am persuaded, admitted at Petersburg. The favourite expression of the First Consul on this occasion is, ' Malheur à ceux qui n'observent pas les traités!'—the natural answer to which is, ' Malheur à ceux dont l'ambition nécessite leur infraction!' The great point to be now carried with regard to Russia is, I apprehend, not so much to engage it in war with us at the first outset—for that, I suppose, would be nearly impossible —but to insure its concurrence in and countenance of our measures and conduct; and that in the Emperor's answer to the First Consul, whether by Monsieur de Colbert or through the regular channel, there should be nothing which can be construed into an approbation of which he would immediately avail himself as a justification to the French nation of the war in which his ambition and violence may plunge it. Such a satisfaction will, I think, not be difficult to obtain from the Emperor Alexander, and from those in whom he places his confidence. It would be conformable to the principles which I have always known them to entertain; and when the question is to be tried of the purity of the views of the two Governments, I trust it is not difficult to foresee on which side the scale will preponderate. The countenance of the Emperor will therefore be of the utmost importance, and indeed have such an influence on the discussion as perhaps to terminate it without a recourse to war, which once begun might not be concluded without involving those who think themselves the most secure. All these arguments will have been suggested to you by Lord Hawkesbury; they will have occurred to yourself, as they must do to everyone who thinks soberly on this business. I will not, however, apologise for the repetition of them, but conclude with sincerely hoping that they will have that effect on the decision of the Emperor which his own dignity and the security of what remains of Europe still independent of France so evidently demand.

Lord Hawkesbury to Lord Whitworth.

Downing Street, March 15, 1803.

I send your Excellency a copy of the note presented to me by General Andréossy on the 10th inst., and a copy of the answer which I have this day by his Majesty's commands returned to it. I have only to desire that in all your communications with the French Government you would endeavour to conform yourself as much as possible to the language and sentiments contained in the answer to that note. It is of the utmost importance that the French Government should not be led to believe that the island of Malta is the sole, or even the chief, cause of the differences subsisting between the two countries, but that you should impress upon them that their acts of aggression and views of aggrandisement have principally occasioned the present situation of affairs, and that in every discussion which may take place between your Excellency and the French Government you should bring forward all the grounds of complaint which his Majesty feels he is warranted in giving against them.

To General Andréossy.

The undersigned, his Majesty's principal Secretary of State for Foreign Affairs, has laid before the King the note of his Excellency the French Ambassador of the 10th inst. In obeying the commands of his Majesty, by returning an official answer to this note, the undersigned feels it necessary for him to do little more than repeat the explanations which have been already given on more than one occasion by himself verbally to General Andréossy, and by Lord Whitworth to M. Talleyrand, on the subject of the note, and of the points which appear to be connected with it. He can have no difficulty in assuring the French Ambassador that his Majesty has entertained a most sincere desire that the Treaty of Amiens might be executed in a full and complete manner; but it has not been possible for him to consider this treaty as having been founded on principles different from those which have been invariably applied to every other antecedent treaty or convention,—namely, that they were negotiated with reference to the actual *state of possession* of the different parties, and of the *treaties* or *public engagements* by which they were bound at the time of its conclusion, and that if that state of possession and of engagements was so materially altered by the act of either of the parties as to affect the nature of the compact itself, the other party has a right, according to the law of nations, to interfere for the purpose of obtaining satisfaction or compensation for any essential difference which such acts may have subsequently made in their relative situation; that if there ever was a case to which this principle might be applied with peculiar propriety it was that of the late Treaty of Peace, for the negotiation was conducted on a basis not merely proposed by his Majesty, but specially agreed to in an official note by the French Government, viz. *that his Majesty should keep a compensation out of his conquests for the important acquisitions of territory made by France upon the Continent.* This is a sufficient proof that the compact was understood to have been concluded in relation to the then existing state of things; for the measure of his Majesty's compensation was to be calculated with reference to the acquisitions of France at that time. And if the interference of the French Government in the general affairs of Europe since that period; if their interposition with respect to Switzerland and Holland, whose independence was guaranteed by them at the time of the conclusion of the Treaty of Peace; if the acquisitions which have been made by France in various quarters, but particularly those in Italy, have extended the territory and increased the power of France: his Majesty would be warranted, consistently with the spirit of the Treaty of Peace, in claiming equivalents for these acquisitions as some counterpoise to the augmentation of the power of France. His Majesty, however, anxious to prevent all ground of misunderstanding, and desirous of consolidating the general peace of Europe as far as might be in his power, was willing to have waived the pretensions he might have a right to advance of this nature; and as the other articles of the Definitive Treaty have been in a course of execution on his part, so he would have been ready to have carried into effect an arrangement conformable to the true intent and spirit of the tenth article, the execution of that arrangement according to its terms having been rendered impracticable by circumstances which it was not in his Majesty's power to control. Whilst his Majesty was actuated by these sentiments of moderation and forbearance, and prepared to regulate his conduct in conformity to them, his attention was particularly attracted by the very extraordinary publication of the report of Colonel Sebastiani to the First Consul. This report contains the most unjustifiable insinuations and charges against his Majesty's Government, against the officer commanding his forces in Egypt, and against the British army in that quarter—insinuations and charges wholly destitute of foundation, and such as would have warranted his Majesty in demanding that satisfaction which, on occasions of this nature, independent Powers in a state of amity have a right to expect from each other. It discloses, moreover, views in the highest degree injurious to the interests of his Majesty's dominions, and directly repugnant to and utterly inconsistent with the spirit and letter of the Treaty of Peace concluded between his Majesty and the French Government. His Majesty's Ambassador at Paris was accordingly directed to make such a representation to the French Government as his Majesty felt to be called for by imputations of the nature above described, by the disclosure of purposes inconsistent with good faith, and highly injurious to the interests of his people; and as a claim had recently been made by the French Government on the subject of the evacuation of Malta, Lord Whitworth was instructed to accompany this representation by a declaration on the part of his Majesty that before he could enter into any further discussions relative to that island it was expected that satisfactory explanations should be given upon the various points respecting which his Majesty had complained. This representation and this claim, founded on principles incontestably just, and couched in terms the most temperate, appear to have been wholly disregarded by the French Government: no satisfaction has been afforded, no explanation whatever has been given; but, on the contrary, his Majesty's suspicions of the views of the French Government with respect to the Turkish Empire have been confirmed and strengthened by subsequent events. Under these circumstances his Majesty feels that he has no alternative, and that a just regard to his own honour and to the interests of his people makes it necessary for him to declare that he cannot consent that his troops should evacuate the island of Malta until substantial security has been provided for those objects which, under the present circumstances, might be materially endangered by their removal. With respect to several of the positions stated in the note, and grounded on the idea of the tenth article being executed in its literal sense, they call for some observations. By the tenth article of the Treaty of Amiens, the island of Malta was to be restored by his Majesty to the Order of St. John, upon certain conditions. The evacuation of the island at a specified period formed a part of these conditions; and if the other stipulations had been in a due course of execution, his Majesty would have been bound, by the terms of the treaty, to have ordered his forces to evacuate the island. But these conditions must be considered as being all of equal effect; and if any material parts of them should have been found incapable of execution, or if the execution of them should from any circumstances have been retarded, his Majesty would be warranted in deferring the evacuation of the island until such time as the other conditions of the article could be effected, or until some new arrangement could be concluded which should be judged satisfactory by the contracting parties. The refusal of Russia to accede to the arrangement, except on condition that the Maltese Langue should be abolished; the silence of the Court of Berlin with respect to the invitation that has been made to it, in consequence of the treaty, to become a guaranteeing Power; the abolition of the Spanish Priories in defiance of the treaty to which the King of Spain was a party; the declaration of the Portuguese Government of their intention to sequestrate the property of the Portuguese Priory, as forming a part of the Spanish Langue, unless the property of the Spanish Priories was restored to them: these circumstances would have been sufficient, without any other special grounds, to have warranted his Majesty in suspending the evacuation of the island. The evacuation of Tarentum and Brindisium is in no respect connected with that of Malta. The French Government were bound to evacuate the Kingdom of Naples by their treaty of peace with the King of Naples, at a period antecedent to that at which this stipulation was carried into effect. The French Government were likewise, by engagements with the Emperor of Russia, to respect the independence of the Kingdom of Naples. But even admitting that the departure of the French troops from Tarentum depended solely on the article of the Treaty of Amiens, their departure is, by the terms of the treaty, to take place at the same period as the other evacuations in Europe—namely, one month after the ratification of the Definitive Treaty, at which period both Porto Ferrajo and Minorca were evacuated by his Majesty's forces; whereas the troops of his Majesty were in no case bound to evacuate the island of Malta antecedent to the period of three months after the ratification of the Definitive Treaty; and even in that event it must be considered as depending upon the other parts of the arrangement being in a course of execution. With respect to the assertion in the note, that the Neapolitan troops were to form the garrison of Malta until the period when the arrangements relative to the Order could be carried into effect, it will appear by a reference to the article, that by the preliminary paragraph the island was to be restored to the Order upon the condition of the succeeding stipulations; and that it was only from the period when the restitution to the Order had actually taken place that, by the twelfth paragraph, the Neapolitan troops were to form a part of the garrison. The undersigned has thus stated, with all the frankness which the importance of the subject appears to require, the sentiments of his Majesty on the note delivered to him by General Andréossy, and on the points in discussion between the two countries. His Majesty is willing to indulge the hope that the conduct of the French Government on this occasion may be influenced by principles similar to those which have invariably influenced his own; that as far as possible all causes of distrust and every impediment to a good understanding between the two countries may be completely and effectually removed; and that the peace may be consolidated on a secure and lasting foundation. The undersigned requests General Andréossy to accept the assurances of his high consideration.

LORD WHITWORTH TO LORD HAWKESBURY.

Paris, March 17, 1803.

I called yesterday on M. de Talleyrand, to converse with him on the subject of what had passed on Sunday last at the Tuileries. He had been since that day so fully occupied with his expeditions to different foreign Courts, that I had no opportunity of seeing him sooner. I told him that I had been placed by the First Consul in a situation which could neither suit my public nor my private feelings; that I went to the Tuileries to pay my respects to the First Consul and to Madame Bonaparte, and to present my countrymen, but not to treat of political subjects, the discussion of which was better suited to the cabinet than to a public assembly; and that unless I had the assurance from him that I should not be exposed to a repetition of the same disagreeable circumstances I should be under the necessity of discontinuing my visits to the Tuileries. M. de Talleyrand assured me that it was very far from the First Consul's intention to distress me, but he had felt himself personally insulted by the charges which were brought against him by the English Government, and that it was incumbent upon him to take the first opportunity of exculpating himself in the presence of the Ministers of the different Powers of Europe. He assured me that nothing similar would occur. Such is the explanation given of this highly unjustifiable conduct of the First Consul. He now affects to pass over as a premeditated declaration what was the effect of petulance and ill-humour. The fact is, they are heartily ashamed of it; and as the First Consul will have three weeks to reflect, I trust I shall find him more temperate the next time we meet in the same place. M. de Talleyrand did not neglect this opportunity of entering into a discussion on the present posture of affairs. He assured me that the First Consul lamented the lengths to which they were likely to lead as much as any individual in France; that for his part he could not comprehend what could be the motive of the uneasiness we expressed, or, indeed, what was the discussion from which such serious consequences could be apprehended. He gave me 'his word of honour' (and I must declare that I have in this instance no reason to doubt it) that no armaments capable of giving us the least uneasiness were carrying on in the ports of France; that as for those in the Dutch ports, their destination was notorious. What, then, had we to apprehend? For we could not suppose the First Consul to be so wanting in common honesty and lost to shame as to meditate an attack in the midst of peace. I told him that if he had read with attention his Majesty's message, and the explanation which has been given of it by his Majesty's Ministers, he would not have attributed the measure of precaution which had been taken to a want of confidence in the First Consul. No such thing had been asserted or even alluded to. All that had been said, and that in the plainest terms, was that a discussion of great importance, the result of which was uncertain, was on foot between the two Governments; that the nature of this discussion, of which he declared himself to be ignorant, was neither more nor less than this: By the Treaty of Amiens, England is bound to evacuate Malta when certain stipulations are fulfilled. England now refuses to do so upon the plea, firstly, that since the conclusion of the treaty the conduct of France had been such as to justify England in seeking a counterpoise; and, secondly, that the First Consul's views on Egypt, and consequently on his Majesty's possessions in India, have been so plainly manifested, both in direct opposition to the letter and spirit of the treaty, as not only to justify England in keeping Malta, but even to render such a measure absolutely necessary for the preservation of his Majesty's dominions. This, then, was the nature of the discussion, and he would not, I trusted, dispute its importance; that in the meantime a very considerable armament was preparing in the ports of Holland, obviously with a view to the colonies. But who could say that that armament might not be directed towards the coasts of England, from which it was but the distance of a day and a half's sail, should this important discussion lead to hostilities; and in that event what would be our situation? They would find both the coasts and the country perfectly unprepared. And I appealed to him whether his Majesty's Ministers would have been worthy of the confidence they possessed had they incurred the most remote risk of such an order of things. They had done the only thing they had to do: they had advised his Majesty to embody the militia, and to take such other constitutional measures of defence as the circumstances seemed to require. M. de Talleyrand could not but admit the force of this argument. He contented himself, therefore, with protestations of the First Consul's sincere desire of peace; at the same time, however, that he was determined on war rather than suffer any infraction of the Treaty of Amiens. He dwelt a considerable time upon the subject without advancing anything new, or giving me reason to suppose that the First Consul was more disposed to compromise than he was a week ago. It is, however, certain that he had no desire to go to war. He feels that he has nothing to gain from us, and he feels that the whole country is against it. How far these motives will operate, supported by a continuation of the same calm and dignified firmness with which his Majesty's Government has hitherto proceeded, and which, whatever may be the feelings of the First Consul and of those of his generals who urge him on, is properly appreciated by the public, a short time will show. In the meantime, I think I can say with certainty that no armaments of any consequence are carrying on in the French ports. Orders were given (as I mentioned to your Lordship in a former despatch) a fortnight ago to equip what there was in the different ports; but the total want of naval stores, and the absence of by far the greatest part of the naval force, render such an order almost nugatory. A messenger has, however, been despatched to Madrid to require twelve sail of the line and twenty-four thousand men, by virtue of the treaty subsisting between the two Governments. It has also been signified to the Court of Naples, that, as the English Government refuses to fulfil the Treaty of Amiens, it will be incumbent on the First Consul to place himself, with regard to his Sicilian Majesty's dominions, in the situation he was previous to the conclusion of the treaty. The Americans, whose fears never suffered them to doubt the professed destination of the armaments in the Dutch ports, are now delivered from their apprehensions. They are sanguine enough to hope that they shall hear no more of the threatened exchange of the Floridas, or even of the projects on Louisiana. It is certain that M. de

Talleyrand has given the American Minister reason to suppose that these projects will be deferred, and he trusts to the chapter of accidents for the rest.

Paris, March 18, 1803.

I received your Lordship's despatch, with its enclosures, this morning early, and I learnt at the same time that a messenger had arrived from General Andréossy to M. de Talleyrand. Shortly after, M. de Talleyrand sent to desire I would call upon him, which I accordingly did. He told me that he had not only received your Lordship's note to the French Ambassador, but also the sentiments of the First Consul upon it, which he was desirous to communicate to me before he re-despatched the messenger. This he did; and I refer your Lordship to the communication which General Andréossi will make according to his instructions without loss of time. From the tenor of this note your Lordship will be convinced that this Government is not desirous to proceed to extremities—that is to say, it is not prepared so to do; and therefore it expresses a willingness to enter on the discussion of the point which appears, according to their conception, or rather to the interpretation they choose to give it, the most material. This of course is the safety of Egypt. On this the First Consul declares in the note, as M. de Talleyrand did repeatedly to me, that he would be willing to enter into any engagement by which such a security as would fully quiet our apprehensions might be given on the part of the French Government. On the subject of Malta, the First Consul maintains that he cannot listen to any compromise. He is bound in honour to require the full execution of the Treaty of Amiens, and therefore cannot in honour give up the point. With regard to Egypt, for the preservation of which we say it is necessary we should keep possession of Malta, he is willing to enter into any engagement which may be thought sufficient. I told him that he had departed from the letter and the sense of your Lordship's note by confining the question to Malta alone. That note had comprehended other most important considerations: that the best method of bringing the discussion to a speedy conclusion, such as his Majesty's Government appeared to wish, was to take it up on a broader scale; but that at the same time his Majesty's Government would not refuse to lend itself to anything reasonable which might be suggested. There was, however, I told him, one distinction to be made in the situation of the two Governments in the discussion of this question. France had no other ground than the maintenance of its honour, whilst England had the same, with the addition of its security. By our possession of Malta France was not threatened; but the reverse was the case should the access to Egypt be opened by its evacuation. I declared to him, therefore, that I saw no means of coming to an understanding, unless Malta was conceded to us, if not in perpetuity, at least for a definite term—such as might insure a long continuance of peace. This, he assured me, would not be possible to obtain; and I did not touch on any other mode. In this state the business is referred to your Lordship. And I think we may fairly attribute even this disposition to accommodation to the vigorous measures which have been adopted by his Majesty's Government, aided by the unprepared state of this country. I re-despatch this messenger without loss of time, to prepare your Lordship for the communication which General Andréossy will have to make. I should observe that M. de Talleyrand said to me, as a proof of the First Consul's earnest desire to conciliate, that he had refrained from everything which could look like a demonstration of hostilities. No orders had yet been given to arm in the ports, no troops ordered to march to the coasts. This, however, is not to be taken literally. It is certain that the greatest activity and bustle prevail in the naval and military departments at Paris, whatever may be the case in the ports and provinces.

Paris, March 18, 1803.

Captain Wright arrived this morning by the way of Havre with your Lordship's letter of the 16th. I shall of course be very happy to avail myself of this gentleman's aid and information; but I fear he is too well known to be of any material service; and I will confess to your Lordship that I am not without apprehension that, in a moment of irritation like the present, it may be recollected that he was a prisoner here, and that he escaped from prison. I cannot but think a less remarkable person, however intelligent Captain Wright may be, might have been equally useful, without incurring the risk of adding another *pierre d'achoppement* to the many which we may expect to find in our way. I have, however, told him he might remain here for the present, and see his old friends, if they were willing under the present circumstances to renew their acquaintance—which I very much doubt. For the rest, he has seen nothing at Havre which can be construed into an armament; and I verily believe this is the case in every port of France. They doubtless will now begin; but their means are so slender that their progress can be neither quick nor alarming. On the subject of my despatch I have little to add. It is evident that the First Consul is under considerable embarrassment. I have no reason, however, to imagine that he is more disposed than he was to renounce Malta; but yet I do not think even this a desperate case. But, at the worst, such arrangements may be made for the security of Egypt as may appear best to answer our purpose, short of the actual possession of Malta. I am at the same time persuaded that, had it not been for the tone which his Majesty's Government has assumed, we should not have met even with a disposition to give us satisfaction on this head. Much will doubtless depend on the line which Russia may adopt. It will be endeavoured here to give the Emperor the mediation, and nothing will be spared to gain the mediator. Should the determination be such as we could wish, and as we have a right to expect, I think we may look with a well-grounded hope to the possession of the object in dispute, if not in perpetuity, at least for such a number of years as might answer our purpose. But then we must do as others do, and trust a little to the chapter of accidents—*faire ce qu'on peut* is the next to *faire ce qu'on veut.*

Copie d'une Lettre à M. Talleyrand.

Lundi, 16 Mars à minuit.

Je reçois à courant un mot de Joseph Bonaparte, et voici ce mot : *Il n'y a rien à faire pour le moment.* Après vous avoir quitté à 4 heures, mon cher Monsieur, je me suis rendu chez moi, où j'ai écrit au Lord Whitworth correctement et littéralement mes deux conversations du jour—la première avec Joseph, la seconde avec vous. Je lui ai marqué que vous m'aviez expressément dit de lui *donner ma parole d'honneur* que demain il me seroit expédié d'ici une dépêche qui me parviendroit dans la suite du mardi ou mercredi, que cette dépêche porteroit vraisemblablement une proposition pour rapprochement et dans l'esprit de l'ultimatum d'Angleterre. J'ai lu ma lettre à M. Talbot, secrétaire d'ambassade, qui a fait partir un courrier pour la porter. Cette lettre parviendra demain à midi, et ma parole d'honneur annonçait décidément une dépêche officielle. Je suis comme assuré que my Lord Whitworth attendra jusque'à mercredi, à moins qu'il n'ait trouvé à Calais des instructions positives pour mettre à la voile. Dans cette situation, veuillez vous mettre franchement à ma place. Ce mot : *Il n'y a rien à faire pour le moment,* me prescrit d'envoyer un second courrier pour révoquer ce que j'ai dit par celui de ce soir. Mais comme je me suis appuyé de votre nom, je pourrois être doublement compromis si je faisois partir ce second courrier sans vous en prévenir, et sans vous prier au préalable de me donner l'explication de ces deux mots si douteux. J'attends votre réponse, et d'après ce que vous me marquerez pour faire cesser la cruelle incertitude où je suis, j'enverrai mon second courrier ou j'y renoncerai.

Recevez, Monsieur, &c.

LORD WHITWORTH TO LORD HAWKESBURY.

Paris, March 21, 1803.

I have no material change in the aspect of affairs here to announce your Lordship since my letter of the day before yesterday. The First Consul is undecided on the line of conduct he shall pursue; his passions urging him one way, and his reason, backed by the representations of his family, another. In this dilemma, he appears to have made a most dangerous experiment—that of calling to his most intimate confidence those who are his most rooted enemies, and who consequently will advise him to what they wish most likely to lead him to ruin: these are Fouché and Masséna. I have reason to believe they were both for war. The thinking part of those who are in the service of Government are, however, very far from following the same course. The general opinion is against it. General Berthier, the War Minister, has, I am assured, declared his determination to resign should hostilities be resolved on; and many others will follow his example. In short, Bonaparte finds no encouragement but from the needy and hot-headed aides-de-camp who are in his ante-chamber. In his heart he is averse to the war, from the same reasons which alarm so much his family; so that, though he will endeavour to put a good face upon it, with a view to his dignity, he will, I am persuaded, at last do much to avoid it. Everything, therefore, points out the necessity of a steady and temperate perseverance; for we may be assured that, whether we are to attain our object by force of arms or by any other means whatever, this Government and this country must be convinced that we are in earnest; that we have not adopted the present vigorous measures with a view solely to intimidate, but that our unshaken resolution is Malta or war. To impress on this country such a conviction, no means should be neglected; and, were such a thing practicable, every newspaper even which finds its way here should repeat to them, Malta or war. In the meantime, what is most to be feared is that this situation may last too long without coming to a crisis. We shall, it is true, remain in possession of Malta; but at the same time we shall be at the expense of a war establishment without the means of keeping alive the spirit of the country. Such an order of things would well suit the policy of the First Consul. At a very trifling expense he would oblige us to incur a very heavy one, and if he could not exhaust our resources he might at least wear out our patience. The Neapolitan Ambassador has required the support of the Russian Minister, by virtue of the Emperor's guarantee, in his representations against the threatened aggression on the Neapolitan dominions. And the latter has declared that his Court would not see such an infraction with indifference. Russia is therefore already engaged in the discussion; and I think we are justified in hoping that the part which the Emperor may be still further induced to take will be so decisive as to afford us a prospect, at the same time that we attain our individual object, of consolidating a better system for Italy. Sienna and the Presidi of Tuscany have not been accepted by the Russian Minister: he has submitted the proposal to his Court, but is inclined to think that, in the present situation of affairs, it would not be prudent to conclude.

Lord Hawkesbury to Lord Whitworth.

Downing St., March 22, 1803.

Your Excellency's several despatches to No. 26 inclusive have been received and laid before the King. With respect to the subject of your Excellency's despatch No. 24, I have it in command to signify to you his Majesty's pleasure that you take the earliest opportunity to represent to M. de Talleyrand the surprise with which his Majesty has learnt the conduct which the First Consul had observed towards your Excellency in the instance to which that despatch refers; and you will add that as his Majesty has a right to expect that his Ambassador should be treated with the respect and attention due to the dignity of the sovereign whom he represents, it will be impossible for you to present yourself on any days of ceremony to the First Consul unless you receive an assurance that you will never be exposed to a repetition of the treatment which you experienced on the occasion in question, and which is so entirely different from the manner in which, under the same circumstances, his Majesty thought it proper to conduct himself with respect to General Andréossy. Although your Excellency appears to have anticipated this instruction in one of your most recent conversations with M. de Talleyrand, I nevertheless think it right to enable your Excellency to state to that Minister the sense which the King entertains of this transaction.

Lord Whitworth to Lord Hawkesbury.

Paris, March 24, 1803.

I have no commands from your Lordship since my last; neither have I anything very material to add to those despatches. It should seem that the First Consul is more composed than he was; but I rather attribute this change to the expectation which seems to have prevailed within these few days, and which has been encouraged by some people here, who disgrace the name and character of Englishmen, of the present vigorous measures being meant merely as a menace to which no effect will be given. These people have asserted to M. de Talleyrand—but I do not believe they have convinced him—that his Majesty's Ministers will not venture to declare the ground on which they would renew the war, and will ultimately accept of any compromise rather than submit the matter to investigation. I have repeatedly represented to M. de Talleyrand the views of these gentlemen in holding such language, and the danger in suffering it to have any influence on the determination of this Government. I trust I have not been unsuccessful; but the expectation thus held out is too favourable to their wishes not to be attended to with some degree of satisfaction, although on reflection they must be sensible of its futility. Various motives are assigned in the public prints for this hostile appearance on the part of England; and the First Consul has been himself at the pains of writing a paper for the 'Publiciste,' in which it is asserted that it is to be considered only as a measure of policy for the purpose of getting rid of a number of dangerous people complicated in the treason of Colonel Despard; and this tale, ridiculous as it is, finds credit with many. In the meantime the utmost tranquillity is affected. No menacing articles, either of defiance or of preparation, appear in the public prints; and this with a view to prove to the country that whilst England breathes jealousy and hostility the First Consul is all moderation and forbearance. Few are the dupes of this manœuvre. The preparations are, however, at the same time going on. A considerable body of troops is ordered to march towards the coasts, and will assemble in the neighbourhood of Dunkirk and Boulogne. Orders are given for building boats and other small craft at these ports and those of Havre and Cherbourg, and the military people here affect to talk with confidence of an invasion. Their confidence, however, is, I am persuaded, not founded on so desperate an undertaking, but rather on the hope of being employed again in Holland and Italy, the invasion of which countries would be attended with little danger, and where it is expected they may yet find wherewithal to gratify their love of plunder. So much do they affect to depend on the resources which they will afford, that the First Consul has declared that the day he is forced to go to war he will remit twenty millions of taxes. Although I have but little faith in their menaces against his Majesty's dominions, I am not so secure with regard to those of the King of Naples and of the Dutch Republic. It is on those devoted countries that all the vexation of the First Consul at not being able to give effect to his hatred against us will probably fall; and unfortunately he will meet with no resistance in either. I can with the utmost confidence assure your Lordship that I see no ground for despondency. I am persuaded, as I have been from the beginning, that by firmness and perseverance we shall attain our object. We owe already two favourable symptoms to the attitude we have taken: the first, a disposition to join in any measure of security for Egypt; and the second—although it has not yet been mentioned to me I know it to be in contemplation—an idea of satisfying us by conceding on the subject of Louisiana. I am sensible that nothing can satisfy us short of Malta; and I am at the same time satisfied that such is the jealousy of our retaining any possession in the Mediterranean, that to induce us to leave it no sacrifice would be thought too great. It is that which checks the favourite pursuit, and, considered as such, it is the only point worth contending for. I cannot refrain from concluding this despatch as I did my last, by repeating that, by whatever means we are to effect our purpose, this Government must be convinced that the question is—Malta or war.

Paris, March 24, 1803.

The expedition to India, consisting of one of the sail of the line and three frigates, has at length sailed from Brest; but not till several days after its departure had been announced in all the newspapers. Generals St. Suzanne and Decaen are gone with it, and with them a man by the name of Roger, who has passed most of his life in India. It is he who is particularly charged with the political concerns, such as gaining over the native princes, and of exciting jealousy and mistrust against us. I am told that this man is well suited to such purposes. According to the plan of this Government, every French, Spanish, or Dutch ship going to India is to take a certain number of troops, which are to be in the pay of France from the moment of their embarkation; and it is hoped by these means in the course of two or three years to assemble a considerable European force in that country without exciting alarm. A considerable number of officers of all descriptions are gone with the expedition from Brest; but I am assured there are not more than a few hundred men. The general of division Montchoisi is appointed Captain-General of the 'Isles de France et de la Réunion,' and the general of division Ernouf to the same situation at Guadeloupe. M. de Talleyrand announced to me yesterday that the sailing of the expedition from the Dutch ports, which was to have taken place about this time, is now countermanded; and he at the same time informed me that it was the intention of the First Consul to make an excursion this spring to Belgium and along the coast. This journey is, I suppose, meant as a demonstration; but I confess I see nothing very alarming should he carry it into effect. Antwerp is said to be the principal object of this journey, and of the First Consul's attention. It is to be made a naval arsenal for ships of war as well as of commerce, and the most skilful engineers are now there for that purpose. Officers of the same description are at this moment taking surveys in Switzerland; and such is the independence of Holland, that it is actually included in the statistical account of the French Republic lately published by the Minister of the Interior. A second messenger was despatched two days ago to Madrid in order to prepare that Court for the measure of shutting the ports of Spain to the English trade on the first appearance of a rupture with France. And the same measure has been strongly recommended to the Court of Berlin. Your Lordship need not, I suppose, be told that the note lately presented to your Lordship by M. Schimmelpenninck was fabricated in M. de Talleyrand's chancery. He communicated it to me two days ago, and left me no doubt whatever that he himself is the author of it. I should mention to your Lordship that the order from this Government prohibiting the exportation of coin has found the sum of 500,000 dollars belonging to the East India Company in the hands of Thornton and Power, English bankers in this city. They are taking means to remit them with as little expense and delay as possible. The dismay of the public here, and more particularly of those who are anywise engaged in commerce, is not to be told. They consider war as the ruin of their hopes, which were just beginning to revive. The same sentiment prevails all over France, and will, I have no doubt, be conveyed to the First Consul. The Five-per-Cents. Consolidated are at something less than fifty-six; but every livre at the disposal of Government is employed for the purpose of supporting them.

Lord Whitworth to Mr. Hammond.

Paris, March 24, 1803.

It is right that I should explain to you my motive for sending on the messenger Hunter to London. It is not, as you will perceive, on account of the extraordinary importance of the despatches with which he is charged—although the newspapers will not fail to attribute to it something of that kind—but for the purpose of conducting to us the Duke of Dorset, whom, notwithstanding the short time he, or indeed we, may remain in this country, I have promised to allow to come to us for his holidays. I have further to request that you would give him an order for an extra packet for his return. I have nothing to add to my despatch. It is difficult to foresee how all this will end; but I cannot repeat too often that it is absolutely necessary that we should stick to our text in order to do away with the impression which some of our rascally countrymen here have given. I have for this last fortnight shut my door to Lord Lauderdale and all those of his stamp with which this city swarms. It is rather singular that Lord Moira should have given me as warm a letter of recommendation as if it had been for his own brother, to a Mr. Devereaux, an Irishman, and one whom Lord Loftus assures me he knows to have been throughout one of the foremost in the rebellion.

Lord Hawkesbury to Lord Whitworth.

Downing St., March 25, 1803.

Your several despatches to No. 27 inclusive have been received and laid before the King. I herewith enclose to you for your Excellency's information the copy of a confidential communication which I made to Count Woronzow on Monday last. I think it right to apprise your Excellency that I have not as yet received from General Andréossy any answer to the note which I delivered to him on the 15th of this month; but I conclude that this answer will not be much longer delayed.

Lord Whitworth to Lord Hawkesbury.

Paris, March 26, 1803.

It is, I suppose, in order to attach some importance to the paper which accompanies this that M. de Talleyrand has desired I would forward it to your Lordship by a special messenger. And as Lieutenant George Jenkinson is returning to-day to England, I entrust it to him. The style and the spirit in which it is conceived leave no doubt of its origin; and indeed, were there no other reason for supposing it to be the production of the First Consul, the solemnity with which it has been communicated and recommended to me would justify the suspicion. I could not, however, agree with M. de Talleyrand on the great importance of the matter contained in this note. I observed to him that, in the situation in which the two Governments stood with regard to each other at this moment, none of the charges, supposing them to be facts, could afford much surprise; that with regard to the persons landed on the coast of France, whose claim to the title of *brigands* I should not dispute, it would, I made no doubt, appear that they were Frenchmen and others sent into England on no friendly errand, and who, having excited the attention of the police, had been conveyed back to the country from whence they came; that as to the second charge, it could not be wondered at if under the present circumstances the armament carrying on in the Dutch ports should be watched very closely by his Majesty's cruisers; and that on the subject of what might appear in the public prints I could only repeat what I had so often said, that his Majesty's Ministers could not be responsible for any reports which they might propagate. After having said this much on the several charges contained in the paper, I confess I could not refuse myself the pleasure of observing to M. de Talleyrand, on the subject of the extreme moderation which the First Consul attributes to himself, that I was glad he had limited the term to fifteen days, since if he had added only two more to the number I should have been obliged myself to testify against him. M. de Talleyrand sent to me at ten o'clock at night to communicate to me this curious paper. His impatience to see me had led me to expect something more important. He did not seem much disposed to talk on the subject of the discussion between the two Governments, but asked me what was my idea of the result. I told him that for my own part I was very sorry to see no probability whatever of its ending as we both wished, since it was quite impossible his Majesty should recede without obtaining that satisfaction which his dignity as well as the security of his dominions demanded, and he had given no reason to suppose that the First Consul was disposed to satisfy either. This brought on a repetition of professions of forbearance and moderation on the part of the First Consul, but nothing to the purpose. He told me that an answer to your Lordship's last note had been sent two days ago to General Andréossy, and I am to go to him this evening for the purpose of its being communicated to me. I received yesterday your Lordship's despatch No. 4 of the 22nd instant, and I shall this day communicate the purport of it to M. de Talleyrand. Although I have in fact anticipated your Lordship's intentions, yet the stating to that Minister the sense which his Majesty entertains of the conduct of the First Consul cannot but be attended with good consequences.

M. DE TALLEYRAND TO LORD WHITWORTH.

Le soussigné, ministre des Relations Extérieures, est chargé de demander à Monsieur l'ambassadeur d'Angleterre une explication catégorique sur la violation du territoire françois qui vient d'avoir lieu par le débarquement de quatre-vingts brigands entre Ostende et Dunkerque, lesquels ont été jetés sur la côte par des bâtiments de Sa Majesté Britannique. On est instruit, de plus, qu'un brick du Roi a également mouillé dans la rade d'Ostende; qu'il a obligé une chaloupe française de porter à terre seize étrangers qui ont servi dans les rangs de l'armée britannique; et l'on se demande avec étonnement qui a pu porter à violer ainsi le territoire de France et à faire jeter sur ses côtes les mauvais sujets de tous les pays. Plusieurs frégates angloises se sont présentées à Helvoetsluys, elles croisent devant la rade, et les capitaines ont déclaré à tous les bateaux du pays auxquels ils ont pu parler qu'ils étaient chargés d'empêcher la sortie des bâtiments français. On a fait répondre dans les journaux de Londres une prétendue lettre du Premier Consul au Roi d'Angleterre, ainsi que la nouvelle de l'échouage de plusieurs bâtiments chargés de cent mille armes pour l'Irlande et portant les couleurs des Irlandais Unis. Toutes ces clameurs paraissent avoir évidemment pour objet d'irriter la nation française et de la mettre dans l'obligation de repousser la force par la force. Cette marche du gouvernement britannique n'est pas digne de sa puissance. Si, en effet, Sa Majesté Britannique veut déclarer la guerre, elle doit le faire loyalement et ne pas se permettre, tant que la guerre ne sera pas déclarée, de violations de territoire et de pavillon. La conduite du Premier Consul, depuis quinze jours qu'il est provoqué de toutes les manières, a été pleine de franchise, de loyauté et d'une extrême modération; mais l'on se tromperait étrangement si on pensait que cette modération peut s'étendre à voir, de sang froid, des violations de territoire et de pavillon. Le soussigné prie Monsieur l'ambassadeur d'Angleterre de recevoir l'assurance de sa haute considération.

CH. MAU. TALLEYRAND.

Paris, le 4 Germinal, an XI.
A S. E. Lord Whitworth,
Ambassadeur de Sa Majesté Britannique.

LORD WHITWORTH TO LORD HAWKESBURY.

Paris, March 31, 1803.

I have to acknowledge your Lordship's despatch No. 5 of the 25th instant, with the copy of a confidential communication of the 21st from your Lordship to Count Woronzow. This paper has been transmitted by Count Woronzow to M. de Marcoff, by whom it had been communicated to me; and your Lordship will have perceived by my despatch of the 21st instant that the Russian Minister had not waited for this suggestion to remind the First Consul of the engagements which subsisted between the Emperor of Russia and his Sicilian Majesty, and consequently that any aggression on the part of France on his Sicilian Majesty's territories would be a violation of the Emperor's guarantee. The answer made to the Russian Minister by M. de Talleyrand was evasive, though couched in terms of high respect for the Emperor of Russia. It by no means satisfied him, and he assures me that he has made his report to his Court accordingly. It is, however, not to be doubted that should the present discussion lead to hostilities, not only the dominions of his Sicilian Majesty, but also Portugal and the Batavian Republic, would be invaded. Such plans are generally spoken of as the only ones by which this Government can find an indemnity for the expenses of a war; and if they have no other security than the morality or moderation of this Government, their case may be considered as desperate indeed. I have little to add to my last despatch on the subject of the question in dispute. It is calculated that an answer to the note, which must have been presented by

General Andréossy two days ago, may arrive to-morrow or next day; and from this answer they expect to learn what they are to depend upon. As far as my private opinion can go, I have not concealed that if it is expected that his Majesty will be induced to recede from his just demands they will be deceived. In the meantime the preparations for war do not correspond with the firmness of the language held by the First Consul and his Ministers. They affect to rest their claim on the impossibility of its being disputed. This is the language which is constantly held. Although no troops, at least to any considerable amount, are in motion, eventual orders are given for forming a camp in the neighbourhood of Breda, another near Dunkirk, another near Bayonne, and a fourth near Verona. The situations of these camps point out the countries against which it is meant to act. As may be naturally expected in this moment of crisis, all negotiations relating to the King of Sardinia are suspended. His Sardinian Majesty's acceptance of the terms which were offered would have been of no avail, since it was clogged with a refusal to renounce his former possessions. It is most ardently to be wished, not only on account of the interest which the situation of his Sardinian Majesty must naturally excite, but also as a measure of gratifying the Emperor of Russia, that some advantage may result to him from the present discussion. On the subject of the Indian fleet which sailed from Brest a short time ago, I have to add that the number of troops on board was about fifteen hundred. Amongst the preparations for war, I should not omit the orders which have been signified to Prussia, to the Batavian Republic, to Spain, to Italy, and to Portugal to shut their ports to his Majesty's flag on the first news of a rupture. The difference between this country and the Dey of Algiers, as your Lordship will have seen by the public papers, is adjusted, and ostensibly without the usual present from this Government; but in fact presents are preparing at this moment for the Dey—probably with a view of conciliating that Power under the existing circumstances.

Paris, March 31, 1803.

I have the honour to enclose your Lordship an official note which I received yesterday from M. de Talleyrand, and also the answer which I returned to it this morning. Ignorant as I am of the transaction, I could of course give no satisfactory answer; though I will confess to your Lordship that in the conversation I had with the several members of this Government I have not hesitated to declare, as far as my private opinion went, that Malta was the only point which his Majesty had determined to retain. I beg, however, your Lordship to understand that you are nowise committed by anything I have advanced. I at the same time enclose an answer which I have received from M. de Talleyrand on the subject of the British claimants. About three weeks ago I gave in a list of the claimants, with the nature and amount of their claims; and at the same time I represented to M. de Talleyrand, as well as to the *Grand Juge*, in whose department the decision ultimately rests, that it would considerably facilitate the expedition of this business if commissioners were appointed on the part of the claimants as well as on the part of the French Government for its discussion and arrangement. It should seem that this is likely to be adopted, subject, however to your Lordship's approbation.

M. DE TALLEYRAND TO LORD WHITWORTH.

Paris, le 9 Germinal, an XI.

J'ai reçu la lettre que vous m'avez fait l'honneur de m'adresser en me transmettant la liste de sujets des S. M. Britannique qui réclament en France la restitution de leurs propriétés. Je vais présenter au Premier Consul la proposition que vous faites de nommer pour l'examen et la reconnaissance des titres sur lesquels ces prétentions sont appuyées une commission nommée moitié par le Gouvernement françois et moitié par les réclamans. J'aurai l'honneur de vous faire connaître la décision qui sera prise à cet égard. Recevez, my Lord, les assurances de ma haute considération.

Lord Whitworth to M. de Talleyrand.

Paris, ce 31 Mars 1803.

Le soussigné, ambassadeur extraordinaire et plénipotentiaire de S. M. Britannique, a l'honneur d'accuser la réception de la note par laquelle le citoyen ministre des Relations Extérieures lui demande des explications sur une capitulation, prise des gazettes, d'après laquelle le cap de Bonne-Espérance seroit encore en la possession des troupes britanniques. Le soussigné n'a d'autres notions de cette affaire que celles qu'il a tirées de la même source que le Gouvernement françois, et par conséquent se trouve sans moyen de donner l'explication désirée. Il ne manquera pas de transmettre la note à sa cour et s'empressera de faire connoître la réponse au citoyen ministre des Relations Extérieures aussitôt qu'il la recevra. En attendant il a l'honneur de lui renouveler l'assurance de sa haute considération.

(Signed)   WHITWORTH.

Note.

Les gazettes viennent de publier une prétendue capitulation entre les troupes anglaises et hollandaises, d'où il résulteroit que le cap de Bonne-Espérance seroit encore en la possession des Anglais. Quoique le Premier Consul n'ait pu ajouter aucune foi à la nouvelle d'une violation aussi extraordinaire du traité d'Amiens, les bruits qui courent à cet égard sont tellement accrédités, surtout à Londres, et les détails de la capitulation sont si explicites, que le soussigné se voit chargé de demander à Monsieur l'ambassadeur d'Angleterre des explications qui puissent dissiper tous les doutes sur un fait aussi grave. Le soussigné prie Monsieur l'ambassadeur d'Angleterre d'agréer l'assurance de sa haute considération.

Ch. Mau. Talleyrand.

A Son Excellence Lord Whitworth,
    Ambassadeur de S. M. Britannique.

Lord Hawkesbury to Lord Whitworth.

Downing St., March 31, 1803.

I transmit to your Excellency herewith the draft of a note in answer to that delivered to you on the 25th instant by M. Talleyrand, and I am to desire you will communicate it to that Minister either in French or English, according to the language in which your Excellency has hitherto corresponded with M. de Talleyrand.

The undersigned, his Britannic Majesty's Ambassador Extraordinary, having transmitted to his Court a copy of the note which was delivered to him on the 25th instant by M. Talleyrand, has been directed to inform his Excellency that his Majesty's Government have no knowledge whatsoever of either of the two facts which are stated in the first part of that note, and which are represented as a violation of the territory of France. They have, however, thought it their duty to employ all the means in their power for the purpose of ascertaining the existence either of these facts, or of any circumstances to which such a construction could be given, and in the meantime the undersigned requests M. Talleyrand to furnish him with any information which he may have received upon this subject. With respect to the British vessels alleged to be cruising off the ports of the Batavian Republic, his Majesty has several ships of war in the seas adjacent to those ports; but if their commanders have made any movements or held any language which could be regarded as being of a hostile nature, their conduct has been in direct opposition to the tenor of their instructions. His Majesty has received assurances from the French Government that it is not their intention that the expedition to Louisiana should proceed to its destination under the present circumstances; in which assurances his Majesty places the most entire confidence. On the subject of the articles which have appeared in the English newspapers, the undersigned can only repeat what he has frequently stated—that his Majesty's Government cannot conceive themselves to be responsible for any articles that may be inserted in any other newspaper than the one which alone is published by their authority, under the title of the 'London Gazette.' The undersigned esteems it to be unnecessary for him to make any professions of the sincerity and moderation of his Majesty's Government, as he can assert with confidence that the discussions which have lately arisen have been conducted on their part with temper and candour, and with an anxious desire to avoid anything which could bear the appearance of animosity. The undersigned requests M. Talleyrand to accept the assurances of his high consideration.

To M. Talleyrand.

Lord Hawkesbury to Lord Whitworth.

Downing Street, April 4, 1803.

It is become essential that the discussions which have been for some time subsisting between his Majesty and the French Government should be brought to an issue within as short a time as is consistent with the deliberation which must be given to objects of so much importance. The last note presented to General Andréossy in the name of his Government, in answer to my note of last month, evades all explanation, and even all discussion, of the points on which complaint has been made to his Majesty. If the French Government should seriously persist in this course of proceeding, there can be no hopes of a successful termination to the present negotiation. It is important, therefore, that you should ascertain distinctly from the French Government, in the first instance, whether they are disposed to enter into explanation on the points on which his Majesty has complained, and to come to such an arrangement as may be calculated to adjust the differences at present subsisting between the two countries; and for this purpose you will present a note to the effect of that which is herewith enclosed. It is possible that the French Government may continue to evade all discussion on the points in question, and confine themselves to a categorical demand that Malta should be immediately evacuated. In that case it is his Majesty's pleasure that you should declare the impossibility of the relations of amity continuing to subsist between the two countries, and the necessity that you will be under of leaving Paris within a certain time. But if, on the other hand, they should show a readiness to enter into a discussion and to give reasonable satisfaction and explanation, it is important that you should be informed, without loss of time, of the sentiments of his Majesty's Government as to what might be considered as an equitable adjustment of the differences between the two Governments at this moment. I have therefore, by his Majesty's command, enclosed the project of an arrangement which, under the present circumstances, would meet the ideas of his Majesty's Government, which would afford security for those objects which are considered as endangered by the unequivocal disclosure of the views of the First Consul, and which at the same time might entirely save the honour of the French Government. If you should find insurmountable objections made to this proposition, and an arrangement founded upon it to be impracticable, you should in that case call upon the French Government to suggest some other *equivalent security* by which his Majesty's object in claiming the permanent possession of the island of Malta may be accomplished, and the independence of the island secured conformably to the spirit of the 10th article of the Treaty of Amiens. The justice of the principle on which his Majesty proposes this arrangement cannot be disputed, viz. security for those objects which must have been considered as secure at the time of the conclusion of the Treaty of Amiens, but which have been endangered by the proceedings of the French Government since that period. His Majesty relies on the zeal and diligence of your Excellency in endeavouring to bring these discussions to a speedy conclusion, and on such terms as may be consistent with the honour of his crown and the interests of his dominions. Your Excellency should understand that, in the event of the project in question being acceded to as a basis of negotiation, his Majesty has no doubt that the French Government will be disposed to satisfy him by disavowing any intentional insult on their part towards his Majesty in some of their late official publications, and particularly in that of the report of Colonel Sebastiani.

The undersigned, his Britannic Majesty's Ambassador Extraordinary, has received the orders of his Court to make the following communication to the French Government. His Majesty has perceived with great regret that the French Government continue to withhold all satisfaction and explanation on the points on which he has complained; that at the time when they evade all discussion on the subject of his representations they persist in their requisition that the island of Malta should be forthwith evacuated by his forces. His Majesty can never so far forget what is due to himself and to his people as to acquiesce in such a course of proceeding. He has therefore commanded the undersigned to ascertain distinctly from the French Government whether they are determined to persevere in withholding all satisfaction and explanation upon the points on which his Majesty has complained, or whether they are disposed, without delay, to give such satisfaction and explanation upon the present state of affairs as may lead to an arrangement which may be calculated to adjust the differences at present subsisting between the two Governments. It is his Majesty's anxious desire that by adopting this mode of proceeding an end may be put to that state of suspense and uncertainty which must be so injurious to the interests of both countries, and that the two Governments, actuated by the same principles of justice and moderation, may be led to concur in such measures as are most likely to conduce to their permanent tranquillity.

Heads of an Arrangement to be concluded by Treaty or Convention between his Majesty and the French Government.

Malta to remain in perpetuity in the possession of his Majesty.

The Knights of the Order of St. John to be indemnified by his Majesty for any losses of property which they may sustain in consequence of such an arrangement.

Holland and Switzerland to be evacuated by the French troops.

The island of Elba to be confirmed by his Majesty to France, and the King of Etruria to be acknowledged.

The Italian and Ligurian Republics to be acknowledged by his Majesty, provided an arrangement is made in Italy for the King of Sardinia which shall be satisfactory to him.

Downing Street, April 3, 1803.

I enclose to your Excellency for your information copies of the official note delivered to me on the 29th ultimo by General Andréossy, and of the answer which, by his Majesty's command, I this day returned to that communication.

The undersigned, his Majesty's principal Secretary of State for Foreign Affairs, has laid before the King the note of his Excellency General Andréossy of the 29th of last month. His Majesty has been induced, by that spirit of moderation and forbearance which has invariably governed his conduct in every part of his communications with the French Government, to abstain from making any observations which the perusal of this note may naturally have suggested to his mind. His Majesty has perceived with great regret that the French Government continue to withhold all satisfaction and explanation on the points on which he has complained, and that at the time when they evade all discussion on the subject of his representations they persist in their requisition that the island of Malta should be forthwith evacuated by his forces. His Majesty can never so far forget what is due to himself and to his people as to acquiesce in such a course of proceeding. He has therefore judged it expedient to give instructions to his Ambassador at Paris to ascertain distinctly from the French Government whether they are determined to persevere in withholding all satisfaction and explanation on the points on which his Majesty has complained, or whether they are disposed, without delay, to give such satisfaction and explanations upon the present state of affairs as may lead to an arrangement which may be calculated to adjust the differences at present subsisting between the two Governments. It is his Majesty's anxious desire that by this mode of proceeding an end may be put to that state of suspense and irritation which must be so injurious to the interests of both countries, and that the two Governments, actuated by the same principles of justice and moderation, may be led to concur in such measures as are most likely to conduce to their permanent tranquillity.

The undersigned requests General Andréossy to accept the assurances of his high consideration.

Downing Street, April 3, 1803.

Downing Street, April 4, 1803.

Your Excellency's several despatches to No. 31 inclusive, together with your separate despatch of the 31st ultimo, have been received and laid before the King. With respect to the note from M. Talleyrand, enclosed in the last-mentioned of those despatches, relative to the continuance of the occupation of the Cape of Good Hope, I have to signify to you his Majesty's pleasure that you deliver to that Minister an answer in writing to his note in which you will state that orders were transmitted on November 20 directing the immediate evacuation of the Cape of Good Hope by his Majesty's forces, and that consequently no doubt can now be entertained of that settlement having been for some time past in the possession of the Batavian Republic.

Lord Whitworth to Lord Hawkesbury.

Paris, April 4, 1803.

I have the honour to acknowledge your Lordship's despatch No. 6 of the 31st ult., and will take the earliest opportunity of communicating to M. de Talleyrand a translation of the note in answer to that delivered to me by that Minister on the 25th. I wish most sincerely that the fair and candid manner in which your Lordship has condescended to reply on this occasion may secure us from a repetition of such frivolous charges. I have little to add to my former despatch on the subject of the negotiation. I am waiting for the reply to General Andréossy's last note, which your Lordship announces as likely to be forwarded to me in a very few days. And I shall not fail in the interval to endeavour to insure it at least a temperate reception, if such a one could be expected from the irascible character to which it is addressed. The Corps Diplomatique were assembled yesterday at one o'clock for the purpose of paying their compliments to the First Consul. He was, however, occupied from that time till five in the evening in inspecting the knapsacks of about eight thousand men assembled in the court of the Tuileries. When that ceremony was performed he received us, and I had every reason to be satisfied with his manner towards me. General Duroc is expected to return to Paris to-day. I understand that he is to bring nothing decisive, the Court of Berlin having founded a pretext for delay by a reference to the Emperor of Russia. I am happy to find, however, that the point at issue is likely to be decided one way or the other before the effect of such a reference, which might probably lead to a joint mediation, can be known; since there is every reason to fear that anything which might be proposed by mediation so partial, at least as far as relates to Prussia, would in fact leave the question in no greater state of security than they found it. The effect of the present state of affairs has been felt at Madrid, and that Court has assumed courage to declare to this Government that it cannot on any consideration consent to the proposal for the exchange of the Floridas. I have the honour to send enclosed to your Lordship the substance of a report made by M. Blanchot, who has been charged by the French Government to take possession of the island of Goree according to the stipulations of the Treaty of Amiens, and of his correspondence with Colonel Fraser on this occasion.

It is well known that by one of the articles of the Treaty of Amiens it was stipulated that the island of Goree, on the coast of Africa, should be restored to France. The Government has just received despatches on this subject, dated January 26, from M. Blanchot, Commandant of Senegal, by which it appears that under various pretexts the British Governor refuses to deliver up that island. The following is an extract of the correspondence between the French Commandant and the English Governor. M. Blanchot, in a letter of October 30, acquaints Colonel Fraser, the British Governor, that he has instructions to take possession of the island in his quality of Commissary of the French Republic, enclosing at the same time his Britannic Majesty's orders to give up that island, and requesting to be informed when these orders might be put into execution. The Governor, in his answer of November 9, says that he is ready to deliver up the place the moment that the transports which he is expecting shall arrive, to convey from it the garrison stores, provisions, &c.; adding that he had taken such measures as would insure the speedy arrival of the transports. On the 18th M. Blanchot despatches the corvette 'L'Impatiente' pressing the restitution of the island. He writes thus to the British Governor: 'As the waiting for the transports which you expect would cause a delay in the execution of our respective instructions that might draw upon us a degree of blame which we certainly can have no desire to merit, I have the honour to observe to you that we can still execute the evacuation of the island before the arrival of the transports, by taking such measures of precaution as you may think proper to adopt for the preservation of the stores, &c., which are to be sent away in them. One of the vessels that will accompany me shall take the garrison to Sierra Leone, and another shall be employed for yourself and baggage.' Colonel Fraser replies, on November 22, 'that he regrets being the cause of any fresh delay; that, to his utter astonishment, the transports which he expected had not arrived; and that there was no instance of a British garrison having evacuated an island given up by treaty, under any other flag than their own; that he might be severely reprimanded if he were to quit the place in this manner; and that he cannot give a definite answer till after the return of a vessel that he had just despatched to Sierra Leone. November 30 and December 12, fresh applications on the part of M. Blanchot. December 21, the British Governor writes to M. Blanchot: 'I have the pleasure to inform you of the return of the vessel that I had despatched to Sierra Leone. It brings me letters from the Governor, in which he acquaints me that he has freighted a transport of sufficient tonnage to take on board the troops, provisions, &c. This vessel was to sail from Sierra Leone on the 4th or 5th of this month, so that I expect it every moment: and upon its arrival I will immediately despatch to you a courier fixing a day for the evacuation of the island.' The 26th, the Governor acquaints M. Blanchot that this transport, although hourly expected, had not yet arrived, but he had just been informed that a ship would be immediately sent from England to embark the garrison, and that it might be necessary perhaps to wait the arrival of this vessel before he gave up the island. January 5, M. Blanchot, in his reply to the Governor, presses for the evacuation of the island. Colonel Fraser, in his answer of January 14, says that it is impossible for him to dispense with the arrival of the ship from England, adding with the utmost politeness: 'As you have expressed a fear that the delay in the restitution of the island of Goree might bring upon us a reprimand from our respective Governments, I shall be myself ready to do you justice on this occasion, and to become personally responsible for all the blame.' M. Blanchot here terminates the correspondence by communicating to Colonel Fraser that he had taken such precautions as would put him out of the reach of all blame.

Paris, April 7, 1803.

I received your Lordship's despatches of the 4th instant by Wagstaff, with their enclosures, yesterday evening, and shall probably in the course of the day have an opportunity of communicating to M. de Talleyrand the note (No. 1), which I shall translate for that purpose. I hope this evening to be able to give your Lordship some information as to the effect it may have produced. In the meantime I cannot but rejoice that the discussion is likely to be brought to a speedy issue. It is on every account important that it should, whether with a view to relieving the country from a state of painful suspense, or of not losing this favourable opportunity of striking the blow, should it be necessary. The language now held by the First Consul to his intimates is that he has made up his mind to see us destroy that part of his fleet which is abroad, and even to regain perhaps possession of his colonies; but that if they succeed in their attempts to invade England they shall quickly repair all their losses and revenge themselves completely. This project of invasion is, however, considered by everyone, in the present state of their navy, as totally impracticable, and is, I am persuaded, held out as a demonstration with a view to excite anxiety in England, and to put us to the expense of a defensive system, whilst this Government will incur no more than what must attend the marching of troops to the coast, or to the countries which are destined to be its victims. It is really painful to see to what a state of depravity the leading men of this country are reduced. So far from feeling the least shame or remorse at such an ungenerous and unmanly method of retaliating upon us, they not only excuse but applaud it. General Duroc returned on Thursday night. The chief objects of his mission were to engage the Court of Berlin to accede immediately to the guarantee of Malta, and to make a demonstration against his Majesty's electoral dominions. On the first of these points the Court of Berlin has, if we may give credit to the 'Moniteur,' conceded; and to the second it is answered that, in the present state of affairs, his Prussian Majesty does not feel justified in taking steps which might tend to disturb the tranquillity of Germany. At the same time that the Court of Berlin evades coming forward as a principal, it expresses great readiness to undertake the office of mediator. This mission has, therefore, not satisfied the expectations of the First Consul. It remains to be seen, though I most anxiously hope the business may be settled before any answer can arrive from thence, what will be the language of the Court of Russia. It appears to me that Count Marcoff is endeavouring—or, more properly, is following—the bent of his natural character by steering a middle course. He has, in the different conversations I have held with him, always appeared most anxious to know what would be the idea of his Majesty's Government with regard to the Order of Malta in the event of that island remaining in our possession; whether it was to be preserved, and retain a settlement on the island (which, he declared, would be most agreeable to the Emperor), or whether it would be driven to the necessity of looking for shelter elsewhere. The language which I have always held is that on this, as on every other point, his Majesty would probably concert with the Emperor, provided he should, as I made no doubt he would, approve the line of conduct which his Majesty had been obliged to pursue in order to retain possession of a point so essential to the safety of his Majesty's dominions. I yesterday saw M. de Talleyrand for the same purpose as I had visited Joseph Bonaparte the day before—namely, to prepare him, and through him the First Consul, for the important communications which I have now received from your Lordship. After assuring me that nothing should be wanting on his part which might conduce to the temperate discussion of the question, a conversation took place which I think right to communicate to your Lordship. In remarking on the armaments which were carrying on in England, he said he could not yet comprehend why and with whom we meant to go to war; for, says he, the First Consul is so convinced it cannot be with him that he has not yet expended a single shilling in preparations. I will confess to your Lordship that I was piqued at this mode of reasoning; and upon his repeating the question I told him that in a very few days I should, in all probability, be furnished with instructions which would satisfy his doubts; that his Majesty's Government would state plainly and openly what were the points necessary to restore confidence and to maintain peace; that if the French Government acquiesced in them, peace, and what had been hitherto wanting to it—good harmony—would be the consequence; but that if our disposition to conciliate should not be met with an equal one on their side, then war became inevitable, and in that case we should, of course, pursue such measures as might render it most effectual; that their naval force might be still further disabled, their colonies wrested from them, their commerce, and that of their allies, would fall a prey to our cruisers; and in addition to all this we should, at the conclusion of the war, negotiate upon fresh ground, and, if it were successful, which I trusted such a war would be, we might pretend to much more for the security and tranquillity of ourselves and Europe than we now required. He still affected to dispute the ground of the jealousy which we had conceived, and seemed on the whole less conciliating than I had yet found him. This must be attributed to the dread which he and all those who have to do with the First Consul have of the violence of his temper. If your Lordship take the trouble of reading the French papers, you will have perceived that in a discourse of Regnault de St. Jean d'Angely, in which he had occasion to advert to the flourishing state of France, he lamented that the fair prospect he described was threatened by a probability of war. The First Consul sent for him the next day, and, reprimanding him for touching on that point, said: 'Il faut que nous prenions garde dans notre position de ne pas avoir l'air de croire la guerre possible, puisque nous ne demandons rien que l'exécution du traité.' I trust the ground which his Majesty's Government has taken will induce him to give more extension to his means of defence.

Paris, April 7, 1803.

My Lord,—Since writing the preceding despatch I have seen M. de Talleyrand and communicated to him the enclosed note, which, I trust, your Lordship will find as close a translation as possible of that which I received from your Lordship. He read it over with much attention, and when he had done he appeared to be in expectation of some other communication. Upon my desiring he would explain himself, he said that he was in hopes I should have furnished him with the heads of those points on which it was affirmed in the note that the French Government had so repeatedly refused all explanation and satisfaction. I told him that it would have been entirely useless to repeat what had been so often urged in vain; that he could not but know that the explanation required referred to the conduct of the French Government and the system of aggrandisement which it had constantly pursued since the conclusion, and in direct violation of the spirit, of the Treaty of Amiens, founded as it indisputably was on the state of possession of the two countries at the time; that with regard to the satisfaction, it evidently referred to the unjustifiable insinuations and charges against his Majesty's Government, against the officer commanding his forces in Egypt, and against the British in that quarter, contained in the official report of Colonel Sebastiani. He was by no means disposed to admit that either of these cases could justify the assertion of the French Government having refused explanation and satisfaction, on the ground that no notice had been taken of these transactions but in a very cursory manner, nor had any explanation ever been required as to any particular transaction, whether in Italy or elsewhere, and if it had been required it would immediately have been given, and that the language of Colonel Sebastiani was not to be put in any comparison with that used by

Major Wilson in his account of the campaign of Egypt. I urged the difference of a common publication like that to which he alluded, and a report to the First Consul, published by him in his official paper. On this occasion M. de Talleyrand was disposed to call in question the authenticity of the 'Moniteur.' In short, the most ungrounded assertions were substituted for arguments, and amongst these I cannot but place that so often repeated, of the First Consul's having entirely given up all idea whatever of Egypt, consequently we could have no pretext for retaining Malta. He assured me, for the rest, that he would communicate it this evening to the First Consul, and that to-morrow he should in all probability have a communication to make in return. He gave me no hope, from anything which occurred in the course of the conversation, that our demand would in the first instance be acquiesced in, but assured me that every security and satisfaction might be obtained, short of the actual possession of Malta. Thus the business rests for the moment. It remains to be seen what course will be taken. But it evidently appears that their object is to gain time; and in this I am afraid they will succeed in spite of all we can do. I shall keep the messenger Wagstaff, in order to despatch him should anything occur before the regular day of the post.

Le soussigné, Ambassadeur Extraordinaire et Plénipotentiaire de Sa Majesté britannique, a reçu ordre de sa cour de communiquer ce qui suit au Gouvernement de France.

Sa Majesté a vu à regret que le Gouvernement de France continue à refuser toute satisfaction et toute explication sur les objets dont elle a à se plaindre, et qu'en évitant toute discussion de ce qui fait le sujet de ses représentations, il persiste néanmoins à demander l'évacuation de l'île de Malte par les forces de Sa Majesté. Sa Majesté sait trop ce qu'elle se doit à elle-même et à son peuple pour acquiescer à de pareils procédés. En conséquence elle a ordonné au soussigné de savoir distinctement du Gouvernement de France s'il est déterminé à persévérer dans son refus de toute satisfaction et de toute explication sur les objets de Sa Majesté, ou bien s'il est disposé à donner sans délai cette satisfaction et cette explication sur l'état actuel des affaires, de manière à pouvoir conduire à un arrangement qui seroit de nature à ajuster les différends qui actuellement existent entre les deux Gouvernemens. Sa Majesté désire sincèrement l'adoption de ce moyen, qui mettroit fin à un état de suspension et d'incertitude si nuisible à l'intérêt des deux nations, et de voir que les deux Gouvernemens, agissant par les mêmes principes de justice et de modération, puissent s'entendre pour concourir aux mesures les plus susceptibles de leur assurer une tranquillité permanente. Le soussigné prie Son Excellence, Monsieur de Talleyrand, d'agréer l'assurance de sa haute considération.

(Signed) WHITWORTH.

LORD HAWKESBURY TO LORD WHITWORTH.

Downing Street, April 7, 1803.

Intelligence was received two days ago at the Admiralty from the officer commanding his Majesty's ships in the North Seas, that a movement had taken place of the French frigates and transports in the port of Helvoetsluys, as if they were intending to proceed on their destination. His Majesty is unwilling to suppose that, after the assurances given to him by the French Government, the armament which is in the port will put to sea under the present circumstances. He has, however, thought it his duty to reinforce his squadron in the North Seas for the purpose of watching more closely the operations of the French squadron. I lose no time in informing your Excellency of this circumstance, that you may know what language it is proper for you to hold on this subject.

Lord Whitworth to Lord Hawkesbury.

Paris, April 9, 1803.

In my conversation yesterday with M. de Talleyrand, I found him, after he had seen the First Consul, more disposed to contest the substance of the note which I had presented the day before than to afford any further explanation. He said that in order to proceed regularly it would be necessary that the French Government should be informed precisely what were the objects which had created such uneasiness and on which it was alleged all explanation had been refused; that although this had perhaps been touched upon in general conversation, yet no specific charge had been adduced in such a formal manner as to demand a formal explanation. I told him that if the object of the French Government was to protract the present state of suspense and uncertainty, that object might be answered to the extent, indeed, of a very few days, by forcing me to such a reference; but I must at the same time declare to him that it could be productive of no advantage, and would serve only to provoke such a recapitulation of the system and conduct which France had pursued since the Treaty of Amiens as would have all the appearance of a manifesto, every item of which would carry conviction to the heart of every individual in Europe; that it appeared therefore more likely to answer the end which both parties proposed—that of hastening the conclusion of an amicable arrangement—to take up the business on the basis which I should propose, and by which they would admit no more than what was incontrovertible, namely, that if the French Government exercised a right of extending its influence and territory, in violation of the spirit of the Treaty of Amiens, Great Britain had, if she chose to avail herself of it (which I was confident she would not do further than was necessary as a measure of security), an undoubted right to seek a counterpoise. He did not seem inclined to dispute this position, but rather to admit that such a right did exist, and might be claimed in consequence by the acquisitions which had been made by France. On the point of satisfaction I found him much more obstinate. He said that the First Consul was hurt at the expression 'satisfaction,' to which he gave an interpretation I had never understood belonged to it, as implying superiority, so that if the British Government required satisfaction of the French it arrogated to itself a superiority. I told him, what certainly must be understood by everyone, that the demand of satisfaction implied that one party had been offended by another, and of course had a right to demand such satisfaction; that an inferior had an equal right with his superior to demand it; but in the case in question there was perfect equality, and consequently there was no offence to be found but in the conduct which rendered such an appeal necessary. He endeavoured to get over this difficulty as well as he could. He disputed the authenticity of the 'Moniteur,' which, he said, was not entirely official; and, in short, attempted to make the best of a bad business. He feels the folly of the publication, but trembles before the violence of the First Consul. I must not, however, omit that he endeavoured to extenuate the fact by retorting upon us. He said that a publication has appeared in England in which the most horrid charges had been brought against the First Consul; he did not say this had been published in the 'London Gazette,' but he had it, he said, from the best authority that it had been presented publicly to his Majesty. I told him I could not dispute this fact, as nothing of the kind had ever come to my knowledge: I only knew that publications were very frequently presented to his Majesty at his *levée*; but I had never understood that his Majesty or his Government were committed by the condescension of his Majesty in receiving them, or that they acquired any degree of authenticity by such an acceptance; therefore, supposing the fact to be so, there could be no parallel. The discussion of this point took up a considerable time, without producing anything decisive; but I told him that if the bare refusal of satisfaction for an offence to his Majesty's Government, his army, or any of his officers should be made the ground of a rupture, there was not a hand or heart in England that would not be united to enforce it. We at last came to the main point of the business, and on this I cannot say any real progress has been made. M. de Talleyrand repeated to me that the First Consul had nothing more at heart than to avoid the necessity of going to war, and that there was no sacrifice he would not make, short of his honour, to obtain this end. If, said he, the English Government insists absolutely on breaking the Treaty of Amiens, the First Consul is determined to go all lengths to maintain it. If the English Government is determined to keep possession of Malta, the First Consul will suffer himself to be cut in pieces rather than consent to it—not so much on account of the importance of Malta in itself, as that he is bound in honour to maintain the inviolability of the Treaty of Amiens. To this I answered that if the First Consul was so determined I feared we were both losing our time in the discussion, for that I must tell him that his Majesty's Government was as firmly determined to retain possession of it as a measure of defence and precaution, rendered indisputably necessary by the views which had been manifested by the First Consul. I was as explicit on this subject as possible. 'But is there,' said M. de Talleyrand, 'no modification, no means of satisfying both parties? for at the same time that the First Consul insists, and will always insist, on the full execution of the treaty, he will not object to any mode by which you may acquire the security you think so necessary. You are not satisfied with the independence of Neapolitan troops: what others will answer the purpose?' I told him that he could propose nothing so secure as the garrison which was now in Malta; it was, I feared, to that, and to that only, we could confide it. He then started the idea of a mixed garrison, composed of English, French, Italians, Germans, etc.; but this of course could answer no good purpose. He then was preparing to make the tour of Europe in search of an independent Power; but I told him to take care that by so doing he did not furnish us with even stronger arguments for the measures of precaution we were now taking against the influence and power of France. In short, say what we would, it came always to the point that nothing was secure short of the actual possession of Malta, and that nothing could be proposed or accepted in lieu of it. I must confess that he seemed seriously to lament the difficulty of our coming to an understanding; but he never gave me the least reason to hope that the First Consul would ever consent to our acquiring the possession of the point in dispute. He repeatedly told me that, short of that, everything might be done. He begged that I would refer once more to your Lordship, and submit the paper which he drew up in my presence to the above effect. I told him that we were only losing time by such a reference; that my instructions were positive, and had certainly not been sent me without the fullest consideration; that your Lordship could say no more than had been said, and which even he must admit, viz. that nothing would be deemed secure short of actual possession. I could not, however, refuse what he so earnestly required, and your Lordship will see by the paper how the matter rests after this first conference. I will confess to your Lordship that my motive for consenting to forward this sort of proposal to your Lordship is, that supposing we should find the First Consul as obstinate as he now appears to be on the point of abandoning Malta to us in perpetuity, and that a temporary possession might be considered as the next best thing, something of this kind might derive from it. It appears that what the First Consul is most anxious about is the full acknowledgment of the Treaty of Amiens, but that he is ready to make any arrangement or concession by a particular convention between the two Governments. I am perfectly aware that, whatever concession he may be inclined to make, we can never give up the actual possession of Malta, either in perpetuity or for whatever term of years may be agreed upon; and if we could get it for any term not less than eight years I think we might without imprudence trust to the chapter of accidents, and at the worst to our endeavours to enable the Maltese themselves to preserve their own independence. Your Lordship will, therefore, understand that I have not, by consenting to refer his proposal to your Lordship, given up in any degree whatever the ground we have taken in the first instance. But I must confess that, however determined we may be to maintain it, the First Consul (for I confine it to him) appears to be no less so to support the Treaty of Amiens. In the conversation I had the night before last with Joseph Bonaparte I found him disposed to hold the same language as M. de Talleyrand: determination on the part of his brother not to admit the infraction of the Treaty of Amiens, but every disposition to come to an understanding on the subject with his Majesty's Government. In looking over the Mediterranean for a place which might afford an equivalent security he mentioned Candia and Corfu. I told him that such situations would in no degree answer our purpose, nor indeed could I see anything short of Malta which could. It is to this, and this only, that we must strictly adhere; and if we act up to the full extent of the demonstration we have made, and convince these people that we are determined to fight for the security we require, I think we shall obtain it, if not in perpetuity, at least for such a term as may answer our purpose. I believe that there is no doubt that they are making the greatest efforts in the port of Toulon. I am informed that they are well supplied there with timber and stores of every kind; that a very considerable number of workmen are employed; and that they are building four sail of the line—two of eighty, two of seventy-four—and three frigates of forty guns. This will, I think, point out still more strongly the necessity of our keeping up a sufficient force in the Mediterranean.

La conversation avec M. de Talleyrand aujourd'hui nous a conduit à ce résultat. Tout ce qui a pour but de violer l'indépendance de l'ordre de Malte ne sera jamais consenti par le Gouvernement français. Pour ce qui peut convenir ou être agréable au Gouvernement anglois pour terminer les présentes difficultés, et qui ne seroit pas contraire au traité d'Amiens, le Gouvernement françois n'a aucune objection pour faire une convention particulière à cet égard. Les motifs de la convention seroient renfermés dans le préambule et qui porteroient sur les griefs respectifs sur ce que les deux Gouvernemens croiroient utile de s'entendre.

Paris, April 11, 1803.

I have little to add to my despatch of the 9th instant. The overture which I then transmitted to your Lordship, though not coming up to our ideas, might nevertheless be considered as a concession, from which some advantage might be derived; and I am anxious to have your Lordship's opinion of it. I feel as strongly as possible the importance of not suffering the negotiation to be too long protracted but at the same time your Lordship would not authorise me to hurry it on, so as to subject me to the reproach of precipitation or petulance. According to your Lordship's instructions contained in your despatch No. 7, I might, on finding this Government determined not to come to such an arrangement as might be calculated to adjust the differences at present subsisting between the two Governments—and the project which accompanied these instructions points out the possession of Malta in perpetuity, or an equivalent security, as the only arrangement which can be acceded to—I might, I say, have been justified in giving them to understand that it was impossible that the relations of amity should continue to subsist between the two countries, and that I should be under the necessity of leaving Paris within a certain time. By this means I might certainly have brought the matter to a point at once; and we have still the same means in our power, whenever your Lordship shall think proper to give me an ultimatum. But I confess I should not without such an authority feel myself justified in precipitating the business in such a manner as to forego the expectations I may have, if not of obtaining all we demand, at least sufficient to answer our purpose. And the paper which I drew up with M. de Talleyrand and transmitted to your Lordship with my last despatch did appear to me to offer an opening for such an arrangement. It remains to be seen—but in this I must be rather a listener than a proposer—what effect they mean to give to this opening. It occurred to me that if it should appear that the First Consul has in fact made up his mind to risk a war rather than consent to our possession of Malta in perpetuity, the possession of it for a term of years might be the next best thing, and this I proposed to your Lordship. On searching further for modifications which might satisfy both parties—that is to say, Great Britain, by leaving it in possession of a point deemed essential to her interests, and France as preserving the Order of Malta and the sovereignty attached to it, both provided for by the Treaty of Amiens—it has occurred to me that an arrangement might be made by which we should hold the forts of Malta necessary for the security of the harbour, and the Order be put in possession of the remainder of the island, with the sovereignty, under the existing guarantees. By this means we should hold Malta as we do Gibraltar, and retain in fact all we want, which is not sovereignty but a secure point in our hands from whence to observe the motions of France in the Mediterranean. I wish your Lordship to consider of this idea. It seems to me to have fewer objectionable parts than any other. Russia and the other guaranteeing Powers would have little reason to complain. The Order which they have guaranteed would exist, and be in fact stronger and more respectable than ever. I should be glad to have your Lordship's sentiments upon it, so that I may be prepared to close with such a proposal should it be made to me. The general idea is here that the First Consul is determined not to give way, and that he has made up his mind to sustain the first shock of a rupture in the hope of revenging himself in future. This is the language he held yesterday to some persons who were deputed to him on the concerns of the bank. He told them that if war should be the result of the present discussion it must be considered as a war of aggression on the part of England; that, notwithstanding the interpretation that England might endeavour to give it, it was evident that the acquisition of Malta was the sole object;

that he was the first to declare that the insignificant island of Malta was not worth contending for, but, when it was considered that by giving way in this first instance the English Government would only be encouraged to come forward with some new pretension, he trusted there was not a man who did not agree with him that the first claim should be resisted; that he was perfectly aware how vulnerable they were at this moment, but he was at the same time certain that such a mode of attack by invasion might be carried on against the very existence of England as would at once deprive the English Government of all their means of disturbing the general tranquillity. Such is the language the First Consul holds, but he meets with few who are disposed to sacrifice their present existence to the hope of a future triumph. I do not apprehend that it is meant to suffer the squadron to leave Helvoet; at all events, I think it will be advisable to mention the subject of your Lordship's despatch of the 7th instant to M. de Talleyrand.

P.S.—Since writing the above despatch I have had a conversation of some length with Joseph Bonaparte. I cannot say that it has produced anything beyond a very faint symptom of a desire to conciliate. He pressed me repeatedly to suggest some modification, which I as often protested I was unable to do, keeping as I must do in view the equivalent security prescribed to me by my instructions. He mentioned the idea of substituting a Russian instead of a Neapolitan garrison; but I could not, I told him, consider any such substitution as an equivalent. He repeated the proposal of Candia, or of Corfu, or of any other position in the Archipelago. He assured me, however, that he mentioned these matters entirely unauthorised, and in the hope solely of at last suggesting something satisfactory. The impression which this conversation has left upon me is that they will at last come down to something on which we may build such an arrangement as may answer our purpose.

Lord Hawkesbury to Lord Whitworth.

Downing Street, April 13, 1803.

Your Excellency's despatches to No. 34 inclusive have been received and laid before the King. His Majesty has observed with great satisfaction the admission by the French Government of the justice of his claim to some compensation in consequence of the increased power and influence of France since the period of the conclusion of the Definitive Treaty, and it is important that you should lose no proper opportunity of taking full advantage of this admission. Although under the circumstances of your conversation with M. Talleyrand, and particularly after the *note verbale* which he gave to you, it might have been expedient that you should have deferred presenting the *projet* contained in my despatch No. 7 in the form of a *projet*, it is desirable that you should communicate without delay in some mode or other the contents of that *projet* for the purpose of ascertaining distinctly whether the conditions are such as to induce the French Government to give way upon the question of Malta. These conditions appear to his Majesty so well calculated to save the honour of the French Government on the subject of Malta, if the question of Malta is principally considered by them as a question of honour, and at the same time hold out to them such important advantages, that the success of the proposition is at least worth trying, particularly as the result of it might be productive of the most easy means of adjusting the most material of our present differences. With respect to the assertion so often advanced, and repeated in your last conversations, of the non-execution of the Treaty of Amiens relative to Malta, I have only to observe again that the execution of that article is become impracticable from causes which it has not been in the power of his Majesty to control; that the greatest part of the funds assigned to the support of the Order, and indispensably necessary for the independence of the Order and defence of the island, have been sequestrated since the conclusion of the Definitive Treaty, in direct repugnance to the spirit and letter of that treaty; and that two of the principal Powers who were invited to accede as guarantees to the arrangement have refused their accession except on the condition that the part of the arrangement which was deemed so material relative to the Maltese Langue should be entirely cancelled. The conduct of the French Government since the conclusion of the Definitive Treaty gives his Majesty a right, which is now at length admitted by themselves, to demand some compensation for the past and security for the future. Such compensation could never be considered as obtained by the possession of an island which would entail a very heavy expense on this country; and the degree of security which would be provided by these means would only be such as his Majesty under the present circumstances is entitled to demand. I observe in the *note verbale* of M. Talleyrand he makes use of the expression *the independence* of the Order of Malta. If this is meant to apply to the Order exclusively, his Majesty would be willing, for the preservation of peace, that the civil government of the island should be given to the Order of St. John, the Maltese enjoying the privileges which were stipulated in their favour in the Treaty of Amiens, and that, conformably to principles which have been adopted on other occasions, the fortifications of the island should be garrisoned for ever by the troops of his Majesty. In the event of either of these propositions being found unattainable, his Majesty might be disposed to consent to an arrangement by which the island of Malta would remain in his possession for a limited number of years, and to waive in consequence his demand for a perpetual occupation, provided that the number of years was not less than ten and that his Sicilian Majesty could be induced to cede the sovereignty of the island of Lampedusa for a valuable consideration. If this proposition is admitted, the island of Malta should be given up to the inhabitants at the end of that period, and it should be acknowledged as an independent state. In this case his Majesty would be ready to concur in any arrangement for the establishment of the Order of St. John in some other part of Europe. You will not refuse to listen to any proposition which the French Government may be disposed to make to you with a view to an equivalent security for those objects in regard to which his Majesty claims the possession or occupation of Malta; but the three propositions to which I have above alluded appear at the present moment to furnish the only basis for a satisfactory arrangement, and you will decline receiving any proposition which does not appear to you to offer advantages to his Majesty as substantial as that which I have last stated. It is very desirable that you should bring the negotiation to an issue, if possible, without referring to his Majesty's Government for further instructions after the receipt of the despatch; and if you should be of opinion, in consequence of the necessary communications, that there is no hope of bringing it to a favourable conclusion, you may inform M. Talleyrand of the necessity you will be under after a certain time to leave Paris.

Downing Street, April 12, 1803.

His Majesty has received from his Chargé d'Affaires at Hamburg the most extraordinary account of the conduct of Monsieur Reinhard, the French Minister at that place, with respect to a most gross and unwarrantable libel upon his Majesty's Government. He has been assured that the French Minister having proposed the insertion of that libel in the 'Official Gazette' of the town of Hamburg, and the insertion of it having in the first instance been refused, the French Minister went so far as to demand, in his official capacity, the insertion of that article by order of the Senate. His Majesty is unwilling to believe that the French Government could have authorised so outrageous an attack upon his Majesty and his Government, and so daring a violation of the independence of a neutral state. It is his Majesty's pleasure that you should communicate these circumstances to the French Government, and state at the same time the impossibility of bringing the present discussion to an amicable conclusion unless some satisfaction shall be given to his Majesty for the indignity which has thus been offered to him in the face of all Europe by the French Minister at Hamburg.

Lord Whitworth to Lord Hawkesbury.

Paris, April 14, 1803.

Since my last the negotiation is at a stand, in the expectation, I suppose, of the answer which may arrive to the overture which I communicated to your Lordship on the 9th instant, and which, although founded on a basis diametrically opposite to that of the project which I have received from your Lordship, is expected here to produce a good effect, notwithstanding the little hope I have given. To-morrow I shall in all probability be in possession of this answer from your Lordship, and be enabled to speak still more positively. In the meantime the First Consul is gone to St. Cloud, and Joseph Bonaparte, hurt at the little impression he has hitherto made on the mind of his brother, is likewise gone to his country house in disgust. He does not, however, abandon the contest any more than every individual of the First Consul's family; it remains to be seen how far their importunity will be able to work on his intractable character. In the last conversation I had with Joseph Bonaparte, he mentioned as a reason why the First Consul never could consent to our remaining at Malta that we should from thence be able completely to annihilate their trade to the Levant. I told him that this argument could not hold good, since in time of war, whether we had Malta or not, we should always have cruisers in the Mediterranean, and in time of peace such a commercial arrangement for the Mediterranean might be made, without extending it to a general treaty of commerce, which we know to be subject to almost insurmountable difficulties, as would insure to them all the advantages they could reasonably pretend to, and convince them that in retaining Malta we were in fact actuated by no motive of jealousy, or enmity, or of ambition, but simply that of security, which we had always assigned. This seemed to make an impression, and I am persuaded he will have availed himself of it with his brother. I trust that in holding this language I have expressed no sentiment of which your Lordship does not approve. It has been suggested to me that as a last resource the First Consul will propose giving Malta entirely to the Emperor of Russia. General Bernadotte set off two days ago for America, with every assurance of the sincere desire of the First Consul to conciliate the friendship of the United States. This disposition can scarcely be doubted under the present circumstances. Mr. Munroe, an extraordinary negotiator from the United States, arrived here yesterday. America is the first to reap the fruits of our discussion with this Government, in consequence of which Mr. Munroe finds the difference which occasioned his mission nearly adjusted. It is said that he is destined to relieve Mr. King at the Court of London. The Chevalier Anduaga, Minister Plenipotentiary from his Catholic Majesty to the Court of London, is now here, and will pursue his journey to London to-morrow, notwithstanding the assurances which his countryman the Chevalier Azzara gives of his return in a month in consequence of a rupture. A messenger has gone to Madrid to demand a passage for thirty thousand men, destined, in case of a war with England, to act against Portugal. The Portuguese Minister has received a messenger from his Court with instructions to remonstrate against the conduct of the French Minister, General Lannes. The tone he has now assumed appears to be entirely subversive of every idea of independence. He demands the dismissal of Ministers as the only satisfaction which the First Consul can accept for the indignities with which he has been treated. This Government affects not to justify General Lannes' conduct, but does nothing to *control* it. I hope in a very few days to procure some important details of the state of the French navy, notwithstanding the almost insurmountable difficulties that attend every inquiry on the point. In the meantime I am positively assured, by a person who pretends to be perfectly well informed, that at present they have but forty sail of the line from sixty guns and upwards in all parts of the world—and many of these want the most substantial repairs—and about the same number of frigates. I believe this to be nearly accurate, but I shall in a few days be able to speak more positively. The value of the bank shares is reduced from thirteen hundred and eighty to eleven hundred and eighty livres, partly by the general fall of the funds, but principally by the reduction of the dividend from near ten per cent. to six per cent. The surplus of profit, it is true, will be vested in the Five-per-Cent. Consolidé, and finally give a second dividend; but as that will not be immediately, it enters but little into the calculation of purchasers. On the remonstrance of the persons concerned the Government have at length consented to let eight per cent. be divided for the ensuing three half-years; but a great shock is given to public credit by the example of such an interference of the Government in the affairs of a private company, especially as two other companies are in a great degree sacrificed to the Bank of France.

Paris, April 14, 1803.

I am sorry to be able to give you no more consolation in my private letter than you will be able to collect from my despatch of this date. It is certain that hitherto the First Consul has resisted everything and everybody; but still those who have undertaken the task of reducing him to reason will not abandon it, and I think we may still hope. I trust your Lordship will give me credit for the exertion of everything which zeal and diligence can dictate. In the meantime I cannot but represent to your Lordship the extreme importance of betraying no indecision at the meeting of Parliament, or of giving voice to any debate in which those who would wish to embroil and distress us might give encouragement to this Government to hold out. I am sure General Andréossy does his Majesty's Ministers ample justice in the assurances he gives of their desire to preserve peace; but I have my doubts whether he is equally fair in the statement of their determination to go to war if they do not obtain what they so justly demand. It is absolutely necessary that there should be no doubt on this subject. In the expectation of hearing from your Lordship to-morrow, I am, etc.

Paris, April 18, 1803.

I have the honour to acknowledge the receipt of your Lordship's despatches of the 13th instant, Nos. 10 and 11, on Saturday last. No. 9 reached me on the 10th, and as I had every reason to believe that there was no idea of sending the expedition at Helvoet to sea I have made no use of the instructions therein contained. I saw Joseph Bonaparte immediately on the receipt of your Lordship's despatch, and without troubling your Lordship with a repetition of the arguments I used to hasten the conclusion of the negotiation—amongst which I endeavoured to convince him of the importance of preventing the ultimatum which would inevitably follow the rejection of what I had to propose, and which, I foresaw, must, applied to a character like that of the First Consul, render our hopes almost desperate—I will briefly state that, on finding it perfectly impracticable to establish the principle of our keeping possession of Malta in perpetuity, I delivered to him in writing the second proposal I had to make. He did not fail to observe that by this modification the difficulty which he considered as insurmountable was not removed; that although the Order was restored it could not be considered as independent, and in fact Malta would belong to that Power which had possession of the forts. I told him that my instructions allowed me no greater latitude, nor had I any reason to believe that any more would be given to me. I enforced the adoption of this plan by every reasoning which could serve to recommend it; but the possession in perpetuity was constantly urged as a difficulty which nothing could remove; and he repeatedly told me that he was perfectly convinced that his brother was determined, without being blind to the danger by which himself and his friends might be menaced, to withstand it at every risk. Our conversation lasted near two hours. I confess that I gained no solid hope that the project, which he assured me he would take to his brother at St. Cloud, would be adopted. But he said that he was not without hope that he might be authorised to propose to me the occupation of the fortresses for a term of years. It was my wish that such a proposal should come from him rather than from me. I told him that I did not well see how such a tenure could suit us; that we deemed possession of Malta to be conducive to the preservation of peace, and on that ground we should always abandon it with reluctance; and that as we were actually in possession of it any modification was on our part a concession. But I wished too sincerely to avoid the fatal extremities to which I saw the discussion was tending not to give any reasonable proposal which might be made on their part every assistance in my power. He asked me by way of conversation what term of years I thought would satisfy us, and I immediately told him I did not find anything short of twenty years could answer any good purpose whatever. I will, however, confess to your Lordship that I shall be very well satisfied with half that number. As this proposal originated with him, and was received by me merely as a matter on which I would refer to your Lordship, I did not mention the idea of his Majesty's acquiring the sovereignty of the island of Lampedusa. When I receive the proposal in form, which I hope to do to-morrow, 1 may, if we can agree on any reasonable term of years, tack to my acquiescence the acquisition of the island. I can, however, scarcely hope that the evacuation of Holland and Switzerland, or of either, will be acceded to without drawing the negotiation to such a length, and even then without the utmost hazard of its failure, as must under the present circumstances, if possible, be avoided. If, therefore, I can bring the matter to an immediate conclusion, and without further reference to your Lordship, on the principle of our retaining possession of the fortresses of Malta for a term of years not less than that pointed out by your Lordship (for we cannot wait for the determination of his Sicilian Majesty), that this

Government will not oppose the cession of the island of Lampedusa, I shall, I confess, have great pleasure in announcing to your Lordship such a conclusion. I do not enter into a detail of the conversation which I had the same morning with M. de Talleyrand, immediately upon leaving Joseph Bonaparte, as it differed in nowise from what I have above mentioned. He suggested also the possibility of coming to an arrangement on the ground of a temporary occupation, and I made him the same answer. He seemed, however, not to doubt that his Majesty would be willing to give the same advantages in return which had been held out in the project, alluding to the acknowledgments of the Governments in Italy which had not yet been acknowledged. I told him that such an offer had been made as an inducement to the First Consul to accede to our demand of Malta in perpetuity, and it depended on the First Consul to accept it on the same condition; but that it could not be expected that we should allow the same for a modification as for the whole of the demand, and therefore I could not undertake to listen to any proposal of such a nature. I added, however, that if the French Government was disposed to consent to the claims which relate to the evacuation of Holland and Switzerland, and to make a suitable provision for his Sardinian Majesty, his Majesty might perhaps in that case be disposed to extend his offer of acknowledgment to the modification. This idea, however, is not likely to be adopted. Such is the state of the discussion at this moment. I am in expectation of hearing very shortly either from Joseph Bonaparte or M. de Talleyrand; and I am not without hopes that I may be able to announce to your Lordship that such an arrangement is made as may answer his Majesty's expectations, in a very few days. Your Lordship may be assured that I feel the necessity of the expedition. Were it less urgent, I might perhaps hope to bring the discussion to even a more favourable issue. The report of an embargo in the French ports is premature. The merchants have, however, been invited not to run the risk of sending their property to sea under the present circumstances. No English travellers are allowed to embark at any other port than Calais or Boulogne. But this, as well as the declaring Flushing *en état de siège*, is to be considered only as a demonstration, since it is pretty clearly ascertained that no very formidable preparations are or can be carrying on in the ports of the Channel.

Paris, April 18, 1803.

I did not fail to put into immediate execution the instructions contained in your Lordship's despatch No. 11, on the subject of the libel inserted by the French Minister in the 'Hamburg Gazette.' I represented the outrageous and unprecedented conduct of M. Reinhardt in such terms as it deserves, and fairly declared to M. de Talleyrand until satisfaction shall be given to his Majesty for the indignity which has been offered him by the French Minister in his official character there could be no possibility whatever of bringing the present discussion to an amicable issue. M. de Talleyrand assured me that the French Government saw the conduct of M. de Reinhardt in the same light as his Majesty's Ministers, and that they could not be more surprised than the First Consul had been at seeing such an article inserted by authority; that an immediate explanation had been required of M. Reinhardt five days ago, and if his conduct had been such as had been represented he would doubtless feel the effect of the First Consul's displeasure, and that in the meantime I might inform your Lordship that he was completely disavowed. I told M. de Talleyrand that as the insult had been public it would be necessary that the reparation should be so also. He assured me again that the First Consul considered M. Reinhardt's conduct as so reprehensible that every satisfaction might be expected. Your Lordship may be assured that I shall not lose sight of this business. There can, I think, be no doubt that M. Reinhardt received it from the First Consul for the purpose of insertion, and, I really do believe, without the knowledge of M. de Talleyrand. The agent will, however, be sacrificed, as Sebastiani would have been long ago if a disavowal of his report had been anywise practicable. I am convinced that there are few acts in the First Consul's political life which have been the cause of so much uneasiness to him, or of which he is so much ashamed.

Paris, April 20, 1803.

I had hoped that the first extraordinary messenger I should have had occasion to send would have been to announce to your Lordship that the differences between the two Governments were adjusted on one of the modifications pointed out to me by my last instructions from your Lordship. In this expectation I am deceived. I saw Joseph Bonaparte the night before last, before I had sealed up my despatches of that evening to your Lordship; but as all he said tended only to justify the hope I had given your Lordship in those despatches, I added nothing to them. He assured me positively that I should hear from M. de Talleyrand in the course of yesterday morning, and that a meeting would be appointed in order to settle the term of years for which the First Consul might be induced to consent to the cession of Malta. It is true that he declared that in order to gain his consent it would be necessary to hold out the advantages which the British Government was willing to offer in return, meaning the acknowledgments of the new Governments in Italy. I told him that this offer was made only with a view to the possession of Malta in perpetuity; but after some conversation I gave him to understand that I would not refuse to admit the demand *sub spe rati*, on the condition that the cession should be made for a good number of years, that Holland and Switzerland should be evacuated, and that a suitable provision should be made for the King of Sardinia. He seemed to think there could be no difficulty in this arrangement, and I left him in the persuasion that I should the next day, yesterday, or this morning, receive the summons from M. de Talleyrand which he had given me reason to expect. I am sorry to say that no such summons has been received by me; neither has any further notice been taken of the business. So that I feel that I should betray the confidence your Lordship may place in me were I to delay any longer requesting that I may be immediately furnished with the terms on which his Majesty's Ministers would be willing to conclude, and which probably will not differ much from those above stated, in order that I may propose them in the form of an ultimatum, and that at the expiration of the period allowed for deliberation I may be authorised, not only to declare that I am to leave Paris, but actually so to do, unless in the intermediate time the French Government should accede to our demands. I confess I see no other means of bringing the discussion to an issue, supposing, as there is every reason to presume is the case, that the object here is to protract, for which they have doubtless many urgent motives. Amongst these may be stated the expected disapprobation of our conduct by the Emperor of Russia; but in this I trust they will be deceived. And at all events I do not well see how that can change the state of the question with regard to us. But the chief motives for delay are that they are totally unprepared for a naval war; that the greatest part of their fleet is abroad, and consequently exposed to our attack; that what little commerce they can carry on is for the most part at sea, and that of their Batavian allies in the same hazardous predicament, and to a much greater amount. These are undoubtedly good motives for the line of conduct which they seem willing to pursue; but they are at the same time such as point out to us, added to many others, the necessity of despatch. Under all these circumstances, I do presume to suggest to your Lordship the necessity of an ultimatum. Your Lordship has, it is true, authorised me to declare that on the non-acceptance of the proposal I had to make I should be ordered to leave Paris; but I must have to declare that such an order is actually given, and that in consequence of it I am preparing to carry it into effect. This is our last resource, but I trust it will be an effectual one; and when I am in possession of it I am not without hope that I may, by holding it out in the *in terrorem*, reap the full benefit of it even before I make use of it officially; and I am fully persuaded that nothing short of this will convince the First Consul that the intelligence which they receive from England of his Majesty's Ministers not daring to push the matter to extremities, and to which both their hopes and fears induce them to give credit, is totally unfounded.

LORD HAWKESBURY TO LORD WHITWORTH.

Downing Street, April 23, 1803.

Your Excellency's despatches Nos. 37, 38, and 39 have been received and laid before the King. It is necessary for me to do little more on the present occasion than to refer you to my despatch of April 13, in which I stated to you the several propositions on which alone in the judgment of his Majesty the differences between this country and France could be satisfactorily adjusted. If upon the receipt of this despatch it shall not have been in your power to bring the negotiation to a conclusion on either of the propositions to which I have above referred, it is his Majesty's pleasure that you should communicate officially to the French Government that you have gone in point of concession to the full extent of your instructions, and that if an arrangement founded upon one of these propositions cannot be concluded without further delay, you have received his Majesty's commands to return to England. As there is some reason to believe that you have not distinctly understood the third proposition contained in my despatch, it is important that I should repeat that his Majesty can only consent to relinquish the permanent occupation of Malta by his forces on the conditions that the temporary possession shall not be less than ten years; that the authority civil and military shall during that period remain solely in his Majesty; and that at the expiration of that period the island shall be given up to the inhabitants, and not to the Order, and provided likewise that his Sicilian Majesty shall be induced to cede to his Majesty the island of Lampedusa. It is indispensable that, as a part of this arrangement, Holland should be evacuated by the French troops within a short period (say a month) after the conclusion of a convention by which all those provisions are secured. His Majesty will not insist on the evacuation of Switzerland, or on the article for a provision for the King of Sardinia; but he cannot consent to acknowledge the new Italian States unless stipulations in favour of his Sardinian Majesty and of Switzerland form a part of this arrangement. It is his Majesty's pleasure that you should delay your departure from Paris no longer than may be indispensably necessary for your personal convenience, and that, in the event of the failure of the negotiation, you should in no case remain at Paris after the receipt of this despatch more than seven days.

LORD WHITWORTH TO LORD HAWKESBURY.

Paris, April 23, 1803.

As I heard nothing from M. de Talleyrand, and as Joseph Bonaparte was gone into the country till Friday, I called on Thursday on the former, in order to learn the effect of the proposal which I had made, conformably to your Lordship's instructions, on the basis of a perpetual possession of the forts of Malta, on re-establishing the Order in the civil government of the island. He told me that if I had called upon him sooner he should two days ago have communicated to me the First Consul's answer, which was that no consideration on earth should induce him to consent to a concession in perpetuity of Malta in any shape whatever, and that the re-establishment of the Order was not so much the point to be discussed as that of suffering Great Britain to acquire a possession in the Mediterranean. I told him that I did not call sooner because I had been given to understand that he would have himself proposed it to me for the purpose of communicating the answer of the First Consul; and that it did not in any shape become me to put myself on the footing of a solicitor in this transaction. After some conversation, and finding (what I most sincerely believe to be the case) that the First Consul's determination was fixed on the point of a possession of Malta in perpetuity, I repeated to him what I had previously suggested to Joseph Bonaparte—the modification which I had to propose, namely, that for the sake of peace his Majesty would be willing to waive his pretensions to a possession in perpetuity, and would consent to hold Malta for a certain number of years to be agreed upon, on the condition that no opposition should be made on the part of the French Government to any negotiation his Majesty might set on foot with his Sicilian Majesty for the acquisition of the island of Lampedusa. We discussed this proposal in a conversation of some length, and I made use of all the arguments which have been furnished me by your Lordship, or which occurred to me, in its favour. I begged him particularly to recollect that we were in actual possession of the object, and that therefore every modification tending to limit that possession was in fact a concession on the part of his Majesty, and a proof of his desire to sacrifice to his love of peace the just claim which he has acquired in consequence of the conduct of France, and which had recently been admitted, of a much more considerable compensation and counterpoise. M. de Talleyrand did not seem disposed to dispute any of my positions, and I left him, I confess, fully impressed with the idea that the next day (Friday) I should find him prepared to treat on this ground, and that the only difficult point to be arranged would be the number of years for which Malta should be ceded to his Majesty. What, then, must have been my surprise when, on seeing him the next day, he told me that although he had not been able to obtain from the First Consul all we wished, still the proposition he had to make would, he trusted, be such as fully to answer the purpose! He then said that the First Consul would on no terms hear either of a perpetual or of a temporary possession of Malta; that his object was the execution of the Treaty of Amiens; and that, rather than submit to such an arrangement as that I had last proposed, he would even consent to our keeping the object in dispute for ever—on the ground that in the one there was an appearance of generosity and magnanimity, but in the other nothing but weakness and the effect of coercion; that therefore his resolution was taken, and what he had to propose was the possession we required of the island of Lampedusa, or of any other of the small isles, of which there were three or four between Malta and the coast of Africa; that such a possession would be sufficient for the object we had in view, which was a station in the Mediterranean as a place of refuge and security for any squadron we might find it convenient to keep in the sea. I suffered him to expatiate a considerable time and without interruption on the great advantages we were to derive from such an acquisition, as well as on the confidence which the First Consul reposed in our pacific intention in lending a hand to such an establishment. He concluded by desiring I would transmit this proposal to your Lordship. I told him I was extremely sorry indeed to find that we had made such little progress in the negotiation; that my orders were positive—that I could hear of nothing short of what I had proposed, neither could I possibly undertake to make such a proposal to his Majesty, since every word of my instructions (from which I certainly should not depart) applied positively to Malta, unless an equivalent security could be offered, and surely he would not pretend to tell me that Lampedusa could be considered as such; that the possession of Malta was necessary for our security, and was rendered so not from any desire of aggrandisement on the part of his Majesty, but by the conduct of the French Government, and that so strongly were we impressed with this necessity, that rather than abandon it we were prepared to go to war; that it was on this ground I must declare to him that I could neither take upon myself to forward such a proposal as he had made to me, or, indeed, anything short of what I had last proposed as a fair equivalent. I will confess to your Lordship that I was nettled at hearing such a proposal; and I could not refrain from adding that he might perhaps think me an improvident negotiator in declaring to him in the manner I had done the utmost extent of my instructions in the outset of the conversation, but that he would in return find me a firm one, for I should most certainly not recede from the ground I had taken; that in so doing I acted in conformity to his Majesty's views, who would most assuredly disapprove of my conduct were I, by unnecessarily protracting the negotiation, to add one day or one hour, if it could be avoided, to the suspense and anxiety under which his own subjects and all Europe must labour at such a crisis; that I had hoped the French Government, actuated by the same generous motives, would have acted in the same manner; that it might by pursuing a contrary line of conduct gain still a few days, but I must declare that in a very short time I should have to communicate to him those very terms from which his were so wide, but to draw nearer to which was perhaps the object of his negotiating, in the form of an ultimatum, which would at least have one good effect, that of bringing the matter to an issue; and the certainty even of war was preferable to the present state of indecision. To all I could say M. de Talleyrand objected the dignity and honour of the First Consul, which could not admit of his consenting to anything which might carry with it the appearance of yielding to a threat. I told him that it never could be admitted that the First Consul had a right to act in such a manner as to excite jealousy and create alarm in every State of Europe, and, when asked for explanation or security, say that it was contrary to his honour or his dignity to afford either. Such arguments might perhaps do when applied to those Governments with which France had been accustomed to treat, or more properly to dictate to, but never could be used to Great Britain; that his Majesty had a right to speak freely his opinion, and possessed also the means, whenever he chose to employ them, of opposing a barrier to the ambition of any individual or of any state which should be disposed to threaten the security of his dominions or the tranquillity of Europe. I was nettled at this affected assertion of dignity on all occasions, and could not help expressing myself rather warmly on the subject. Our conversation concluded by M. de Talleyrand's assuring me that he would report the substance of it to the First Consul in the evening, and that he should probably have occasion to see me on the following day.

Paris, April 25, 1803.

The conversation I had on Saturday morning with M. de Talleyrand has produced nothing from which I can draw a more favourable conclusion as to the result of the negotiation than when I last addressed your Lordship. He told me that although he had seen the First Consul the night before he had nothing to add to what he had communicated to me on Friday; that the First Consul was determined not to give his consent to our retaining Malta either in perpetuity or for a term, although of the two he would prefer the former tenure, as the less repugnant to his feelings; that he was therefore ordered to repeat the proposal he had lately made me—of acceding to our demand of Lampedusa or any of the neighbouring islands, and that, as our object was to obtain a settlement in the Mediterranean, he imagined that which we ourselves had pointed out would answer every purpose we might have in view; but that at all events the First Consul neither could nor would relinquish his claim to the full execution of the Treaty of Amiens. To this I could only repeat what I had already said to him on the inadequacy of such a proposal, and of the impossibility in which I found myself to transmit it to your Lordship. I lamented the course which the negotiation was taking, and that the First Consul should have so little regard to the dreadful consequences which must ensue as to suffer them to be outweighed by a mistaken notion of dignity. In answer to an observation of M. de Talleyrand, from which he gave me to understand the First Consul could never submit to what he considered as an act of violence, I told him it was but too true that in the late transactions with other Powers the First Consul had been so little accustomed to meet with contradiction that it was natural he should not well distinguish between any opposition to his will and an act of violence, but that his Majesty was not to be classed with those Powers, and the French Government must therefore not be surprised if, when his Majesty's dignity, his honour, or the safety of his dominions were threatened, the most effectual means would be used to secure them; and I added, that notwithstanding the acquiescence which he might have met with from others, the plea of its being incompatible with the dignity of the French Government to give satisfaction or security, when both might with justice be demanded, could never be admitted by Great Britain. M. de Talleyrand heard everything I could say, and seemed unwilling to break up the conference. He constantly brought forward the same inadmissible proposal, requesting that I would at least communicate it to your Lordship. This I told him I could not refuse to do, since everything which passed between him and me must of course make the subject of my reports to your Lordship. I declared, however, at the same time, that I should not think myself by any means authorised to suspend the execution of any instructions I might receive tending to bring the negotiation to an issue, in the expectation of any change which such a proposal might produce. All I could do, and that I would certainly do, would be to communicate the ultimatum, if his Majesty should think proper to furnish me with it, confidentially to M. de Talleyrand before I presented it officially to him as Minister for Foreign Affairs. He assured me that he should consider such conduct as a further proof of my desire to conciliate, and that he could not yet forbear hoping that the differences might be adjusted. I repeated that if his hope was founded on the expectation of his Majesty's being induced to recede from his demand it would be deceiving himself to cherish it. The remainder of the conversation turned on the calamities which would follow the failure of our endeavour to avoid a rupture. He insinuated that Holland,

Naples, and other countries connected with Great Britain would be the first victims of the war. I told him we doubted not the disposition of this Government to extend the miseries of war or its means of carrying such an inclination into effect; but I asked him whether he thought that such conduct would add to the glory of the First Consul, or whether the falling on the innocent and defenceless would not rather tarnish it and ultimately unite against him not only the honest men in his own country, but every Government in Europe; that it certainly would excite more detestation than terror in England, at the same time that it would serve to impress upon us still more strongly the necessity of omitting no means of circumscribing a power so perniciously exerted. M. de Talleyrand observed that he believed that even in England there were persons impartial enough to admit that France had not only acted with good faith towards us, but that she had since the conclusion of the Treaty of Amiens manifested but one idea—that of cultivating the best understanding. I said that I was at a loss to guess who those persons could be to whom he alluded; that those with whom I was in the habit of conversing, amongst whom were people of all parties, were not of that opinion, but were rather convinced that if more provocation had not been given we were more indebted to our own vigilance than to the forbearance of the First Consul—alluding to the project, of the existence of which none could doubt, of invading Egypt in the course of the month of October last, had not the British fleet been, contrary to expectations, at that period in the Mediterranean. I could not help adding that although no act of hostility had actually taken place, yet the inveteracy with which our commerce, our industry, and our credit had been attacked in every part to which French influence could be extended did in fact almost amount to the same, since it went to prove, in addition to the general system of the First Consul, that his object was to pursue under the mask of peace the same line of conduct on which the preceding Governments had acted, tending to the subversion of every regular one in Europe. In the course of this conversation

I am not conscious of having omitted any arguments which might serve to convince M. de Talleyrand, and through him the First Consul, of our determination to adhere to our demand, and at the same time show that we were not imposed upon by their specious professions. In my preceding conversation I had intimated to M. de Talleyrand that if he was bent upon making that proposal to your Lordship which I had declined accepting he might do it through the medium of General Andréossy. M. de Talleyrand now told me that the First Consul had ordered him to assure me that he would make use of no other channel than mine; that he was convinced no one was more desirous than I was of conciliating all differences, and he trusted to my exertions. I will confess to your Lordship that I do not feel much elated with this mark of confidence; neither, indeed, do I well know whether I am to consider it as a compliment. Whatever it be, it cannot render me more conscious than I am to avoid the extremity of war, or less zealous for the honour and dignity of his Majesty, which, I hope and trust, will never be impaired by any transaction of mine. I am sorry to have to inform your Lordship that the further discussion of this business has been taken from Joseph Bonaparte, on the supposition of his not doing sufficient justice to the arguments and pretensions of the First Consul. The whole is now to go through the regular channel of the Minister for Foreign Affairs. Although this change has taken place, I am perfectly sure none will have taken place in Joseph Bonaparte's sentiments, and that he will, in his daily intercourse with his brother, lose no opportunity of serving our cause, which he considers as the cause of peace. M. de Talleyrand can act no otherwise than he does, but I am perfectly sure he coincides in opinion with him, as does every thinking man in the country. The measures which we are pursuing will be considered as political and just; whilst those of the First Consul exhibit a picture of despotism, violence, and cruelty, at the contemplation of which humanity sickens. This I do firmly believe to be the general impression of those who see deeper into the state of Europe than through the medium of the

French papers. It is said since Friday that a messenger is arrived from Petersburg, and that the accounts which he brings are not so favourable to the views of the First Consul as he expected. Should this be the case, we may perhaps reap some benefit from it; but I confess to your Lordship that the intractable character of the First Consul leaves me but little hope. I trust entirely to the effect of the ultimatum, which will at least convince him that we are in earnest, and that he has nothing to expect from protraction. I shall not, however, as I said before, make use of this arm officially until I have tried its effect in a more conciliatory manner. We will convince even the First Consul that nothing has been left unattempted for the preservation of peace. It will be no matter of surprise to your Lordship to learn that the Court of Berlin has engaged—if any credit is to be attached to the assurances of M. de Luchesini—to adopt the views of the First Consul should hostilities take place. I trust, however, that this cannot take place, unless the Emperor of Russia should adopt the same disgraceful line of conduct. On the preparations which are carrying on I have little to say. It is not until within these three days that they have worn any serious aspect. Troops are marching towards the coast, particularly to the neighbourhood of Cherbourg, where General Suchet is appointed to command them. The generals affect to hold out the certainty and the success of an invasion, which few others believe. And it is said that General Moreau should look forward to being at the head of an army; but I believe he does so with views very different from those which are assigned. More troops are ordered to Holland, and everything points out their intention of threatening us with an invasion. Their works in the dockyards do not, I am assured, keep pace with the activity displayed in the marching of troops. Your Lordship knows how difficult it is, not to say impossible, to procure intelligence on these points. Such a system of vigilance and suspicion prevails that money even proves ineffectual. I am, however, persuaded that one great motive of this extraordinary caution is that we may not see their poverty, and be convinced that nothing effectual has been done, or is doing, towards the regeneration of their navy, or even to give the least degree of probability to the success of the threatened invasion. I have always thought it next to impossible. The First Consul has told me himself that he considers it in the same light. I do not believe that he or any one else has any real intention of ever making the attempt. It is on those devoted and defenceless countries which lay open to his attack that his rage will fall: they will be the victims to his insatiate but impotent hatred of us.

P.S.—Your Lordship's despatches Nos. 12, 13, and 14 of the 23rd, with their enclosures, were delivered to me by Shaw this evening at nine o'clock. I shall see M. de Talleyrand to-morrow morning, and I trust your Lordship will not disapprove my following the line of conduct I had proposed, and which I have mentioned to your Lordship, of informing him of the nature of my instructions a few hours before I carry them officially into execution. All I can say at this moment is, that, if I may give credit to those who pretend to be well informed, the First Consul is determined not to comply with our demands. I have, however, reason to believe that he did not expect to be so closely pressed as he now will be.

Paris, April 27, 1803, six o'clock in the evening.

I avail myself of the opportunity of a messenger passing through from Constantinople and Vienna to inform your Lordship of the state of the negotiation at this moment. I communicated to M. de Talleyrand the purport of my instructions of the 23rd yesterday at four o'clock. I prefaced this communication by telling him that I was not unmindful of the engagement I had contracted, of consulting him confidentially on the purport of those instructions before I made the communication in form; and, as I mentioned to your Lordship in a former despatch, I was induced to do so in order that there might be no further expectation of our receding from our demand, and if possible to give an opportunity of adjusting the differences without having recourse to an extremity which might, with a character like that of the First Consul's, increase the difficulties. M. de Talleyrand cut the matter, however, very short. He asked me if the possession of Malta was insisted upon. I told him most certainly it was; and I repeated to him the particulars of the terms on which it was yet possible to conclude the business; that these were, the possession of Malta for ten years, during which period the authority, civil and military, was to remain solely in his Majesty, and that at the expiration of that term it was to be given up to the inhabitants, and not to the Order; provided also that his Sicilian Majesty shall be induced to cede to his Majesty the island of Lampedusa, that Holland should be evacuated by the French troops within a month after the conclusion of a convention by which all these provisions shall be secured; and that his Majesty would further consent to acknowledge the new Italian States, provided stipulations were made in favour of his Sardinian Majesty and of Switzerland. I had no sooner made known these conditions than M. de Talleyrand told me it would be perfectly unnecessary to delay the official communication, for, as the possession of Malta was still insisted upon, although for a term, the First Consul would not consent to them. I accordingly did repeat them to him in the manner he desired, when he told me that he comprehended perfectly what we required, but in similar cases it was usual to state the demand in writing, and he desired I would give him a note upon the subject. I told him that I was by no means authorised so to do; that if he desired it I would repeat to him once more, or as often as he pleased, the express terms which I had stated to him, but that it was not in my power to make any communication in writing; and that as my communication to him was verbal I should of course be content with an answer in the same form. He expatiated much on the irregularity of such a proceeding; but as I could give him no further satisfaction he consented at length to receive it, and to communicate to me the First

Consul's answer as soon as possible. I desired that he would recollect that Tuesday next must be the day of my departure; and I left him, I confess, with no very sanguine hope of success, although not with the degree of despondency with which he evidently meant to impress me. I had in the meantime written to Joseph Bonaparte, who was at his country house near Chantilly, to desire he would return for the purpose of making a last effort on the First Consul. He returned late in the evening, and I have seen him this morning. I told him everything which had passed, and I confess that he has raised my expectations of a favourable issue, by acknowledging, although unintentionally, that in his conversations with the First Consul the number of years for which Malta might be ceded had been discussed, and that the First Consul had said that, let what would happen, he never could consent to more than three or four. I told him that my instructions were so positive as to preclude all further negotiation on that point. But I consider such a confession on his part as a very favourable symptom, since it proves to me that the First Consul is not so stout as M. de Talleyrand had represented him to be on the subject of a temporary possession. After some conversation, tending to convince me that he would employ himself zealously for the favourable conclusion of the business, he left me to go to St. Cloud. About half an hour after he had been gone I received an intimation, from a private but sure hand, that M. de Talleyrand had not made use of my communication in the form of an ultimatum, or at least that the First Consul did not, or, what I believe is nearer the truth, would not, receive it as such. The pretext is that it is not formal unless in writing. And of this I was still further assured by the return of Joseph Bonaparte, who came from the First Consul to tell me that no ultimatum had been given, since nothing verbal was considered as such. I explained again to him the nature of my instructions, declaring that I was not authorised to give anything in writing, but that I could repeat it as often as he pleased. He told me that the First Consul was much embarrassed how to act; that he certainly was disposed to avoid a rupture, if it could be done without dishonour; that if an ultimatum had been given in writing he would perhaps submit it to the Council of State and let that determine on the conduct which he should pursue. I gave it as my opinion that although it was not given in the manner which, according to the opinion of the First Consul, would have been more formal, yet it was sufficiently explicit not to be misunderstood; and that we should, I feared, lose only time, which was extremely precious, in disputing on a point on which I could give them no satisfaction. With this he immediately returned to St. Cloud, and I have heard no further from him or M. de Talleyrand. As I have two extraordinary messengers with me, I shall have sufficient opportunities of communicating to your Lordship the further progress of the negotiation. I forward this with the messenger from Vienna, in order that your Lordship may be informed as early as possible of the state of the business at this moment. There certainly exists a strong disposition to negotiate. It may be for the purpose of delay; but in this they cannot now succeed, since I have given it clearly to be understood that my departure must be regulated by the receipt of your Lordship's instructions which reached me on Monday night. I have just heard that M. Lauriston set out for London at twelve o'clock last night, with despatches to General Andréossy, and possibly for the purpose of seeing your Lordship. I have lately had reason to suppose that the First Consul considers his Ambassador in London as too partial. It is calculated that Lauriston may return before I leave Paris. Joseph Bonaparte on coming from his brother seemed very anxious to know the precise time of my departure, and I told him that it would not be protracted beyond Tuesday next. He asked me if in the case of my leaving Paris the French Ambassador would not be allowed to remain in England, for the First Consul would probably not recall him. I told him I did not well see how that could be; that when I should be recalled from hence it would of course be intimated to the French Ambassador to return, should he not receive orders to that effect from the Government. From this your Lordship will see how disposed they are, by every artifice, to gain time. I should also mention, that on his asking me why his Majesty's Ministers could object to my delivering in writing what I was already authorised to give verbally, I told him that, although no reason had been assigned, yet it appeared to me that it would be difficult in an official note to specify the demand which his Majesty made, amounting to an infringement of the letter of the Treaty of Amiens, without at the same time enumerating the motives, arising from the conduct of the French Government since the conclusion of the treaty, which had rendered such a demand necessary as a measure of reciprocity and of precaution; that this would of course include a great deal of matter, and, in fact, would amount to a manifesto before the necessity of such a measure. He seemed to think this explanation not unreasonable, and I trust it will not be found so by your Lordship.

Paris, April 28, 1803.

Since my letter of last night by Lord Elgin's messenger, I have learnt nothing that can add either to your Lordship's hopes or doubts on the result of the negotiation. The First Consul is, as I am given to understand, in a state of extreme agitation; and those who have conversed with him in the course of yesterday left him with the impression that, of the two, he is more disposed to resistance than conciliation. This is also the language of M. de Talleyrand—not expressed to me, for I have not seen him since the day before yesterday, but conveyed to me with a view probably of exciting alarm by persons deputed for that purpose by him. I have not learnt the motive of M. de Lauriston's mission. It may be to ascertain whether any diminution can be obtained in the term of years for which the possession of Malta is required; and I am inclined to believe this to be the case, as Joseph Bonaparte, on my mentioning ten years, immediately observed that your Lordship had told General Andréossy (I suppose some time ago) that seven years would be accepted. If the First Consul determines to submit the case to the decision of the Council, it will probably not be the Council of State, but a Privy Council, provided for by the Constitution, and composed of the three Consuls, two Ministers, two Councillors of State, two Senators, and two Chiefs of the Legion of Honour. Should such a reference be resorted to, there can be little doubt of the result; for, as I have had frequent opportunities of saying to your Lordship, there is scarcely a man of any consequence employed in the Government, with the exception of a few generals, who would not consider the renewal of a war as the severest calamity which could possibly befall this country. At all events, it is imagined that no decision will be taken, or at least communicated to me, until the return of M. de Lauriston, who, it is calculated, may be back Sunday night or Monday morning. In this case it will run very hard on the term prescribed by your Lordship for my stay at Paris; and without knowing the object of his journey I have given it plainly to be understood that my departure, with that of the mission in general, must take place on Tuesday next unless the modification which I have proposed and from which it is vain to hope that we shall recede shall in the intermediate time be adopted. Enclosed is the Project which I read to M. de Talleyrand, in consequence of your Lordship's instructions of the 13th inst., and from which your Lordship will see that I did not either misunderstand or misapply the letter or the spirit of those instructions. The term of years was left in blank, as no positive term had been specified. I should, had this Government been disposed to negotiate, have insisted on sixteen or fourteen years, and in no case have fallen lower than ten, the number now adopted in the ultimatum.

Projet.

L'île de Malte restera en possession de Sa Majesté Britannique pour l'espace de. . . . À la fin de ce terme elle sera rendue aux habitans, et elle sera reconnue comme état indépendant. Dans ce cas Sa Majesté se prêteroit à un arrangement pour l'établissement de l'ordre de St. Jean dans quelque autre partie de l'Europe. Le Gouvernement françois ne s'opposera pas à la cession de l'île de Lampedusa à Sa Majesté, pourvu que l'on obtienne le consentement de Sa Majesté le roi des Deux-Siciles, moyennant un dédommagement convenable. La Hollande et la Suisse seront évacuées par les troupes françoises. Sa Majesté reconnaîtra le roi d'Etrurie, ainsi que les républiques italienne et ligurienne, à condition qu'il soit fait un arrangement en Italie satisfaisant à Sa Majesté le roi de Sardaigne.

Paris, April 29, 1803.   Friday evening.

Although I can yet say nothing positive, or indeed scarcely form an opinion, as to the event of the negotiation, I think it my duty not to suffer two days to pass without communicating with your Lordship. Were I to give credit to the public report, I should have very little hope of an amicable arrangement. All those who judge from appearances, and from loose expressions dropped—in all probability intentionally—by the First Consul, assure me that he is determined at all events to resist our demands, and to suffer me to depart; and it is certain that a considerable degree of preparation would seem to justify such an opinion. Expresses are continually sent to the ports, troops are marching towards the coast, and the project of invasion is announced as the only measure by which what they term the arrogant and turbulent spirit of Great Britain can be subdued. This is language held by the vulgar; but I may add that none but the vulgar attend to it. It is felt by those who are capable of reasoning that it is much easier to make a demonstration than to carry into effect a project for which everything is wanting, excepting soldiers, most necessary for its execution. And, indeed, it is this deficiency of means which encourages me to hope that matters may yet be accommodated. My last letter to your Lordship was of yesterday evening. This morning a person came to me, whom I suspect of being employed by the First

Consul for the purpose of ascertaining my sentiments (this person is M. de Perregaux, my banker), and told me that I should in the course of the day receive a letter from M. de Talleyrand, drawn up under the inspection of the First Consul, which, although not exactly what I might wish, was, however, so moderate as to afford me a well-grounded hope, and might certainly be sufficient to induce me to delay for a short time my departure. I told him that it would be a matter of great satisfaction to me to perceive a probability of bringing the negotiation to a favourable issue, and that I should be extremely sorry to spoil the business by any useless precipitation; but it must be recollected that I acted in conformity to instructions, that these instructions were positive, that by them I was enjoined to leave Paris on Tuesday next unless in the intermediate time certain conditions were agreed to, and that I could not possibly disobey those instructions unless in the letter which he mentioned, or in any other, such assurances were given of the acceptation we required as would justify me in the eyes of his Majesty for not conforming implicitly to his orders. This declaration seemed to make an impression upon him. He expatiated on the moderation of the letter, which, however, he had not seen, and also of the sincere wish of the First Consul to avoid a war. I could only tell him that if the First Consul did so sincerely wish to avoid a war the means of so doing were in his power, and not in ours, unless we were disposed—which I could not think very likely to be the case—to give up both our honour and our security at the same time. I repeated that nothing would induce me to prolong my stay short of a fair and unequivocal declaration of their acceptance of our just demands. Upon this he left me. No letter came in the course of the day, and I suppose the manner in which I received this insinuation may have suggested the necessity of some further consultation. About four o'clock, however, I went to M. de Talleyrand and I found him at home. I told him that my anxiety to learn whether he had anything favourable to tell me brought me to him, and, in case he had not, to recall to his recollection that Tuesday was the day on which I must leave Paris, and to request that he would have the necessary passports prepared for me and my family. He appeared evidently embarrassed, and after some hesitation observed that he could not suppose I should really go away, but that at all events the First Consul never would recall his Ambassador. To this I replied his Majesty recalled me in order to put an end to the negotiation, on the principle that even actual war was preferable to the state of suspense in which England, and indeed all Europe, had been kept for so long a space of time; and that consequently when I left Paris it would, should the First Consul not think proper to recall his Ambassador, be intimated to him that he could no longer be considered as a public character, although perhaps he might, if he pleased, be allowed to remain in a private one; but his functions would of course cease with mine. He then reverted to the surprise of the First Consul at the difficulty I made of giving our conditions in writing, observing that from conversation or verbal communication nothing specific could be collected; and to illustrate his argument he again mentioned the difference which appears in my demands to the terms held out in conversation with the French Ambassador. I told him I could say nothing to this: that in my instructions there had been no deviation; they had been positive and left me no doubt, and I repeated to him what I had said to Joseph Bonaparte in order to satisfy him that our motives for not giving in writing were good—that a note of the nature he required must of necessity be neither more nor less than a manifesto. From the tenor of his conversation, I should rather be led to think that he does not consider the case as desperate. Upon my leaving him he repeatedly said, 'J'ai encore de l'espoir.' I learn from different quarters that it is the determination of the First Consul to avoid a rupture if he possibly can. All I can possibly say to this is, that he knows the terms on which it might be avoided, and from these terms it is impossible his Majesty can recede. It is said to-day that Lauriston is not gone to England, but to the Hague, where some difficulties have arisen on the subject of the influx of French troops on the Republic. M. de Talleyrand, on my questioning him, did not deny his mission to England, but he did not avow it. At all events, his return is expected on Sunday night. Accounts of a very disagreeable nature have been received from St. Domingo. They amount to the total annihilation of the French army by the blacks, to whom a considerable number of whites, driven to despair by the extortions and indiscipline of the army, had joined themselves. I could wish at this particular moment that the hopes of reducing that colony might not be considered as desperate. Joseph Bonaparte went out of town again on Wednesday evening, but returns to-morrow morning.

Saturday evening.

This day has passed without any occurrence whatever. The letter in question is not yet arrived; but I was informed this morning that in consequence of my observations yesterday it had been necessary to make some alterations. I confess I have no great hopes from it, or indeed of anything conciliatory. But at all events, nothing can be expected until the last moment. On Monday morning I shall send to M. de Talleyrand for my passports, and on the following evening I shall, according to your Lordship's instructions, leave this place. I shall send off a messenger on Monday. An assembly at the Tuileries has been announced for to-morrow; but, in the present state of things, I trust your Lordship will approve my not attending it. I shall in the morning write an excuse to M. de Talleyrand on the score of health. I find always that great stress is laid on General Andréossy's remaining in London, even in the event of my leaving Paris; and it is even pretended that the object of Lauriston's journey, if he is gone to England, is to order the French Ambassador not to depart unless he should be absolutely forced so to do. The policy of this measure is obvious. No messenger is yet arrived from Petersburg. M. de Marcoff received despatches yesterday from his Court by the post, written after his Majesty's message was known there; and, as far as I can pick up from M. de Marcoff, for he is not communicative on the subject, of a nature not quite in the sense of this Government. I am much afraid he will not make all the use he might of this favourable circumstance. I am sorry to say that those whom I have had occasion to see in the course of this day give no good ground to hope a favourable issue to the negotiation. I shall not, however, despair till the very last moment. And should any proposition be made of a nature to justify my deviating from the strict line of my instructions, I shall instantly forward it to your Lordship by a messenger.

Lord Whitworth to Mr. Hammond.

Paris, April 30, 1803.

In answer to your inquiries respecting M. St. Quentin, I have every reason to believe that he did arrive here on Sunday last, and that what he brought was delivered at the Department of Foreign Affairs. I am further assured that the nature of his intelligence was such as to encourage an idea here of his Majesty's Ministers not being supported by the public in the present measures. M. de Talleyrand knows our country too well to trust to such reports; but as you know that a drowning man will catch at a straw, it is not impossible it may have had some effect on the First Consul, whose endeavours and hopes all tend that way. I don't know whether you will be able to form an idea of the result of the negotiation from my despatch of this date. It rests entirely on the determination of one individual, and what that will be I verily believe no one in the country but himself knows at this moment. I have till now been counting by days, but now must begin to reckon by hours. It is now Saturday night, and in the course of Tuesday I must be off, unless very good reasons are assigned for my stay. I have not been very expeditious in my preparations for the journey, as you may well believe.

In the *hope* of seeing you soon, but rather as the messenger of peace than of war, I am, &c.

LORD WHITWORTH TO LORD HAWKESBURY.

Paris, May 2, 1803.

Another day has passed over without producing any change. I mentioned to your Lordship in my last that under the present circumstances I did not think myself justified in attending the audience of yesterday at the Tuileries. Late in the preceding evening a person came—deputed, I believe, by Talleyrand—to suggest to me that by absenting myself on this occasion I might unintentionally give offence, and so increase the difficulties which I had to encounter. My answer was, that after what had passed I could not take upon myself to expose his Majesty's dignity and my own feelings to the danger which must be expected from the violence of the First Consul's temper, irritated as it now is even beyond its usual pitch; that if I went I should feel it incumbent upon me to assume an air of calmness and composure; and that such an air at this particular moment might be misunderstood, and operate more to the detriment of the business than my absence could possibly do. To this no reasonable reply could be made, and in the morning early I wrote M. de Talleyrand a note, of which I enclose a copy, as well as to the Prefect of the Palace, declining the invitation to the circle and to the dinner. The event has given me no reason to repent this determination; for, by all accounts, such a scene of unguarded passion has not been often witnessed. On his first appearance in the room the observation he made was: 'Ainsi donc, M. l'ambassadeur d'Angleterre ne vient pas aujourd'hui; c'est qu'il fait probablement ses paquets.' He then went on in such a strain of invective as indicated a most disordered state of mind, and the audience passed under every appearance of agitation. To all those to whom he addressed himself he made some observation reflecting on England or his Majesty's Government. After dinner the same scene was repeated, but not quite so publicly. He engaged soon in a conversation of considerable length with M. de Marcoff, and when the assembly broke up he took him with him into his cabinet, where he remained with him a considerable time. This was reported to me soon after; and I confess I was in some expectation that (supposing, as I have reason to believe is the case, that M. de Marcoff knows the feelings of his Court on this occasion to go with us, and would endeavour to oppose some reason to the passions of the First Consul) such a conference might be productive of good. My expectations were still further raised when in the morning I received from the Russian Minister the note which I enclose. He followed soon himself; and all I could collect from him was that the First Consul had, as on every former occasion, endeavoured to justify himself completely, and to throw the whole odium of the business upon us. It is therefore useless to repeat to your Lordship the details of such a conversation. He told me, however, that before he came away the First Consul had complained heavily of my precipitate departure from Paris, as precluding all possibility of adjusting the points on which we are at issue. If I may credit M. de Marcoff, he did justice upon this occasion to our motives and conduct. He told the First Consul that I had three weeks ago announced the possibility of the positive instructions which I should soon be furnished with, and that in fact I had formally and officially communicated them near a week ago. This drew from the First Consul some reflections on the unprecedented mode of negotiation by verbal communication; and I am afraid M. de Marcoff did not urge on this occasion all the reasons which he might have assigned, and which a few hours ago I repeated to M. de Talleyrand. As, however, the First Consul declared that he might have made proposals had he not been so pressed, I determined to go myself to M. de Talleyrand and to deliver, instead of sending, the enclosed letter. I told him that it was with great reluctance that I came to make this last application to him; that I had long since told him the extent of the term which had been assigned for my stay at Paris, and that as I had received to this moment no answer whatever to the proposal I had repeatedly made, I could no longer delay requiring him to furnish me with the necessary passports for the return of myself, my family, and the remainder of the mission to England. Upon this I gave him the letter, a copy of which I enclose, and on reading it he appeared somewhat startled. He lamented that so much time had been lost, but said that enough remained if I was authorised to negotiate upon other terms. I could of course but repeat to him that not only I had no other terms to propose, but that most assuredly I should have no other whatever, and that, therefore, unless the First Consul could so far gain upon himself as to sacrifice a false punctilio to the certainty of a war, of which no one could foresee the consequence, nothing could possibly prevent my departure to-morrow night. He hoped, he said, this was not so near; that he would communicate my letter and what I had said to the First Consul immediately, and that in all probability I should hear from him this evening. I thought it right, however, to apprise him that it was quite impossible I could be induced to disobey his Majesty's orders and protract a negotiation on terms so disadvantageous to ourselves, unless he should furnish me with such a justification as would leave me no room to hesitate, and that I did not see that anything short of a full acquiescence in his Majesty's demands could have that effect. He repeated that he would report to the First Consul, and that I should shortly hear from him. In this state the business now rests, and I am expecting either a proposition or my passports. I prepare myself, I confess, rather for the latter, and am consequently taking every measure for setting out to-morrow night. If I determine under these circumstances to send your Lordship a messenger, it is only that your Lordship may know day by day how we proceed. Were I to give implicit credit to all the reports which reach me from all quarters of the First Consul's resolution to maintain his ground, I should certainly have no hope whatever of anything in the shape of conciliation. But I see so much passion, and in fact attach so little importance to all the violence of the First Consul, that I cannot help nourishing a hope that at last he will give way. I am inclined to think that M. de Marcoff knew more than he chose to express to me, and that he is aware of a proposition being about to be made by M. de Talleyrand. In all this, however, it is very possible I may listen rather to my wishes than to my expectations; but at all events four-and-twenty hours must now decide the question. It is, I am persuaded, in the breast of the First Consul, and as yet communicated by him to no one.

P.S.—Since writing the above I have learnt from a person well informed that the answer which I am likely to receive this night or to-morrow morning is so short of everything which we have required, and so evidently calculated to gain time, that it cannot be considered as any justification to me for not carrying his Majesty's commands into effect. Should, therefore, this answer be not more favourable than it is represented to be, nothing will prevent my leaving this place to-morrow night or the following morning at farthest.

LORD WHITWORTH TO M. DE TALLEYRAND.

Paris, ce 2 Mai 1803.

Monsieur,—Quand j'ai eu l'honneur, mardi passé, de vous communiquer officiellement les dernières propositions que j'ai été chargé par ma cour de soumettre au Gouvernment françois dans la vue d'aplanir les présentes difficultés, j'ai eu l'honneur de vous annoncer qu'en cas que le Premier Consul n'agréât pas ces propositions, je me verrois dans la nécessité de quitter Paris en huit jours. Nous touchons à la fin de ce terme, sans que j'aie reçu la moindre réponse à cette communication. Il ne me reste donc qu'à obéir aux ordres du Roi mon maître de retourner auprès de lui, et pour cet effet je vous prie, Monsieur, de vouloir bien me fournir les passeports nécessaires.

1. Un pour moi, Madame la duchesse de Dorset et notre suite.

2. Un pour les enfans avec leur suite.

3. Un pour Monsieur Talbot, secrétaire d'ambassade, et ses domestiques.

4. Un pour Monsieur Mandeville, secrétaire, avec son domestique.

5. Un pour Monsieur Hodgson, aumônier.

6. Un pour Monsieur Maclaurin, médecin, avec sa famille et ses domestiques.

Je saisis cette occasion pour renouveler à Votre Excellence l'assurance de ma haute considération.

WHITWORTH.

LORD WHITWORTH TO M. DE TALLEYRAND.

Paris, ce 30 Avril 1803.

Monsieur,—Une indisposition me prive de l'honneur de présenter mes respects au Premier Consul demain. J'ose vous prier, en cas que le Premier Consul me fasse l'honneur de remarquer mon absence, de vouloir bien avoir la bonté d'être l'interprète de mes regrets.

Agréez, Monsieur, les assurances de ma haute considération.

WHITWORTH.

LORD WHITWORTH TO M. LE PRÉFET DU PALAIS.

Paris, ce 1 Mai 1803.

Monsieur,—Une indisposition m'empêche de rendre mes devoirs au Premier Consul aujourd'hui aux Tuileries. Je vous prie, en cas que le Premier Consul me fasse l'honneur de remarquer mon absence, de vouloir bien être l'interprète de mes regrets.

Agréez, Monsieur, l'assurance de ma haute considération.

WHITWORTH.

The Préfet du Palais to Lord Whitworth.

Ce dimanche, 1 Mai.

Vous m'avez annoncé, milord, que votre intention étoit d'envoyer demain dans la matinée demander vos passeports. Ne pourriez-vous pas retarder cette démarche jusqu'à ce que nous nous soyons vus? J'ai quelque chose à vous communiquer qui pourra peut-être influer sur votre détermination. Marquez-moi l'heure à laquelle je pourrai vous voir, soit chez vous, soit chez moi, à votre choix. Je vous souhaite bien le bonsoir et vous assure de mon bien sincère attachement.

Lord Whitworth to Mr. Hammond.

Paris, May 2, 1803.

Although I am still at Paris, I cannot but consider my stay for more than twenty-four hours as so precarious as not to take every measure of precaution. I have therefore to request that you will immediately be so good as to give orders for two Government packets to be on Friday next at Calais, in order to take me and my family, which is very numerous, over. It is possible, as the children travel with us, that we may not reach Calais till Saturday; but, in order to be sure, I could wish the packet-boats not to be later than Friday. I have ordered Shaw, who takes my despatch of this date, to return from Calais should he find anything there, as this despatch will go as quick without him and perhaps cause less speculation. I shall send him or another on before me to London with an account of my last moments, unless something very unexpected should yet keep me here.

Lord Whitworth to Lord Hawkesbury.

Paris, May 4, 1803.

I have this moment learnt that the First Consul sent off a messenger at ten o'clock last night to Madrid to declare that the negotiation was entirely broken off and hostilities inevitable. From all I learn since my conversation with M. de Talleyrand, it should seem that had I persisted in my refusal to take charge of this proposal my passports were to have been immediately given me, and I should have been suffered to depart. On returning to the charge (as I have no doubt it will be necessary to do) we shall at least have given such incontestable proofs of our moderation as will deprive the First Consul of many of those who are disposed to approve his measures. It might be essential, also, to stipulate with this Government, previous to any overture whatever to Russia, that the First Consul shall begin by agreeing to our possession for the term of ten years, in the event of the Emperor of Russia refusing to take charge of Malta; and that we can consent to its being offered to none other. Should it be determined to set this proposal entirely aside, and to instruct me to leave Paris immediately on our ultimatum being refused, orders may at the same time be given to prepare for the commencement of hostilities, so that as little time as possible may be lost.

M. Huber to Lord Whitworth.

Paris, May 3, 1803.

If it was possible that anything could add to my ardent wish of serving England, it would be the confidence you honour me with, and the flattering approbation you have been pleased to give to the efforts I have made for seconding your Lordship's views at Paris. Your departure, my Lord, must and will be lamented, not only by the friends of England, but by the real friends of France also. The want of your presence and support would greatly diminish my courage; but I am so sincerely devoted to the cause of peace, that as long as my services may be thought of the least use, and through your Lordship be made acceptable to the British Cabinet, they are at your disposal. My opinion is, however, that I can be of use only by remaining on the Continent during the war, and that my abode should be in Switzerland; from whence I could with facility, and better than from any other country, correspond, without danger or inconvenience, both with England and with France. As in this renewed contest (forced on England by the wretched temper and ambition of the Consul) peace must be the constant object in view, it is to be hoped that every incident of some importance will furnish the ground of fresh negotiation. On every such occasion the few men who have in vain laboured to prevent a renewal of war now will vigorously and constantly exert themselves to determine and operate an accommodation. Your Lordship knows that, combining together character, situation, and abilities, they form a very strong phalanx and a very desirable association. Joseph Bonaparte (the best of his family) has, on account of his morality and good conduct, a constant, and *at times* successful, influence on his brother. Regnault de St. Jean d'Angely, his intimate friend and confidant, and a Councillor of State, is a man of excellent, unsullied character and eminent abilities, and under the several points of view a man of real importance, as well as a very rising man, being high in the favour of the First Consul. M. Malouet, a man whose moral character and talents are well known in England, and are here in high and general estimation—he is an essential member of this little phalanx. Fouché, Senator, a very different man from those just named in point of morality, stands notoriously high in point of abilities, energy, and independence of mind; he has on this occasion been a bold and loud advocate for peace, and alone has dared repeatedly to combat the Consul's mistaken pride and ambition. Some of his expressions to him deserve to be kept in memory, and may be relied on: 'Vous recommencez un procès qui étoit jugé. Vous êtes vous-même, ainsi que nous, un résultat de la révolution, et la guerre remet tout en problême. On vous flatte en vous faisant compter sur les principes révolutionnaires des autres nations; le résultat de notre révolution les a anéantis partout. L'esprit public en France est tout contre la guerre; elle ne sera point nationale. On vous craint et on ne vous aime pas.' Notwithstanding (and perhaps because of) such proof of his independent mind, such is the confidence of the Consul in his tried energy and abilities as Minister of the Police formerly, that he has offered him that place again in case of actual war; and nobody doubts his being named to it, in spite of all the generals, who dread in him so avowed and so intrepid an advocate of peace, and in spite also of the present Ministers, who dread his known influence on Bonaparte. As to Talleyrand, you know, my Lord, that his interest as Minister and his interest as an individual are so decidedly connected with peace, that his vote and support may be relied on whenever incidents give him that influence which his want of energy refuses him. These different men (each of whom I have thought it right for your Lordship's recollection hereafter to place in his true light), knowing my political creed and relying on me in every respect, seem earnestly desirous that I should continue to be a medium between England and them. In the course of my co-operation with them I have found such unanimity in principles, opinion, and action (I mean essentially Joseph Bonaparte, Regnault, and Malouet) as to be seriously encouraged and justified in my confidence in their public views; and looking upon them collectively (as long as the Bonaparte family retains the power) as the decided and sure channel to peace whenever the moment arrives, I am very ready to remain in any auxiliary situation, provided I am placed in a convenient and safe post. As long as the ground is tenable here for the English, I mean to stay and observe, and I shall go on to Switzerland whenever Fouché advises it, which may probably be soon. From thence I shall have the honour of writing to your Lordship; there would be too much danger in doing it from this place, unless perhaps through the Portuguese Minister, if he had any despatches to send to England by a safe conveyance.

Permit me now, my Lord, in concluding this letter, to repeat the expression of my regret at seeing unrewarded by success the very able means for conciliation which your Lordship has displayed in this most difficult country, and to which the First Consul himself (in his lucid moments) has repeatedly and publicly done justice.

Lord Whitworth to Lord Hawkesbury.

Paris, May 4, 1803.

The following is the substance of the First Consul's plan of operations in case of a rupture, as communicated by him in conversation yesterday evening to General Masséna:—

To assemble the army of Holland at Nimeguen. On the declaration of war, to march to the attack of Hanover; a division of this army to take possession of Hamburg; to treat that city in the same manner as Leghorn was treated, by confiscating all British property, the whole to be given to Prussia.

Under the pretence of placing Corsica in a state of defence a body of troops is to be sent to that island, part of which shall take possession of Sardinia. Thirty thousand men are to enter the kingdom of Naples, and the King to be prohibited from admitting British ships into his ports; on his refusing to comply that kingdom is to become a republic. Similar demands are to be made to the Court of Lisbon, and in case of non-compliance an army is to take possession of the country to enforce these measures. Portugal is afterwards to be annexed to Spain. Row-boats are to be built without delay in all the ports. Bonaparte concluded by declaring that he would acknowledge no neutral Powers, that all must be either friends or foes. General Masséna's observation to the person to whom he repeated this conversation was *que l'homme a perdu la tête.*

Paris, May 4, 1803.
Wednesday morning.

Your Lordship will be surprised, after the little hope I was enabled to give in my last despatch of a favourable issue to the negotiation, to find that I am still here. It is necessary for my justification to state to your Lordship what has occasioned this delay. Soon after I had despatched the messenger the night before last with my despatches of the 3rd I received a communication from M. de Talleyrand, of which I enclose a copy, the purport of which was so completely wide of everything which could be satisfactory, or which even afforded the least ground on which to build any hope whatever, that I did not think myself authorised to enter into any discussion on the points stated; and as early as I could on the following morning, I returned, by a note also, the answer, of which the enclosed is a copy. I hope your Lordship will feel, as I do, that this was a sufficient reply to M. de Talleyrand's communication. It might, it is true, had it been worth commenting upon, have been completely refuted, and the total want of veracity, excepting in what regards the main object of our demand, would have exposed it to the ridicule it deserves. I contented myself, therefore, with briefly stating what were his Majesty's motives in accelerating the progress of the negotiation, and that my instructions left me no power to hear of anything which might tend to defeat his Majesty's purpose. I could not, however, avoid taking notice of one error relative to the difficulty I had made of giving written notes, by stating that I had no positive instructions on the subject, and consequently did not feel myself authorised to do so. After this I concluded, of course, that there was an end to the negotiation; and, indeed, all those whom I saw in the course of the day, amongst whom were all the Foreign Ministers and many others, gave me every reason to imagine that there was no hope whatever of the First Consul's conceding. I had for some days past been preparing for my departure, and on this every measure was taken for setting out at four o'clock this morning. All my domestic concerns were arranged, all our friends had been to take leave of us, and we were expecting only the passports which I had demanded for the purpose of ordering the post-horses. The day and the evening passed without any passports making their appearance; and whilst we were debating the motive of such a delay, about twelve o'clock a servant came into the room to say that a person wished to speak to Mr. Huber, who was still with us. He immediately went down to the foot of the stairs, and there he found Monsieur Malouet, who told him Regnault St. Jean d'Angely was at the door in his carriage, and wished to speak to him on very urgent business. He came, he said, from Joseph Bonaparte to make through him, Mr. Huber, a proposal to me, which, if I agreed to, might bring the business to a conclusion in the course of a few hours; and this was, that we should consent to put Malta into the hands of the Emperor of Russia. Mr. Huber came upstairs to communicate to me this proposal, and I can take no great merit to myself for having immediately and without the smallest hesitation declined it. I desired him to say simply that it was for ourselves and for our own security that we required the temporary possession of Malta, and not for any other Power, however friendly that Power might be; and that any proposal of such a nature could never be considered by me as a justification for the smallest breach of his Majesty's commands. This answer was delivered, and the two gentlemen returned to Joseph Bonaparte, who lives only at the distance of two doors from me; but he was already gone to bed. This step, although not official, convinced me that it was not meant to give me my passports without another attempt; and I was therefore not surprised when, about one o'clock, I received the enclosed note from M. de Talleyrand. It is probable that the business of great importance to which he alludes is the very proposal that has been suggested to me, and I am consequently prepared to receive it in the same manner. It appeared rather remarkable that M. de Marcoff, who came to take leave of me between nine and ten, remained till near twelve and evidently in expectation of something which would retard my departure. When he took leave of me, however, he did so as if we were not to meet again, and the whole tenor of my conversation went to impress him with the conviction that we should not do so, unless his Majesty's proposal was acceded to by this Government. It is very probable that this plan may have been arranged, partly for the purpose of protraction, and partly as an expedient more palatable than that of giving Malta to us, between the First Consul and M. de Marcoff in the conversation which I mentioned in my last report to your Lordship. And M. de Marcoff, without any specific instructions to that effect, is extremely likely to have taken the responsibility upon himself, as a thing which would be flattering to the Emperor and not disagreeable to the First Consul. From this remark your Lordship will see that I am not perfectly satisfied with M. de Marcoff's conduct in the course of this transaction. I should, however, be more dissatisfied with myself were I to be so far the dupe of his schemes as to swerve in the smallest degree from my instructions, which, thanks to your Lordship, are sufficiently positive to carry me through every difficulty. In this situation I am waiting the hour of rendezvous with M. de Talleyrand. I cannot, however conclude without observing to your Lordship that, in consequence of my not having left it, Paris is totally changed in its appearance. Yesterday it was all gloom and dejection, and to-day, as I am told, all hope and gladness. Surely after raising so much expectation this Government will not feel itself justified in disappointing it. I enclose to your Lordship a French newspaper containing a paragraph by which it appears that Sebastiani's mission is attempted to be called in question. This would certainly be an evident symptom of weakness, from which no good can possibly come.

M. DE TALLEYRAND TO LORD WHITWORTH.

Note.

Le soussigné a rendu compte au Premier Consul de la conversation qu'il a eue avec Son Excellence Lord Whitworth le 6 de ce mois et dans laquelle S. E. a fait connaître que Sa Majesté Britannique lui avoit donné l'ordre de faire, en son nom, verbalement les demandes suivantes.

1. Que Sa Majesté Britannique puisse conserver les troupes à Malte pendant dix ans.

2. Que l'île de Lampedusa lui soit cédée en toute propriété.

3. Que les troupes françoises évacuent la Hollande. Et que si dans sept jours il n'avoit pas été signé une convention sur ces bases, S. E. Lord Whitworth avoit ordre de cesser sa mission et de retourner à Londres. Sur la demande qu'a faite le soussigné, voulant bien, suivant l'usage de tous les temps et de tous les pays, donner par écrit ce que lui-même a appellé *l'ultimatum* de son Gouvernement, Son Excellence a déclaré que ses instructions lui défendoient expressément de passer sur cet objet aucune note écrite. Les intentions du Premier Consul étant toutes pacifiques, le soussigné se dispense de faire aucune observation sur une manière aussi nouvelle et aussi étrange de traiter des affaires de cette importance.

Et pour donner encore un nouveau témoignage du prix qu'il attache à la continuation de la paix, le Premier Consul a chargé le soussigné de faire, dans le stile et les formes ordinaires, la notification suivante. L'île de Lampedusa n'étant point à la France, il n'appartient au Premier Consul ni d'accéder ni de se refuser au désir que témoigne Sa Majesté Britannique d'avoir cette île en sa possession. Quant à l'île de Malte, comme la demande que fait à cet égard Sa Majesté Britannique changeroit une disposition formelle du traité d'Amiens, le Premier Consul ne peut d'abord que la communiquer à Sa Majesté le roi d'Espagne et à la république batave, parties contractantes au dit traité, pour connoître leur opinion ; et de plus comme les stipulations relatives à Malte ont été garanties par Leurs Majestés l'empereur d'Allemagne, l'empereur de Russie et le roi de Prusse, les puissances contractantes au traité d'Amiens, avant d'arrêter aucun changement dans l'article de Malte, sont tenues de se concerter avec les puissances garantes. Le Premier Consul ne se refusera point à ce concert, mais ce n'est point à lui à le provoquer, puisque ce n'est pas lui qui provoque aucun changement dans les stipulations garanties. Quant à l'évacuation de la Hollande par les troupes françaises, le Premier Consul n'a point de difficulté à faire répéter par le soussigné que les troupes françaises évacueront la Hollande dès l'instant où les stipulations du traité d'Amiens pour chacune des parties du monde seront exécutées. Le soussigné saisit cette occasion de renouveler à Son Excellence Monsieur l'ambassadeur d'Angleterre l'assurance de sa haute considération.

CH. MAU. TALLEYRAND.

Paris, ce 12 Floréal, an XI,
May 2, 1803.

LORD WHITWORTH TO M. DE TALLEYRAND.

Note.

Le soussigné, en réponse à la note que M. de Talleyrand a bien voulu lui transmettre hier au soir, a l'honneur de lui observer qu'en cherchant à accélérer la marche de la négociation, le roi n'a eu d'autre motif que de tirer le plutôt possible les deux pays les plus intéressés, et l'Europe en général, de l'état de suspense dans lequel ils se trouvent. Il n'y voit, à son grand regret, rien qui puisse répondre à cette intention, et par conséquent rien qui puisse le justifier en tardant à obéir aux ordres de sa cour. Il ne lui reste donc qu'à prier M. le ministre des Relations Extérieures de vouloir bien lui en donner les moyens en lui fournissant les passeports nécessaires pour son retour. Il est nécessaire pourtant qu'il rectifie un mésentendu qui s'est glissé dans la note de M. de Talleyrand. Le soussigné n'a pas dit qu'il lui étoit expressément défendu de passer aucune note écrite sur l'objet de la discussion, mais qu'il n'étoit pas autorisé de le faire et qu'il ne vouloit pas prendre cette responsabilité sur lui.

Il saisit cette occasion pour renouveler à Son Excellence Monsieur de Talleyrand les assurances de sa très-haute considération.

WHITWORTH.

Paris, ce 3 Mai 1803.

M. DE TALLEYRAND TO LORD WHITWORTH.

Paris, ce 2 Mai 1803.

Ayant demain matin une communication de la plus grande importance de vous faire, j'ai l'honneur de vous en prévenir sur le champ, afin que vous n'attendiez pas ce soir les passeports que vous avez demandés. Je vous propose de vouloir bien vous rendre demain, à quatre heures et demie, à l'hôtel des Affaires Etrangères.—Recevez, milord, l'assurance de ma haute considération.

CH. MAU. TALLEYRAND.

LORD WHITWORTH TO LORD HAWKESBURY.

Paris, May 4, 1803.
Wednesday evening.

I am this moment come from M. de Talleyrand, and I have to reproach myself with having consented to send a messenger to your Lordship contrary to my own conscience, although it was pressed upon me in such a manner as to leave me scarcely a possibility of a refusal. The enclosed note will show your Lordship that the idea proposed is to give Malta to Russia after the expiration of the term of years for which we are to hold it. I pressed for something positive on the subject of the number of years, which I repeatedly declared could not be less than ten; but this, it was said, might perhaps be the subject of the instructions with which your Lordship would furnish me. It was maintained that a less number of years would content us, when the island was to be given up to such a Power as Russia, than to the Order or to the inhabitants. My only inducement for having undertaken to refer again to your Lordship is to avoid every reproach of precipitation. The difference will be but five days, and I have declared that I see so many objections to the plan, that although I could not refuse their solicitation to send it I could give no hope whatever of its being accepted as a ground of negotiation. I feel all the inconvenience of this delay, short as it is; but I could not, I think, have acted otherwise, at the risk of involving everything. The arguments of M. de Talleyrand went to prove that by giving up Malta to Russia we did not give up our claim to a temporary possession; and that the First Consul, as a principal in the Treaty of Amiens, would never consent to set his name to an act of cession of Malta, unless some other Power, like Russia, would do the same. In order to reconcile this step to myself, I argue that the delay, although it may be inconvenient, is not irremediable, and that we may take up the negotiation on the same ground without having lost any of our advantages. A delay of a few days cannot better the state of the First Consul or make him better prepared for war; it must be one of many, many months that can have any effect. In this respect, therefore, I think we cannot be losers, and we shall have convinced them that we do not act with precipitation. The object gained by this proposal would be that Malta, instead of being in the hands of the Neapolitans, would be placed in those of the most independent Power in Europe after Great Britain, and that England would reserve to herself such a temporary possession as may be agreed upon—and I think that Russia would not make much difficulty on that score. The inconvenience of this proposal arises from the loss of time and the distance to which the negotiation is transferred. Should, however, the proposition on this ground be found inadmissible, the delay will be but five or six days, and we resume the negotiation on the terms we now are, without being exposed to the least reproach of driving it on with intemperance. An ultimatum after this act of complaisance will come with a better effect than it would have had without it. I must, however, say to your Lordship that although I am not perfectly satisfied with myself for having undertaken to connive at this delay, yet I do not see whether I could have answered it to myself to withhold from his Majesty Ministers a proposal of a nature to admit of an honourable and an advantageous adjustment of the present differences. It must at the same time be admitted that upon this ground we should find our situation considerably bettered, inasmuch as Russia is stronger than Naples, and our claim to a temporary possession will not be disputed. The only discussion will be on the term for which we are to hold it. In the instructions with which your Lordship may think perhaps proper to furnish me on this subject, it would be well to bind this Government to accede to whatever terms may be agreed on between Great Britain and Russia not under ten years, and to signify to them that no negotiation would be entered upon with Russia until the First Consul should have entered into a positive agreement that he will be satisfied with whatever arrangement may be made between England and Russia, and will engage to ratify the same. And this to be a previous *sine quâ non* (and if in the form of an ultimatum the better) with France, without which no proposal whatever is to be made to Russia. Whatever your Lordship may think proper to do, I cannot but think myself justified in submitting the proposal. Had I persisted in my refusal to do so, I should have taken upon myself a much greater responsibility, and one pregnant with much more danger. This consideration will, I hope, be admitted as an excuse, if I have occasion for any. Any delay whatever, it is true, may be productive of expense, but it cannot be put in any competition with that of one month of hostility. To all that I have said I have only to add that it is necessary to take the violence of this man's character into the calculation. He certainly does require every degree of management in dealing with him. Were he to be driven to desperation, he might, it is true, do perhaps great mischief to this country and to himself; but it would probably not be without entailing upon us a considerable share also. My position is a very difficult and a very delicate one.

M. DE TALLEYRAND TO LORD WHITWORTH.

Note.

Le soussigné a mis sous les yeux du Premier Consul la note de Son Excellence Monsieur l'ambassadeur d'Angleterre en date du 3 de ce mois.

Après la dernière communication qui a été adressée à Son Excellence, on conçoit moins que jamais comment une nation grande, puissante et sensée pourroit vouloir entreprendre de déclarer une guerre dont les résultats entraîneroient des malheurs si grands et dont la cause seroit si petite, puisqu'il s'agit d'un misérable rocher! Son Excellence a dû comprendre que la double nécessité de s'entendre avec les puissances garantes du traité d'Amiens et de ne pas violer un pacte, dont l'exécution intéresse aussi essentiellement l'honneur de la France, la sûreté de l'avenir et la loyauté des relations diplomatiques entre les nations européennes, avoit fait une loi au Gouvernement françois d'éloigner toute proposition diamétralement contraire au traité d'Amiens. Cependant le Premier Consul, accoutumé depuis deux mois à faire des sacrifices de toute espèce pour le maintien de la pacification, ne repousseroit pas un terme moyen qui seroit de nature à concilier les intérêts et la dignité des deux pays. Sa Majesté Britannique a paru croire que la garnison napolitaine, qui devait être établie à Malte, ne présenteroit pas une force suffisante pour assurer véritablement l'indépendance de cette île. Ce motif étant le seul qui puisse au moins expliquer le refus qu'elle fait d'évacuer l'île, le Premier Consul est prêt à consentir que l'île de Malte soit remise aux mains d'une des trois principales Puissances qui ont garanti son indépendance, soit l'Autriche, la Russie ou la Prusse, bien entendu qu'aussitôt que la France et l'Angleterre seront d'accord sur cet article, elles réuniront leurs demandes pour y porter pareillement les différentes Puissances, soit contractantes, soit adhérentes au traité d'Amiens. S'il étoit possible que cette proposition ne fût pas adoptée, il seroit manifeste que non-seulement l'Angleterre n'a jamais voulu exécuter le traité d'Amiens, mais qu'elle n'a même été de bonne foi dans aucune des demandes qu'elle a faites, et qu'à mesure que la France eût cédé sur un point, les prétentions du Gouvernement britannique se fussent portées sur un autre. Et si une pareille démonstration devoit être requise, le Premier Consul aura du moins donné encore un gage de sa sincérité, de son application à méditer sur les moyens d'éviter la guerre, de son empressement à les saisir et du prix qu'il mettroit à les faire prévaloir.

Le soussigné saisit cette occasion de renouveler à Son Excellence Lord Whitworth l'assurance de sa haute considération.

CH. MAU. TALLEYRAND.

Paris, le 14 Floréal, an XI.

LORD WHITWORTH TO LORD HAWKESBURY.

Paris, May 4, 1803.

I add two lines to my despatches of this date to beg your Lordship to be assured that I would have avoided taking any kind of notice of the proposal made to me this evening could I possibly have done so with any kind of decency. It would in all probability have been considered as such a determination to shut the door to all accommodation as might have driven the First Consul to a state of desperation. I stated, however, plainly, that although I undertook to delay my departure until an answer was received, yet I could not give the smallest hope of the proposals being adopted; and indeed I am very much inclined to believe that it is not expected to have any effect, even by those who make it. I rather consider it a pretext for protraction, in the hope that his Majesty's Ministers may be induced to open a negotiation with Russia; and if they could have found out a Power more remote than Russia they would have given it the preference. Although I am persuaded of this, yet I could not refuse, so urgent were the solicitations of M. de Talleyrand. I comfort myself, however, with the idea that we shall not stand on worse ground a few days hence, and the First Consul on better; and we shall have proved to everyone's conviction that we desire to conciliate, provided it can be done without losing sight of our object. I entreat your Lordship to send back Sylvester with as little delay as possible. I am persuaded that the First Consul is determined to avoid a rupture if possible; but he is so completely governed by his temper that there is no possibility of answering for him. I hope I shall stand excused for what I have done. I have had occasion this evening to converse with M. de Marcoff on the subject of this proposal. He has very candidly told me that he did not believe the Emperor would give in to it, as he had always expressed a decided aversion to taking any forward part in the business. It becomes, therefore, of the utmost importance to secure the acquiescence of the First Consul, let the determination of Russia be what it will. The Duke of Bedford is still here, and conducts himself very properly; I wish I could say as much of many of my countrymen and countrywomen. He seems perfectly aware of the character and projects of the First Consul, and of the necessity (although he exaggerates the danger to ourselves) of imposing some restraint upon him if possible. He appears to me to be one of the most moderate party men I can meet with.

P.S.—It shall be my business in the interval between the departure of this messenger and his return to prepare if possible the First Consul's mind to consider the terms, from which I have not in the smallest degree receded by this step. And this time may therefore be very profitably employed.

Lord Hawkesbury to Lord Whitworth.

Downing Street, May 7, 1803.

Your Excellency's despatches Nos. 45 and 46 have been received and laid before the King. The propositions which have been made to you on the part of the French Government, and which have induced your Excellency to delay your departure until the return of the messenger Sylvester, are in every respect so loose, indefinite, and unsatisfactory as to fall so far short of the just pretensions of his Majesty that it is impossible that the French Government could have expected them to have been accepted. During the whole of the discussions which have lately occurred, his Majesty has had a right to consider himself in the character of the complaining party. No means have been omitted on his part to induce the French Government to make a full and early explanation of their views, and to afford to his Majesty that satisfaction and security to which he considered himself to be entitled. It was in consequence of the apparent determination of the French Government to evade all discussion on points of difference between the two countries, that his Majesty was induced to state the grounds on which, according to his views, an arrangement might be concluded satisfactory to both Governments; and he accordingly authorised your Excellency to communicate the three projects which at different times I had forwarded to you. Until the very moment when your Excellency was about to leave Paris the French Government have avoided making any distinct proposition for the settlement of the differences between the two countries; and when at the very moment of your departure the French Government felt themselves compelled to bring forward some proposition, they confined that proposition to a part only of the subject in discussion, and on that part of it it is wholly inadmissible. The French Government propose that his Majesty should give up the island of Malta to a Russian, Austrian, or Prussian garrison. If his Majesty could be disposed (which, under the present circumstances, he deems impossible) to waive his demand for a temporary occupation of the island of Malta, the Emperor of Russia would be the only sovereign to whom, in the present state of Europe, he could consent that the island should be assigned; and his Majesty has certain and authentic information that the Emperor of Russia would on no account consent to garrison Malta. Under these circumstances his Majesty perseveres in his determination to adhere to the substance of his third *projet* as his ultimatum. As, however, the principal objection stated by the French Government to his Majesty's proposition appears to be confined to the insertion of an article in a public treaty by which his Majesty shall have a right to remain in the possession of the island of Malta for a definite number of years, his Majesty will consent that the number of years (*being in no case less than ten*) may be stated in a secret article; and the public articles may be agreed to conformably to the enclosed *projet*. By this expedient the supposed point of honour of the French Government might be saved; the independence of the island of Malta would in principle be acknowledged, and the temporary occupation of his Majesty would be made to depend *alone on the present state of the island of Lampedusa*. You may propose this idea to M. Talleyrand, at the same time assuring him that his Majesty is determined to adhere to the substance of his ultimatum; and if you shall not be able to conclude the minute of an arrangement on this principle, you will on no account remain in Paris more than thirty-six hours after the receipt of this despatch. I observe by your despatch No. 11 that you did not consider yourself authorised to deliver to the French Government any note or *projet* in writing. The words of my despatch were, that you were to communicate the terms *officially*, which left it at your own discretion to communicate them verbally or in writing as you might judge most expedient. You were certainly right in communicating them in the first instance verbally; but as so much stress has been laid by M. de Talleyrand on this distinction, it is important that I should inform you that his Majesty neither had nor has any objection to your delivering the enclosed

Q

projet as an ultimatum, accompanied by a short note in writing. I cannot conclude this despatch without recalling again your attention to the conduct of the French Minister at Hamburg, and referring you to my instructions, by which you should abstain from concluding the arrangement until you have received from M. Talleyrand an assurance that his conduct would, in some manner or other, be publicly disavowed.

Projet.

1. The French Government shall engage to make no opposition to the cession of the island of Lampedusa to his Majesty by the King of the Two Sicilies.

2. In consequence of the present state of the island of Lampedusa, his Majesty shall remain in possession of the island of Malta until such arrangements shall be made by him as may enable his Majesty to occupy Lampedusa as a naval station; after which period the island of Malta shall be given up to the inhabitants and acknowledged as an independent state.

3. The territories of the Batavian Republic shall be evacuated by the French forces within one month after the conclusion of a convention founded on the principles of this *projet*.

4. The King of Etruria and the Italian and Ligurian Republics shall be acknowledged by his Majesty.

5. Switzerland shall be evacuated by the French forces.

6. A suitable territorial provision shall be assigned to the King of Sardinia in Italy.

Articles 4, 5, and 6 may be entirely omitted or must all be inserted.

(*Secret article.*) His Majesty shall not be required by the French Government to evacuate the island of Malta until after the expiration of ten years.

If the French Government will not consent that the occupation of Malta by his Majesty's forces for ten years should be inserted in the body of the treaty, the secret article must be considered as an indispensable part of the arrangement.

Lord Whitworth to Lord Hawkesbury.

Paris, May 9, 1803.

I need not, I am sure, say how extremely anxious I am for the return of the messenger by whom I accused myself of having acted in opposition to your Lordship's instructions by consenting, instead of leaving Paris on Wednesday last, as I should inevitably have been suffered to do, to receive and submit to your Lordship a proposal, the evident tendency of which was in direct contradiction to the policy which it is our interest to pursue in this negotiation. I will, however, confess that every day convinces me that had I acted otherwise I should have been unworthy of your Lordship's confidence, and that we should at this moment have found ourselves, from the violence and passion of the First Consul, involved in hostilities, when they might, as I trust they will be, by management and temper have been avoided. I do, therefore, consider the resolution I took not to push the matter to extremities in the first instance, however much I may have been inclined to reproach myself for having taken upon myself so much responsibility, as a most fortunate inspiration; and I flatter myself we shall not be many days without reaping the benefit of it. In this little interval nothing has been left unattempted which can work on the mind and influence of the First Consul. His brothers have been indefatigable. It was they who, almost by violence, wrung from him this first concession, and they certainly will not give up the point until they reduce him still further. When the character of the First Consul is taken into consideration, and the shame and vexation he must feel at eating his own words in the face of all Europe, no one, I trust, will deny that the task has been arduous. By the means of the brothers, such other assistance has been gained as must inevitably weaken, if not totally preclude, his further resistance. The daily reports which he receives from the police of the state of Paris are such as to convince him that his popularity depends on peace; and by contrasting, as we have done, our moderation and temperance to his obstinacy and violence, we deprive him of the argument on which he chiefly rests—that Great Britain is determined on war at all events, and shuts the door to every proposal tending to conciliation. I should consider it as a most unfavourable circumstance were he able to impress such an opinion on the public mind. The moderation with which the discussion has been carried on on our part has defeated this policy; and the public begins to feel that if it leads to hostilities, it is to the First Consul, and not to Great Britain, that the calamity is to be attributed. Your Lordship will not fail to appreciate the importance of such an opinion, whatever may be the event. It is, I trust, firmly established, and we may now proceed without the risk of destroying it. In my conversations with Joseph Bonaparte since the departure of the messenger I have fully impressed him with the conviction that, having once taken upon myself to act in contradiction to his Majesty's commands, no second act of complaisance of such a nature can possibly be required of me; and, therefore, that the negotiation must inevitably be concluded forthwith on the tenor of the instructions which I shall receive, or be broken off. I have prepared him for such an ultimatum as will leave us little time for discussion, and made him sensible of the impossibility of our consenting, in the situation in which we are, to transfer to Russia what must be settled between Great Britain and France. In a conversation which I had with him yesterday, before he went to pass the day with the First Consul, I repeated all these arguments, and I make no doubt he will have enforced them. I think, therefore, I may be justified in holding out an expectation of yet bringing the negotiation to a favourable issue. I should, at all events, have no further occasion to refer to your Lordship, and my next letter will be to announce our success or my departure. The Emperor's ratification of the conclusion of the general Diet of the empire was received here on Thursday last. There are still some trifling reserves, which will, however, be acceded to by the First Consul. A reinforcement of about twelve hundred men has been sent to St. Domingo from the port of Havre de Grâce.

Paris, May 9, 1803.

Since writing the above the messenger is arrived with your Lordship's despatch No. 15, of the 7th of May. I am not at all surprised at the judgment your Lordship passes on the proposition which I undertook to transmit to your Lordship. It is perfectly conformable to the opinion I entertained of it myself. But still I cannot repent having acted as I did; and if by so doing I shall have contributed to the restoration of public tranquillity on conditions both safe and honourable to his Majesty I shall have neither his Majesty's displeasure nor the reproaches of my own conscience to apprehend. As soon as I received your Lordship's instructions I prepared a translated copy of the project furnished me by your Lordship, and a short note, with which it is my intention to accompany the communication. I sent immediately to Joseph Bonaparte in order to communicate it to him, before I carried it officially into execution. I received for answer that he was at St. Cloud with the First Consul. I then sent a person to M. de Talleyrand to know when I could see him (although I did not mean to begin by communicating anything to him officially), and I was informed that he also was at St. Cloud. I soon after learnt that both the persons were gone there in consequence of an accident which had happened yesterday to the First Consul, who, probably for the first time in his life, had attempted to drive himself four horses without a postillion. The horses, not being thoroughly broke, or perceiving, perhaps, the want of skill in their conductor, soon ran away, and in turning into the gateway of the palace the carriage struck against it with such violence as to throw the First Consul from the box to the distance of several yards. He was thrown on a part where there was no pavement. He bruised himself a good deal, and spit a considerable quantity of blood. I understand that no bad consequences are likely to ensue, and that he is able to transact business. This, however, I have heard from a person interested in giving a favourable report. In the meantime those with whom I am to communicate are with him, and I cannot expect to see them before to-morrow morning. Although this circumstance may cause a delay of a few hours, your Lordship may be assured that the prosecution of those instructions with which you have furnished me shall not be protracted. I shall leave Paris most assuredly, or have concluded a satisfactory arrangement, within the time specified by your Lordship, reckoning from the moment of my being able to make an official communication rather than from that of the receipt of your Lordship's letter. From what I stated in my preceding despatch, and from what I have since learnt, I do not despair of success, although I do not feel authorised to raise any very sanguine hope. In the meantime I perfectly agree with your Lordship that anything is preferable to this state of uncertainty. I beg leave to mention that Sylvester performed the journey from London to Paris in thirty-five hours. But, notwithstanding this very uncommon expedition, M. de Talleyrand had received from General Andréossy the purport of the project transmitted to me by your Lordship four hours and a half before Sylvester arrived.

Nine o'clock in the evening.

Joseph Bonaparte has been with me, and I have communicated to him the nature of the project I have to propose. Were I to judge from his language, I should consider the business as desperate. He repeatedly assured me that the First Consul would never consent to our possession of Malta unless it were on the ground stated in that part of the project which is meant to be public, and by which such a possession is to be considered as dependent on the works to be carried on at Lampedusa, and not to exceed a year or two. I told him that such a tenure would, if we were not sincere, answer our purpose better than what we had proposed, as an indefinite term might be prolonged until it became a possession in perpetuity; but that we wished for peace, and felt that it could not be enjoyed with such an indefinite tenure, subject always to jealousy and irritation; whilst a definite one, acceded to by the First Consul, would be really productive of peace, with all its attendants of good understanding and harmony. He could not help agreeing with me, but appeared always to doubt the assent of his brother. In the course of the conversation he regretted that we persisted always in demanding so long a term, and said that if it had been for three or four years the First Consul might perhaps have been persuaded to give way. I told him my instructions were positive on this head, and that it did not depend upon me a second time to take any kind of responsibility upon myself. So the business rests. I am to see M. de Talleyrand to-morrow. In the meantime I cannot help entertaining a hope that if they have made up their minds to concede a part they will not contend for the remainder. At all events, I shall conclude or set out on Thursday morning.

P.S.—I have since learnt that the First Consul is entirely recovered from his late accident.

Lord Whitworth to M. de Talleyrand.

Note.

Le soussigné, ambassadeur extraordinaire et plénipotentiaire de Sa Majesté Britannique près la République française, ayant transmis à sa cour la proposition qui lui a été faite par le ministre des Relations Extérieures le 4 du courant, vient de recevoir l'ordre de remettre à Son Excellence le projet de convention ci-joint, fondé sur la seule base que Sa Majesté croit, dans les circonstances actuelles, susceptible d'un arrangement définitif et amical. Le ministre des Relations Extérieures ne manquera pas d'observer jusqu'à quel point Sa Majesté a cherché de concilier la sécurité de ses intérêts avec la dignité du Premier Consul. Le soussigné se flatte que le Premier Consul, rendant justice à ces sentimens, adoptera, d'accord avec Sa Majesté, un moyen aussi propre à rendre une tranquillité permanente aux deux nations et à l'Europe. Le soussigné saisit cette occasion de renouveler à Son Excellence l'assurance de sa très-haute considération. WHITWORTH.

Projet.

1. Le Gouvernement françois s'engagera à ne faire aucune opposition à la cession de l'île de Lampedusa à Sa Majesté par le roi des Deux-Siciles.

2. Vu l'état actuel de l'île de Lampedusa, Sa Majesté restera en possession de l'île de Malte jusqu'à ce qu'il ait été pris des arrangemens pour mettre Sa Majesté à même d'occuper Lampedusa comme poste militaire; après quoi l'île de Malte sera remise aux habitans et reconnue état indépendant.

3. Le territoire de la république batave sera évacué par les troupes françaises dans l'espace d'un mois après la conclusion d'une convention fondée sur les principes de ce projet.

4. Le roi d'Etrurie et les républiques italienne et ligurienne seront reconnus par Sa Majesté.

5. La Suisse sera évacuée par les troupes françaises.

6. Une provision territoriale convenable sera assignée au roi de Sardaigne en Italie.

Article Secret.

Sa Majesté ne sera pas requise par le Gouvernement françois d'évacuer l'île de Malte qu'après l'expiration du terme de dix ans.

LORD WHITWORTH TO LORD HAWKESBURY.

Paris, May 10, 1803.

With regard to the numerous memorials and representations which I had to make to this Government in behalf of those of his Majesty's subjects who have suffered by the detention and confiscation of their vessels and property in the ports of France, I have only to observe that they have, with the exception of one or two instances, remained unanswered. I trust, therefore, no blame can attach to me if my endeavours to carry into effect your Lordship's instructions on this head have not been more effectual.

Paris, May 12, 1803.

The expected messenger with your Lordship's answer to the proposition which I had taken upon myself to transmit on the 4th returned on the 9th at twelve o'clock. I immediately, as I had promised to do, sent to acquaint Joseph Bonaparte of it. He came to me about six, being engaged with the First Consul. I explained to him the nature of the instructions which I had received, and the reasons why the propositions of the First Consul on the subject of Russia could not be admitted. I declared that I had nothing now to do but to take up the negotiation where it had been left off, and require possession of Malta for ten years, etc. etc. We conversed for some time upon the business, and he left me, giving me little hope of a favourable issue. I then wrote to M. de Talleyrand, informing him of the return of the messenger, and desiring him to name an hour when I might wait upon him in order to communicate to him the purport of my instructions. To this letter I received no answer that evening or the following morning. Anxious to execute my orders and to lose no time, I enclosed the project furnished me by your Lordship, accompanied by an official note and a private letter, to M. de Talleyrand, and sent it to the Bureau des Relations Extérieures by Mr. Mandeville, with directions to deliver it to M. de Talleyrand, or, in his absence, to the Chef du Bureau. He delivered it accordingly to M. Durand, who promised to give it to his chief as soon as he came in, which he expected, he said, shortly. At half-past four, having waited till that time in vain, I went myself to M. de Talleyrand. I was told that the family was in the country, and that they did not know when the Minister would be in town. Half an hour after I got home, the packet which Mr. Mandeville had given into the hands of M. Durand was brought to me—I believe by a servant—with a verbal message that as M. de Talleyrand was in the country it would be necessary that I should send it to him there. In order to defeat as much as depended upon me their intention of gaining time, although I am persuaded it was done for the purpose only of combating the perseverance of the First Consul, I wrote again to M. de Talleyrand, recapitulating the steps I had taken since the return of the messengers, and desired Mr. Talbot, the Secretary to the Embassy, to take it himself at nine o'clock at night, when I thought M. de Talleyrand would be at home, to his house at Meudon. He was, however, not at home. Mr. Talbot was told that he was at St. Cloud, where he had been all day, and that he would not be back until very late. He therefore left my private letter with his name, and returned with the packet. It was my intention to have sent it in the following morning to the Bureau, with orders that it should be left there. On its receipt, however, at one o'clock in the morning, I received a note from M. de Talleyrand, accounting for his not having been able to answer me sooner, and appointing me at twelve o'clock at the Bureau des Relations Extérieures. I went at the appointed time. He began by apologising for having so long postponed the interview; which he attributed to his having been the whole day with the First Consul. We then entered upon business. I told him that, limited as I was by your Lordship's instructions, he could not be surprised at my impatience to acquit myself of my duty. I explained to him the nature of your Lordship's observations on the proposal of the 4th, and that it was considered as on one hand impracticable from the refusal of the Emperor of Russia to take charge of Malta, and on the other as being wholly inadequate to his Majesty's just pretensions. I gave him the note in which this was expressed, and the project, on which alone a satisfactory arrangement could be framed. He read them with apparent attention and without any remarks; and after some time he asked me if I felt myself authorised by my instructions to conclude with him a convention, framed on the basis of my project, or, indeed, extending that basis, since the first article of it would be the perpetual possession of Malta to England in return for a consideration. I told him I most certainly was not authorised to enter into any engagement of such a nature, which would make the negotiation one of exchange instead of a demand of satisfaction and security. To this he replied that the satisfaction and security which we required was Malta, and that this we obtained; that the First Consul could not accede to what he considered, and what must be considered by the public and by Europe, as the effect of coercion; but if it were possible to make the draught palatable did I think myself justifiable in refusing to do so? I told him that, acting in strict compliance with my instructions, I could have no need of justification, and that I came to him with the determination of abiding strictly by them. He contended that by communicating a project I merely stated on what grounds we would be willing to conclude; and that a counter-project, founded on the basis of giving us what we required, could not be refused a fair discussion. To this I urged the resolution of his Majesty's Ministers to avoid everything which could protract the negotiation; that I saw no other means of acting up to those views than by taking my stand on the project at all events. I urged him repeatedly to explain himself more fully on the nature of the demand which he should make for Malta; but he could not or would not explain himself. After much contestation it was agreed that the proposal should be submitted to me in the course of a few hours, and that I should determine on the line of conduct I felt myself justified in pursuing—either to sign it, or send it home, or to leave Paris. It was in vain I racked my brain to guess what could be the nature of this new proposal. I felt that it must be advantageous indeed to induce me to suspend my departure; but still I felt that as the basis of it was to put us in possession of Malta I could not do less than see what they might demand, determined to resist every attempt the object of which might be, notwithstanding the specious pretences of M. de Talleyrand, merely to protract, at a moment when everything pointed out to us the advantage, and indeed the necessity, of accelerating, the progress of the negotiation. The remainder of this day passed without receiving any communication from M. de Talleyrand, and it was not until about eleven o'clock that I was informed by a friend of Joseph Bonaparte that I should receive nothing until the following morning, and that then a note would be communicated merely to assert that our information with respect to the disinclination of Russia to take charge of Malta was incorrect. Upon this I immediately determined to demand by an official note my passports. I was told that the day had been passed in much agitation at St. Cloud, and that a council had been held at five o'clock, composed of seven people, amongst whom Joseph Bonaparte and Talleyrand were the only two who voted for peace. The others were more subservient than Talleyrand to the will of the First Consul, and sought to make their court by thus conforming to his wishes. It seems that M. de Talleyrand, in his conference with me, had engaged for more than he was able to accomplish. He had hoped that, with the assistance of Joseph Bonaparte, he should have been able to arrange a proposition in such a manner as to render it acceptable to us and palatable to the First Consul. He was, however, disappointed, and the generals, assisted perhaps by the news which came in the evening from Russia, of the Emperor's having proposed his intervention, succeeded in persuading the First Consul not to accede to our demands and suffer me to depart. Just as I was going to bed I received a message from Joseph Bonaparte requesting that I would come to him. I did not, however, judge it expedient, in the present state of the business, to have the appearance of intrigue or anything which might be construed into so great a solicitude, and I let him know I would call upon him at ten o'clock in the morning. I this morning called upon Joseph Bonaparte at ten o'clock. He told me all that had passed yesterday at St. Cloud, and of the advantage which the war faction had gained. He represented the case as entirely desperate, unless it was presented to the First Consul in such a shape as to lose the appearance of coercion, against which he would recoil at the risk of everything. I repeated to him that I had no other proposal to make; neither could I by any means consent to quit the ground we stood on, which was such as to justify us in the eyes of all Europe. I do not trouble your Lordship with a detail of all the arguments which were urged, since they have been so repeatedly used. The conclusion was that he could not relinquish the hope of preserving peace as long as there was the smallest chance of bringing the First Consul to a fair proposal. He asked me what I would do were he to propose to leave us in possession of Malta on condition that we should not oppose any amicable negotiation the First Consul might open with the Court of Naples for the possession of Otranto, on the same ground as we required the acquiescence of the French Government in any arrangement we might have made with the same Court for the acquisition of Lampedusa. He wished me to understand this as an expedient to save a little the vanity of the First Consul, who might have to say that the acquisition of Malta by us had not been obtained by violence, but by an arrangement. I did not hesitate a moment in declaring to him that I saw no probability whatever of such a proposal being accepted in England, and that I certainly would not suspend my departure a moment in consequence of it. He asked me if I would mention it to your Lordship. I told him I certainly should mention it, or, more properly, be the bearer of it, since I should set out in the evening. He then told me that he knew my passports were ready, and that I should have them when I demanded them. I came home, and immediately sent Mr. Mandeville with an official note requiring my passports, in order that I might leave Paris in the evening. In half an hour Joseph sent to me again to ask me if I would send the proposition by the messenger who was to precede me, provided it came to me officially. He told me that he had no other orders from the First Consul, and that, indeed, he was very uncertain whether he would hear of it in the temper in which he was; but he would go to St. Cloud immediately and make a last effort. I repeated to him what I had said before—that nothing but an acceptation of my project could justify my stay at Paris, and as they had no intention of concluding on that ground I should set out in the evening as I had intended. I told him that it was my duty to report to your Lordship not only anything which came to me officially, but also from a quarter so respectable as his, and that I should do so on the subject of what he had mentioned to me. It is possible, therefore, I may receive such a proposal from M. de Talleyrand, and in that case I shall add it to this despatch, which goes by the messenger who will precede us. Should your Lordship have any orders to give me on the subject, they may, by sending the messenger back immediately, find me this side of Calais. I have not given the least encouragement to hope that any good could derive from it. But your Lordship will naturally weigh it with all the seriousness which must attach to anything which may contribute to the preservation of peace with honour and security. Shortly after I had left Joseph Bonaparte I saw M. de Marcoff by appointment. He had received a messenger from his Court last night, and communicated to me the contents of his despatches. They go to the proposal of an intervention, and express in strong terms the desire of the Emperor to conciliate the differences—in terms, I must confess, rather more favourable and friendly to this Government than I could have wished. M. de Marcoff made many proposals, and communicated to me many projects of this nature, and he hoped to induce me to suspend my departure. Of course I could listen to nothing of this nature. At two I renewed my demand for passports, and was told I should have them immediately. They arrived at five o'clock, and I propose setting out as soon as the carriages are ready. In this despatch I have endeavoured to keep your Lordship informed of the progress of the negotiation, if such it may be called, since Monday. I have only to regret that it has not led to a more favourable result.

Lord Whitworth to M. de Talleyrand.

Note.

Paris, ce 12 Mai 1803.

Ne pouvant plus remettre l'exécution des ordres de sa cour, le soussigné se voit obligé de prier le ministre des Relations Extérieures de vouloir bien lui faire expédier les passeports nécessaires pour son retour en Angleterre.

Il prie Son Excellence de vouloir bien agréer l'assurance de sa haute considération.

WHITWORTH.

Lord Whitworth to M. de Talleyrand.

Paris, ce 10 Mai 1803.

Monsieur,—Pour ne pas perdre un instant d'un tems si précieux, j'ai l'honneur de vous faire parvenir le projet que j'ai reçu de ma cour, avec la note qui l'accompagne. J'aurai celui de me rendre chez Votre Excellence à l'heure que vous m'indiquerez d'après la demande que j'ai faite hier. Mais en attendant vous serez en possession du contenu de mes instructions. Dieu veuille qu'elles soient de nature à assurer la tranquillité des deux pays et de l'Europe! Je saisis cette occasion pour renouveler à Votre Excellence l'assurance de ma haute considération.

Lord Whitworth to M. de Talleyrand.

Paris, ce 10 Mai 1803.

Monsieur,—Ayant reçu hier matin des instructions importantes à vous communiquer, je vous écrivois le soir pour demander à Votre Excellence l'heure où je pourrois avoir l'honneur de m'acquitter de ce devoir. Cette lettre est restée sans réponse. A deux heures après midi aujourd'hui j'ai envoyé M. Mandeville, attaché à l'ambassade, au bureau des Relations Extérieures pour remettre à Votre Excellence, et en son absence au chef du bureau, un paquet cacheté contenant les papiers que j'avois à vous communiquer, et y ajoutant une seconde lettre à Votre Excellence. M. Mandeville a remis ce paquet, en main propre, à M. Durand, qui lui a assuré qu'il vous seroit communiqué sans délai. A quatre heures et demie, ne recevant aucune réponse à mes lettres, je me suis rendu aux Relations Extérieures, et là j'appris que vous étiez à la campagne et qu'on ignoroit quand vous reviendriez en ville. Une demi-heure après rentrer chez moi, on me rapporta les papiers que mon secrétaire avoit pris et délivrés à M. Durand, en me disant qu'il falloit que je les envoyasse au ministre à sa campagne. Dans cet état de choses, puisque Votre Excellence ne me donne pas l'occasion de vous faire cette communication, je n'ai d'autre parti à prendre que d'en charger M. Talbot, secrétaire d'ambassade. Il aura l'honneur de vous remettre le projet de convention, qui, à ce que je l'espère, servira de base à un arrangement amical entre nos deux Gouvernemens. Il ne me reste qu'à ajouter que le terme de mon séjour à Paris est limité, et je dois me mettre en route jeudi matin pour me rendre en Angleterre, si d'ici à ce temps la négociation n'est pas terminée favorablement. Je vous prie, Monsieur, d'agréer l'assurance de ma haute considération.

WHITWORTH.

Lord Whitworth to Lord Hawkesbury.

My dear Lord,—I have been delayed much longer than I wished by the infamous chicanery and difficulties which have occurred. I shall, however, set off in half an hour; and if they have any proposal to make they must send it after me, which many people think will happen. I confess I am not so sanguine. I shall in all probability be at Calais on Sunday, and I hope to find the packets ready to take me over immediately. I am so hurried and tormented that I scarcely know what I write. I shall have no rest till I get out of this bustle, which has already lasted too long.

Thursday evening, May 12.
    Eight o'clock.

Chantilly, May 13.
Ten o'clock A.M.

Agreeable to your Lordship's commands, I send the messenger Shaw to England to acquaint your Lordship that I am so far on my journey. I left Paris last night after many difficulties and delays—first in the delivery of the passports, which were promised me early in the morning; and then in the obtaining post-horses. I thought at one time that it was intended not to suffer me to leave Paris; they came, however, at ten o'clock, and I set off immediately for this place. We propose proceeding, as expeditiously as we can with the incumbrance of a large family, in an hour, and we shall not be able to get further than Breteuil, or somewhere between that and Amiens, to-night. By what I heard from Paris this morning, the conflict was very severe during the whole of yesterday between Joseph Bonaparte and the First Consul. He endeavoured to obtain some specific proposal in the hope of inducing me to forward it to your Lordship. I am given to understand that he has not succeeded, but does not give up the point. Whatever comes to me it is my duty to transmit to your Lordship; but most assuredly nothing short of an acquiescence in our demands can justify my infringing your Lordship's instructions. In a letter which I received from M. de Talleyrand a few hours before my departure from Paris, with my passports, he expressed a hope that I should conform to what he called the established usage, and wait at Calais till General Andréossy should be at Dover, so that we might both set out at the same time; and he added that he supposed of course the persons attached to my mission would not leave Paris until those of the French mission in London should leave that capital. As I never heard of such a usage or of such a necessity unless in transactions between the most barbarous and uncivilised nations, I made no answer whatever to his observations, but contented myself with returning the personal civilities which he had expressed towards me. I shall therefore proceed on my journey, and cross the water without waiting for any

R

proposal from General Andréossy. If he should make any, I shall tell him what are my intentions with respect to the time of my embarking, etc. It was agreed on my leaving Paris that Mr. Talbot, Mr. Mandeville, and the other gentlemen attached to the mission should set out Sunday or Monday. The cyphers will be destroyed, and the archives brought in a carriage by Mr. Mandeville. I have in all these respects endeavoured to make the best arrangement in my power.

I shall have the honour of paying my respects to your Lordship an evening in the ensuing week.

Breteuil, May 14, 1803.
Half-past eight A.M.

Scarcely had I forwarded the French messenger who will bring your Lordship my letter of this date, with a note from M. de Talleyrand, when Mr. Mandeville arrived from Paris with the enclosed papers. My last despatch from Paris will have prepared your Lordship for some proposal of this nature. I refer your Lordship to Mr. Huber's letters to me, and the observation of Regnault d'Angely. The proposition is not precisely what Joseph Bonaparte stated to me. Should, however, the idea be such as to offer anything on which to build a basis, taking it always in the light of an expedient to save the *amour propre* of the First Consul, such alterations and modifications might be proposed as would perhaps render it practicable. I shall proceed as I intended, and should your Lordship have any orders for me they will find me at Calais. Your Lordship will observe that neither the note which has been forwarded nor any other measure of irritation is to be taken here until the event of this proposal is known. The difference between the proposition and that made to me verbally by Joseph Bonaparte consists in his Majesty's being required to barter away what does not belong to him, instead of giving his consent to any amicable and suitable arrangement between the French Government and the King of Naples; and the arrangement is for a limited term, and that all the other demands of his Majesty are wholly omitted. Joseph Bonaparte gives it, however, to be understood that there would be no difficulty in regard to them, or indeed to any modification which might leave the project such an appearance as to satisfy the dignity of this Government.

Projet.

Le Premier Consul de la République française et Sa Majesté Britannique désirant maintenir la paix, heureusement rétablie à Amiens, les plénipotentiaires soussignés conviennent des articles suivants.

Article I.

Malte restera en la possession de Sa Majesté Britannique pendant l'espace de dix ans, au plus.

Article II.

La République française occupera, pendant le même espace de tems, les positions d'Otrante et de Tarente, telles qu'elle les occupait lors de la signature du traité d'Amiens, et qu'elle a évacuées en conséquence de l'article XI du même traité.

Article III.

La présente convention sera ratifiée et les ratifications échangées dans l'espace de quinze jours, et plus tôt si faire se peut.

REMARKS OF JOSEPH BONAPARTE.

Les positions qu'occupait l'armée française sont: La presqu'île d'Otrante, bornée de trois côtés par la mer et de l'autre par les rivières d'Ofanto et de Bradano et une ligne joignant les deux rivières par Venosa. Lord Whitworth a dû recevoir le matin une note dans laquelle on a exprimé les plaintes que l'on croit avoir droit de faire sur la conduite du Gouvernement britannique depuis deux mois. Le Premier Consul a paru sentir vivement la précipitation des démarches qui ont été prescrites à Lord Whitworth. Cependant rien n'est encore désespéré. On peut assurer qu'aucune publication n'aura lieu ici, et qu'aucune hostilité ne sera commencée, moins dans l'espérance de conserver la paix, que dans le désir d'augmenter encore les droits que l'on doit avoir à la considération publique par la modération et la patience que l'on a montrées dans les circonstances. Quelque résolu que l'on soit à la guerre, on désire toutefois la paix, plus qu'on ne l'espère. Si la convention ci-jointe était signée par Lord Whitworth, elle le serait également ici, et l'on garantit sa prompte satisfaction.

Mr. Huber to Lord Whitworth.

Friday, One o'clock P.M.
May 12, 1803.

My Lord,—Just returned from a long conversation with Joseph Bonaparte. I sit down to give your Excellency the particulars of it. I was introduced by his friend and mine, Regnault de St. Jean d'Angely. He received me with great affability, and like a man of whom he had heard a character which invited him to his confidence and to his esteem. My first words were of the disappointment your Excellency had felt at being deprived of the expected pleasure of seeing him on his return from St. Cloud, and at being obliged to set off, even later than you intended, without knowing the success of his visit to his brother. I will, as much as I can, state his own words. 'Je croyois être convenu avec Lord Whitworth de le revoir dans le cas seulement où j'aurais pu lui annoncer la concession de sa demande, savoir une lettre officielle de M. Talleyrand confirmant l'offre verbale que je lui avois faite, le matin même, de terminer la longue discussion des deux cabinets par la prise de possession de notre part du port d'Otrante sans opposition de la part de l'Angleterre, et par la rétention de Malte par cette dernière Puissance comme un équivalent de notre nouvelle acquisition. Lorsque j'ai présenté à mon frère cette idée, qui avoit été traitée précédemment, je m'ai trouvé arrêté par la lettre que le ministre de Russie avoit reçue la veille et lui avoit communiquée, lettre par laquelle son maître consent ou à être simplement médiateur entre la France et l'Angleterre, ou à entrer en possession de Malte pour un terme d'années qui seroit convenu par ces deux Puissances. Le cabinet de St. James a fait annoncer par le Lord Whitworth avoir des assurances et des documents positifs que jamais l'empereur de Russie ne voudra consentir à cette possession temporaire. Entre ces deux assertions opposées, mon frère s'est arrêté à celle qui met la France dans la meilleure position, et il a paru craindre de perdre cet avantage en mettant en avant la prise de possession d'Otrante avant d'être assuré qu'elle seroit consentie par le cabinet britannique. Je vous réitère ce que j'ai eu l'honneur de dire hier à milord Whitworth. C'est que, nonobstant cette nouvelle position du Premier Consul, nonobstant les entraves qu'on a mises ici il y a deux jours au moyen conciliatoire de la compensation de Malte par Otrante (ce qui est assurément bien à notre désavantage), je signerai encore dès ce moment cet arrangement, en m'engageant d'en obtenir de mon frère la ratification, pourvu que l'ambassadeur se croie autorisé à en faire autant de son côté.' My answer was: 'Comme l'affaire d'Otrante en compensation de Malte est une idée absolument nouvelle, elle est et a dû être étrangère aux instructions et aux pouvoirs donnés au Lord Whitworth. Si cette idée devoit donc définitivement faire la base d'une négociation, il me paroît qu'il seroit nécessaire d'avoir de nouveaux pouvoirs. S.E. ne peut la présenter à sa cour sans qu'on lui en donne les moyens d'une manière officielle. Je présume qu'il est des situations où les formes officielles sont d'une nécessité rigoureuse, et doivent faire taire des considérations qui leur sont bien supérieures en elles-mêmes. Tel est le cas présent, où le caractère connu de M. Joseph Bonaparte et la qualité de frère du Premier Consul devroient donner un poids suffisant aux offres dont il le rend l'organe et le garant. Je pense qu'un cabinet ne peut pas délibérer, encore moins décider, sur le simple rapport d'une conversation. Ainsi donc, si, par des raisons qui lui sont particulières, le Premier Consul résiste à ce que cette proposition soit faite officiellement à la cour d'Angleterre, verriez-vous de l'inconvénient, Monsieur, à substituer à la lettre officielle une lettre de vous qui seroit confidentielle et qui porteroit le sceau de votre caractère? Il me semble que ce seroit une pièce suffisante pour autoriser l'ambassadeur à la soumettre à la déliberation du cabinet, pourvu qu'en la lui envoyant vous lui donniez, en même tems, la liberté de le faire. Je crois pourtant devoir au préalable rappeler la condition essentielle que le Lord Whitworth a mise, au nom de sa cour, à la compensation de Malte pour Otrante. C'est que l'arrangement, qui n'exige de l'Angleterre que sa simple adhésion, lui soit présenté revêtu du consentement du roi de Naples. (I said this because two or three words had been dropt which I had rather had not been pronounced, such as 'Lors même que les cours d'Europe trouveroient mauvaise cette nouvelle entrée dans le royaume de Naples, nous avons de quoi leur répondre'; this is an *a parte* which your Excellency is not to hear; for, once more, unless England is bound and determined to defend the King of Naples against any invasion from the French, how can England prevent this transaction taking place at any rate?) Joseph did not reply to my observation. He then asked, 'Dans le cas où ce que vous souhaitez pourroit se faire, pensez-vous que le Lord Whitworth voulût suspendre son embarquement jusqu'à ce qu'il ait reçu de sa cour réponse à la lettre que vous désirez avoir?' My answer was, 'Votre nom donneroit tant de poids à cette lettre que je présume que S. E. ralentiroit sa marche de manière à recevoir cette réponse de Londres.' 'Eh bien!' said Joseph, 'je vais partir pour St. Cloud, et si je trouve mon frère disposé comme je le désire à mon retour ce soir, je rendrai tout de suite réponse à Regnault, qui vous la dira. Croyez-vous, M. Huber, que l'Angleterre veuille la paix de bonne foi? Car nous en doutons encore.' If Heaven ever gave me any energy of feeling and of expression, it was on such a question being put to me by the Consul's brother. I believe my words and my manner bore the evident mark of truth, for he appeared convinced. I left him after expressing my fervent wishes for the success of his journey to St. Cloud, and requested a speedy answer—here I am interrupted by a note from Joseph requesting my immediate attendance.

No. II.

Friday night, Nine o'clock.

My Lord,—I had finished my first letter, marked No. 7, when I received (at five o'clock) a note from M. Regnault intimating that Joseph was just returned from St. Cloud, and wished to see him and me immediately. As Mr. Mandeville sets off as soon as the horses can be got ready, and takes charge of my first letter, and of the *projet d'arrangement* dictated by the First Consul to his brother, I have only to add that everything that I knew to be in your Lordship's breast, and in the principles of the Government of England, arising from the violation of the rights of the King of Naples, has been represented and urged by me to Joseph in the strongest manner; that with his usual candour he has admitted the strength of my plea in many respects; that he has silenced me by saying 'Toutes les objections que vous faites, laissez les faire par l'Angleterre et par le Lord Whitworth. L'Angleterre peut demander une modification des articles pour ce qui regarde le roi de Naples, et je pense qu'on pourrait y avoir égard pour obtenir la paix. Quant au mal qui en peut résulter pour le roi de Naples par l'occupation d'Otrante et de Tarente par des troupes françaises, l'Angleterre a à considérer quel sera l'état de ce même roi si nous ne pouvons pas nous entendre avec votre cabinet. Nous allons tout de suite faire marcher nos troupes de Rimini sur Naples, et nous nous emparerons de la Sicile (si nous pourrons vous empêcher de prendre possession vous-mêmes'). Mr. Regnault, who sits by me whilst I write this second letter, is also writing a note on the points I have just mentioned. I shall therefore say no more on those points. I come to the kind of manifesto which was sent to your Lordship this morning by order of the First Consul. I have told Joseph fairly that if your Lordship has thought it right to forward that manifesto to the Cabinet it may of itself determine war immediately, and in that case every attempt at pacification will prove needless. He (Joseph) began by giving me his word that that performance would not be made public until the answer of England to the present proposal be made known. The Consul has given orders that the communication to the Corps Législatif, etc. etc. should again be adjourned. I come to the last point of this letter. After the Consul had agreed with his brother to this proposal and worded it, he said, 'Il n'y a que M. Huber qui puisse convenablement se charger de porter ce projet à milord Whitworth, dont il a la confiance, et il faut l'en prier.' It was my luck to have by me at dinner Mr. Talbot, to whom, as I ought, I communicated everything that has passed this day. I requested his advice and opinion; and although he sees as strongly as I do myself all the objectionable part of the proposal, yet he thinks as I do, that the whole might be immediately sent to your Lordship. I shall certainly set out to overtake you a few hours after Mr. Mandeville, whose immediate business is, if he is in time, to stop the sending of the manifesto to England; at least, not without the Consul's observation on its non-publication here at present. In great haste.

LORD WHITWORTH TO LORD HAWKESBURY.

Breteuil, May 14, 1803.

The enclosed note reached me at Breteuil, where I passed the night, and I forward it immediately to your Lordship by the same French messenger who brought it from Paris. I see nothing in it the least likely to terminate the present differences. It is evidently the style of the First Consul, and consequently cannot be very conciliatory. I shall proceed with as much expedition as I can to England, and shall be at Calais to-morrow, where, I understand, the packets are ready.

M. DE TALLEYRAND TO LORD WHITWORTH.

Note.

Dans les circonstances importantes et graves où se trouvent les deux nations, le soussigné, ministre des Relations Extérieures de la République française, a reçu l'ordre de mettre sous les yeux du Gouvernement britannique la note suivante. Le 17 Ventose Sa Majesté Britannique fit connaître à son parlement, par un message spécial, que des armements formidables se préparaient dans les ports de France et de Hollande, et que des négociations importantes, dont l'issue était douteuse, divisaient les deux Gouvernements. Cette déclaration extraordinaire et inattendue excita un étonnement général ; mais la situation maritime de la France était patente. L'Angleterre, l'Europe, savaient qu'il n'y avait d'armements formidables ni dans les ports de France ni dans les ports de Hollande. Le soussigné ne rappellera pas à Son Excellence Lord Whitworth tout ce qui fut dit alors. On se demande de quelle source avaient pu sortir des informations aussi mal fondées. Le discernement personnel de Lord Whitworth, la loyauté de son caractère ne pouvaient être un seul instant soupçonnés. L'assertion que la France faisait des armements hostiles était une supposition manifeste et qui ne pouvait en imposer à personne. Son effet naturel devait être d'induire à penser qu'elle n'était qu'un moyen dont voulaient se servir des hommes signalés par leurs opinions perturbatrices, et qui cherchaient avidement des prétextes pour susciter des troubles, pour enflammer les passions du peuple britannique, pour exciter la défiance, la haine et les alarmes. Quant au Gouvernement anglais, si par de faux rapports il avait pu être induit en erreur sur l'existence des armements, il ne pouvait l'être sur l'existence d'une négociation. L'ambassadeur de la République à Londres ne fut pas plutôt informé du message de S. M. Britannique qu'étonné de ce qu'il annonçait l'existence d'une négociation dont il n'avait pas connaissance, il se rendit chez Son Excellence Lord Hawkesbury ; et, devant dès-lors soupçonner qu'un appel aux armes fondé sur deux fausses suppositions pouvait couvrir le projet de violer le traité d'Amiens dans les clauses qui n'étaient pas encore exécutées, il présenta au ministre de S. M. Britannique, le 19 Ventose, une note pour lui demander des explications. En même temps le soussigné eut l'ordre de pressentir Son Excellence Lord Whitworth sur les motifs qui avaient pu déterminer le Gouvernement anglais à l'autoriser dans son message de deux assertions toutes deux également fausses, pour appeler la nation aux armes et rompre le lien de paix qui unissait les deux états.

Son Excellence Lord Hawkesbury remit, le 24 Ventose, au général Andréossi une note vague, aggressive, absolue. Cette note, loin de rien éclairer, jetait de nouvelles obscurités sur le sujet de la discussion. Elle laissait à peine entrevoir la possibilité de l'ouvrir, et bien moins encore l'espoir de la voir terminée par une heureuse issue. La réponse du Gouvernement français, en date du 8 Germinal, fut autant pacifique et modérée que celle du ministre britannique avait été hostile. Le Premier Consul déclara qu'il ne relevait pas le défi de guerre de l'Angleterre, qu'il évitait de peser sur des expressions dont le sens pouvait porter un caractère d'aggression, qu'il se refusait enfin à croire que S. M. Britannique voulût violer la sainteté d'un traité sur lequel reposait la sûreté de toutes les nations. Cette déclaration faite par ordre du Premier Consul provoqua, le 17 Germinal, une nouvelle note, dans laquelle le Gouvernement français ne vit pas sans surprise qu'une demande indéterminée de satisfaction lui était adressée ; le vague de cette demande exprimée sans motif et sans object ne laissait apercevoir distinctement que l'inconvenance de son expression. On manifestait dans cette note l'intention de violer le traité d'Amiens en refusant d'évacuer Malte. On semblait se flatter que le peuple français consentirait à donner satisfaction sur deux faits supposés, sur l'allégation desquels il avait peut-être le droit d'en demander lui-même. En remettant cet office, Lord Whitworth demanda qu'un arrangement fût fait immédiatement sur les bases qui viennent d'être exposées, et il fit en même temps entendre que dans le cas contraire il craignait de se voir obligé par les ordres de son Gouvernement de quitter incessamment sa résidence et de mettre fin à sa mission. Que pouvait répondre le Gouvernement de la République à d'aussi étranges, à d'aussi brusques ouvertures? Il n'y avait qu'un grand amour de la paix qui pût l'emporter sur l'indignation. Pour s'arrêter à une décision froide et calme qui laissât à la raison et à la justice le temps de l'emporter sur les passions, il fallait se pénétrer profondément de l'idée que les nombreuses victimes des discordes des Gouvernements n'ont aucune part aux insultes qui les aigrissent; que les milliers de braves citoyens, qui, dans les vœux de leur héroïque dévouement, versent leur sang uniquement pour leur patrie, n'ont jamais le désir d'offenser un peuple voisin et puissant; qu'ils ne prennent aucun intérêt à des démarches d'orgueil et à de vaines prétentions de suprématie. Il ne fallait pas seulement se pénétrer de cette idée, il fallait s'en laisser maîtriser à chaque instant. Son Excellence Lord Whitworth convint d'écrire à sa cour que le Premier Consul ne pouvait consentir à la violation d'un traité solennel, mais qu'il voulait la paix; que si le Gouvernement d'Angleterre désirait qu'une convention fût faite pour des arrangements étrangers au traité d'Amiens, il ne s'y refuserait pas, et que les motifs de cette convention pourraient être tirés des griefs réciproques. Ces vues étaient justes et modérées. Il était difficile de proposer une négociation sur des bases plus libérales. Il n'est pas hors de propos d'observer ici que c'était six semaines après le message, où une négociation difficile, d'un intérêt grave et d'une issue incertaine mais prochaine, avait été signalée, que les ministres des deux

Gouvernements n'avaient pu encore arriver à ouvrir une véritable négociation. Lord Whitworth reçut de nouveaux ordres. Il présenta successivement deux projets de convention. Par le premier il était proposé que Malte restât sous la souveraineté du roi d'Angleterre ; et cette clause adoptée, Sa Majesté Britannique proposait de reconnaître tout ce qui avait été fait en Europe depuis le traité d'Amiens. S. M. le roi d'Angleterre promettait encore de prendre des mesures pour que les hommes qui, sur les différents points de l'Angleterre, ourdissent des trames contre la France fussent efficacement réprimés. Le soussigné eut l'honneur d'observer à Son Excellence Lord Whitworth que le premier projet de convention était une violation palpable du traité d'Amiens et renversait la base de négociation que Son Excellence s'était chargé de présenter à sa cour ; que quant à la reconnaissance offerte par S. M. Britannique, il n'y avait réellement point d'objet auquel elle pût s'appliquer ; qu'il n'y avait pas de changements en Europe depuis le traité d'Amiens, si ce n'est l'organisation de l'Empire, à laquelle le roi d'Angleterre avait concouru par son vœu comme électeur d'Hanovre, et qui n'était elle-même qu'une suite nécessaire du traité de Lunéville, antérieur de beaucoup au traité d'Amiens. Que les événements relatifs à l'existence politique du Piémont, du royaume d'Etrurie et des républiques italienne et ligurienne avaient leur date avant le traité d'Amiens ; que dans la négociation de ce traité la France avait désiré que l'Angleterre reconnût les trois Puissances ; mais que, comme l'on n'avait pu s'accorder ni sur ce point ni sur les affaires de l'Inde, en ce qui concernait la destruction de quelques états principaux, et les inappréciables acquisitions faites par l'Angleterre dans cette contrée, on en était resté à considérer la discussion de ces objets comme ne tenant pas à l'exécution des articles préliminaires et à l'objet fondamental de la pacification des deux états. Le soussigné observa enfin que le Gouvernement français ne demandait sur ce point aucune approbation ni reconnaissance à S. M. Britannique. Le soussigné ajouta que quant à la république batave elle avait été reconnue par le roi d'Angleterre, puisqu'il avait traité avec elle ; et que, par les traités existant entre cette république et la France, l'arrière-garde des troupes françaises devait évacuer le pays à la nouvelle de l'entière exécution du traité d'Amiens. Quant aux criminels réfugiés à Londres et à Jersey, où ils se livraient à tous leurs penchants pervers, et où, loin d'être réprimés, ils étaient traités et pensionnés par l'Angleterre, le Gouvernement français trouvait que, dans la situation actuelle des négociations, il ne devait y attacher aucune importance. Son Excellence Lord Whitworth proposa un second projet. L'Angleterre demandait que, le Gouvernement civil de Malte étant laissé au Grand-Maître, les garnisons britanniques continuassent d'occuper les fortifications de l'île. Cette proposition était impraticable et inouïe. Comme celle du premier projet, elle était contraire au traité d'Amiens et conséquemment aux bases de négociations offertes par le Premier Consul. Elle avait de plus l'inconvénient irrémédiable de mettre un ordre de chevaliers appartenant à toutes les puissances de l'Europe sous l'autorité et la tutelle arbitraire d'une seule puissance. Elle était enfin par elle-même une offense à l'honneur et à la religion d'un ordre uni, par tous ses éléments, à l'honneur et à la religion de l'Europe entière. Ainsi, dans tous les pas de cette négociation, le Gouvernement de la République était obligé de voir que le Gouvernement anglais n'avait qu'une seule volonté, qu'un seul objet en vue : celui de ne pas remplir les stipulations du traité d'Amiens et de conserver Malte par la seule raison que Malte était à sa convenance et qu'elle appela Malte une garantie suffisante.

Mais quelle est la Puissance de l'Europe, dût-elle se reconnaître inégale, qui pût souffrir de se soumettre aux volontés d'une autre sans discussion de ses droits, sans appel aux principes de la justice ? Quelle est la Puissance surtout, qui, placée comme l'a été la France dans le cours de cette discussion, eût pu se soumettre à des conditions dictées dès le début d'une négociation, et plutôt annoncées au bruit des menaces de guerre, par des préparatifs et des armements, que proposées comme un moyen d'accorder les droits et les intérêts des deux états ? Dans une circonstance à quelques égards analogue, une nation faible, non par son courage, mais par l'étendue et la population de ses provinces, osa braver la puissance anglaise dans sa capitale menacée, exposer la demeure de ses rois, compromettre ses magasins, sa seule richesse, résultat de cent ans de paix et d'une industrieuse économie, plutôt que de se soumettre à des conditions injustes proposées, alors comme aujourd'hui, sur le motif de la convenance de l'Angleterre et appuyées par l'appareil d'un armement considérable. Des braves y périrent; les colonies danoises furent envahies; mais quelque inégale que fût la lutte, l'honneur ne laissait point à cette généreuse nation le choix du parti qu'elle avait à prendre. Dans la discussion présente la politique parle le même langage que l'honneur. Si le Gouvernement britannique est le maître de se conformer ou de ne pas se conformer à ses engagements; s'il peut, dans les traités qu'il a faits, distinguer l'esprit de la lettre; si l'on admet les restrictions autorisées; si les convenances de l'Angleterre doivent enfin expliquer le sens des conventions politiques, quel sera le terme des concessions qu'on se flattera d'arracher successivement à la faiblesse de la France? Quelle sera la mesure des sacrifices et des humiliations qu'on entreprendra de lui imposer? Aujourd'hui la convenance de l'Angleterre exige une garantie contre la France, et l'Angleterre garde Malte. Autrefois la convenance de l'Angleterre voulait une garantie contre la France, et l'on détruisit Dunkerque! et un commissaire anglais donna des loix où flottaient les couleurs françaises! Demain la convenance de l'Angleterre demandera une garantie contre les progrès de l'industrie française, et on proposera un tarif de commerce pour arrêter les progrès de notre industrie. Si nous réparons nos ports, si nous construisons un môle, si nous creusons un canal, si par quelque encouragement nous relevons nos manufactures etc., on demandera que nos ports soient dégradés, que nos môles soient détruits, que nos canaux soient comblés, que nos manufactures soient ruinées. On exigera que la France devienne pauvre et qu'elle soit désarmée pour se conformer aux convenances de l'Angleterre, et donner une garantie suffisante à son Gouvernement. Qu'on considère les principes, ou qu'on examine les conséquences, on est également frappé de l'injustice et du scandale de ces prétentions; on peut se demander : Si elles étaient soumises à un jury anglais, hésiterait-il à les réprouver unanimement? Le Gouvernement de la République a droit de s'étonner que le ministère britannique ait pu se croire autorisé à lui supposer ce degré d'avilissement. Comment a-t-il pu penser que le Gouvernement actuel de la France perdrait, dans un lâche repos, le souvenir de tout ce qu'il a fait et le sentiment de tous ses devoirs? Nos provinces sont-elles moins étendues, moins peuplées? Ne sommes-nous pas les mêmes hommes qui ont tout sacrifié au maintien des plus justes intérêts? et si, après le succès, nous avons fait éclater une grande modération, à quelle autre cause cette moderation peut-elle être imputée, si ce n'est à la justice de nos droits et au sentiment de nos forces? Le soussigné, en exposant à Son Excellence Lord Whitworth ces observations, croit avoir le droit de lui faire remarquer que la conduite modérée de toute l'administration française pendant deux mois entiers, d'une suite de provocations offensantes, et malgré la profonde impression qu'elle en ressentait, doit lui faire apprécier le véritable caractère du Gouvernement français. Cependant, c'est lorsque, par son profond silence sur des insultes répétées, le Gouvernement de la République eut dû s'attendre à voir qu'on chercherait à les réparer ou au moins à y mettre un terme; lorsque, évitant de préjuger la tournure finale que pourraient prendre les affaires, il n'a montré que de l'attention et de l'empressement à examiner les moyens qui pourraient être proposés pour concilier et satisfaire le Gouvernement anglais, c'est alors que, verbalement et sans vouloir consentir à donner aucune déclaration écrite, Son Excellence Lord Whitworth a fait, au nom et par l'ordre de son Gouvernement, le 6 Floréal, au soussigné les demandes suivantes : que l'Angleterre garde Malte pendant dix ans; que l'Angleterre prenne possession de l'île de Lampedusa; que la Hollande soit évacuée par les troupes françaises. Son Excellence Lord Whitworth a de plus déclaré que ces propositions étaient *l'ultimatum* de sa cour, et que sur le refus de les accepter il avait ordre de quitter Paris dans le délai de sept jours. Le soussigné ose dire qu'il n'y a pas d'exemple d'une telle forme donnée à un ultimatum aussi impérieux.

Eh quoi! La guerre ne doit-elle avoir d'inconvénients que pour nous? Le ministère anglais juge-t-il la nation française tellement faible que, dans une circonstance où il s'agit pour elle de la plus importante des délibérations, il ne se croie pas tenu de se conformer, à son égard, aux usages qui sont observés par tous les gouvernements des nations civilisées? Ou bien n'est-ce pas plutôt que le sentiment de l'injustice qui pèse sur la conscience de l'homme public, comme sur celle de l'homme privé, ait empêché le Gouvernement britannique de signer la demande qu'il avait faite, et que, par une marche moins décidée, il a cherché à se réserver pour l'avenir les moyens de faire perdre les traces de ses véritables intentions, et de tromper un jour l'opinion sur l'origine de la rupture? Ou enfin, les ministres de Sa Majesté Britannique, connaissant mal le caractère du Premier Consul, ont-ils espéré, à force de provocations, de l'exaspérer ou de l'intimider, de le porter à oublier les intérêts de la nation, ou de l'exciter à quelque acte d'éclat, qu'ils pourraient ensuite travestir aux yeux de l'Europe en initiative de guerre? Le Premier Consul plus qu'aucun homme qui existe connaît les maux de la guerre, parce que plus que personne il est accoutumé à ses calculs et à ses chances. Il croit que, dans des circonstances telles que celles où nous nous trouvons, la première pensée des gouvernements doit se porter sur les catastrophes et les malheurs qui peuvent naître d'une nouvelle guerre. Il croit que leur premier devoir est non seulement de ne pas céder à des motifs d'irritation, mais de chercher par tous les moyens à éclairer, à modérer les passions imprévoyantes des peuples. Le soussigné, s'arrêtant donc d'abord à la forme de cette communication de Son Excellence Lord Whitworth, le pria d'observer que des conversations verbales et fugitives sont insuffisantes pour la discussion d'aussi immenses intérêts, dont ordinairement tous les motifs sont traités dans les conseils des nations après les plus mûres délibérations. Dans ces conseils et dans de telles circonstances rien n'est jugé indifférent. Les formes, les expressions même, y sont pesées, examinées, débattues, appréciées, et servent toujours à déterminer, comme à justifier, le parti que l'on doit prendre. Si une aussi imprudente, aussi inconvenante violation de toutes les formes avait été faite par la France, que n'aurait-on pas dit, que n'aurait-on pas écrit en Angleterre! Il n'est pas un orateur dans les deux chambres du parlement qui n'eût déclaré que cet écart des règles générales établies entre les nations, dans des circonstances importantes, était un outrage à la nation anglaise. Aux yeux de tous, une telle offense eût été regardée comme un motif suffisant de rompre toute négociation. Quant au fonds de *l'ultimatum* proposé, le soussigné a l'honneur de rappeler à Son Excellence Lord Whitworth qu'il fut chargé de déclarer, par une note qui lui fut remise le 12 Floréal, que le Premier Consul restait impassible aux menaces comme aux injures, et passait par-dessus l'oubli de formes dont il n'est pas d'exemple dans l'histoire qu'aucun gouvernement se soit écarté dans une aussi importante circonstance. Que l'île de Lampedusa n'appartenait pas à la France, qu'elle était sous la souveraineté d'une puissance étrangère, et que sur le désir de S. M. Britannique d'en avoir la possession, le Premier Consul n'avait le droit d'énoncer ni consentement ni refus. Que l'indépendance de l'ordre et de l'île de Malte était le résultat d'un article spécial du traité d'Amiens. Que le Premier Consul ne pouvait prendre à cet égard aucune nouvelle détermination sans le concours des deux autres puissances contractantes à ce traité, Sa Majesté le roi d'Espagne et la république batave. Que l'indépendance de l'ordre et de l'île de Malte avait été garantie par Sa Majesté l'empereur d'Allemagne, et que les ratifications de cette garantie étaient échangées; que Leurs Majestés l'empereur de Russie et le roi de Prusse avaient garanti l'indépendance de l'ordre de Malte; que ces garanties avaient été demandées à ces puissances par l'Angleterre, comme par la France; qu'il était du devoir du Premier Consul de les accepter et qu'il les avait acceptées; que le Premier Consul ne pouvait donc entendre à aucune proposition relative à l'indépendance de l'ordre et de l'île de Malte sans qu'au préalable il eût reconnu relativement à cette indépendance les intentions des gouvernements qui l'avaient authentiquement garantie; qu'un corps peu nombreux de troupes françaises était encore, au moment du message, stationné en Hollande, en vertu d'une convention conclue entre cette république et la France; et que le Premier Consul n'avait point hésité à dire qu'il ferait évacuer la Hollande aussitôt que les stipulations du traité d'Amiens auraient eu leur entière exécution de la part de l'Angleterre. A cette note, qui, dans ses expressions et dans l'exactitude surtout et la précision de ses motifs, ne soupirait qu'équité, paix et modération, Son Excellence Lord Whitworth répondit par une demande péremptoire de passeports, en m'informant qu'il comptait en faire usage mercredi 4 mai à cinq heures du matin. Le Gouvernement français sentit profondément le contraste d'une détermination aussi absolue avec le caractère de bienséance, de justice et de conciliation que, dans toutes les circonstances et principalement dans la dernière, il s'était attaché à donner à ses démarches. Néanmoins il crut devoir faire encore un sacrifice aux intérêts de l'humanité. Il ne voulut abandonner tout espoir de paix qu'au dernier moment, et le soussigné remit à Son Excellence Lord Whitworth une nouvelle note par laquelle la France offrait de consentir à ce que Malte fût remise à la garde d'une des trois puissances garantes, l'Autriche, la Russie ou la Prusse. Cette proposition parut, à Lord Whitworth lui-même, devoir satisfaire les prétentions de sa cour. Il suspendit son départ et prit la note *ad referendum*. En même temps l'ambassadeur de la République à Londres, prévenu de la demande que Son Excellence Lord Whitworth avait faite à Paris de ses passeports pour retourner en Angleterre, eut ordre de se tenir prêt à partir. Il fit en conséquence la demande de ses passeports, qui lui furent accordés sur l'heure. Le *mezzo termine* proposé par le Gouvernement français s'éloignait de l'article du traité d'Amiens; mais il avait le double avantage de se rapprocher le plus possible de son esprit, c'est à dire de mettre Malte dans l'indépendance des deux nations. Il offrait d'ailleurs cette garantie tant réclamée et que le ministère britannique prétendait être le seul de ses alarmes. Le Gouvernement britannique comprit la force de ces raisons, et la malheureuse fatalité qui l'entraîne à la guerre ne lui offrit de réponse que dans de fausses allégations. Le vingt-et-un de ce mois Lord Whitworth remit une note dans laquelle il déclara que la Russie s'était refusée à ce que l'on demandait d'elle. Les puissances garantes étant au nombre de trois, si la Russie s'y était refusée, il restait encore l'empereur d'Allemagne et le roi de Prusse. Mais comment la Russie pouvait-elle avoir fait connaître son opinion sur une proposition nouvelle et faite depuis peu de jours ? Il était à la connaissance de l'Angleterre que la Russie et la Prusse avaient proposé de garantir l'indépendance de Malte avec de légères modifications, et que le Gouvernement français s'était empressé d'accepter ladite garantie ; et par une suite de l'esprit de conséquence et de fidélité à ses engagements qui caractérise l'empereur Alexandre, il n'était nullement douteux qu'il n'acceptât la proposition qui lui était offerte. Mais la Providence, qui se plaît parfois à confondre la mauvaise foi, fit arriver à la même heure, au même instant où Lord Whitworth remettait sa note, un courrier de Pétersbourg adressé aux plénipotentiaires de cette cour à Paris et à Londres, par lequel Sa Majesté l'empereur de Russie manifestait, avec une énergie toute particulière, la peine qu'il avait éprouvée d'apprendre la résolution où était Sa Majesté Britannique de garder Malte ; il renouvelait les assurances de sa garantie et faisait connaître qu'il accepterait la demande de sa médiation qui avait été faite par le Premier Consul, si les deux Puissances y avaient recours. Le soussigné s'empressa, le vingt-deux, de faire connaître à Lord Whitworth par une note l'erreur dans laquelle était sa cour, ne doutant pas que, puisque c'était la seule objection qu'elle avait faite au projet qui avait été présenté, dès l'instant qu'elle connaîtroit la déclaration réitérée et positive de la Russie, elle ne s'empressât d'adhérer à la remise de Malte entre les mains d'une des trois puissances garantes. Quel dut donc être l'étonnement du soussigné lorsque Lord Whitworth n'entrait dans aucune explication et ne cherchait ni à contredire ni à discuter les déclarations qui lui avaient été faites ! Le soussigné fit connaître par une note du même jour qu'aux termes de ses instructions il avait ordre de partir trente-six heures après la remise de sa dernière note, et réitérait la demande de ses passeports : le soussigné dut les lui faire passer immédiatement.

L'ambassadeur d'Angleterre se serait-il comporté différemment si le Gouvernement français eût été assiégé dans une place battue en brèche et qu'il eût été question, non du traité le plus important que le Cabinet britannique ait négocié depuis plus de huit cents ans, mais d'une simple capitulation ? On a fait précéder l'ouverture des négociations par des armements fastueusement annoncés. Tous les jours à toute heure on a signalé la reprise des hostilités. Et quel est cet *ultimatum* qu'on propose au Gouvernement de la République pour être signé dans le délai d'un jour ? Il faut qu'il consente à donner une île qui ne lui appartient pas ; qu'il viole lui-même, à son détriment, un traité solennel sous le prétexte que l'Angleterre a besoin contre lui d'une garantie nouvelle ; qu'il manque à tous les égards dus aux autres puissances contractantes, en détruisant, sans leur aveu, l'article qui, par considération pour elles, avait été le plus longuement discuté à l'époque des conférences ; qu'il manque également à ceux qui sont dus aux puissances garantes en consentant qu'une île dont elles ont voulu l'indépendance reste pendant dix ans sous l'autorité de la couronne britannique ; qu'il ravisse à l'ordre de Malte la souveraineté de l'état qui lui a été rendu, et que cette souverainté soit transmise aux habitants ; que par cette spoliation il offense toutes les puissances qui ont reconnu le rétablissement de cet ordre, qui l'ont garanti et qui dans les arrangements de l'Allemagne lui ont assuré des indemnités pour les pertes qu'il avait éprouvées. Tel est le fonds de cet *ultimatum*, qui présente une série de prétentions toujours croissantes en proportion de la modération que le Gouvernement de la République avait déployée. D'abord l'Angleterre consentait à la conservation de l'ordre de Malte et voulait seulement assujettir cet ordre et ses états à l'autorité britannique. Aujourd'hui et pour la première fois on demande l'abolition de cet ordre, et elle doit être consentie dans trente-six heures. Mais ces conditions définitivement proposées, fussent-elles aussi conformes au traité d'Amiens et aux intérêts de la France qu'elles leur sont contraires, la seule forme de ces demandes, le terme de trente-six heures prescrit à la réponse, ne peuvent laisser doute sur la détermination du Gouvernment français. Non, jamais la France ne reconnoîtra dans aucun gouvernement le droit d'annuler par un seul acte de sa volonté les stipulations d'un engagement réciproque. Si elle a souffert que, sous des formes qui annonçaient la menace, on lui présentât un *ultimatum* verbal de sept jours, un *ultimatum* de trente-six heures et des traités conclus avant d'être négociés, elle n'a pu avoir d'autre objet que de ramener le Gouvernement britannique par l'exemple de sa modération ; mais elle ne peut consentir à rien de ce qui compromît les intérêts de sa dignité et ceux de sa puissance. Le soussigné est donc chargé de déclarer à Son Excellence Lord Whitworth qu'aucune communication, dont le sens et les formes ne s'accorderaient pas avec les usages observés entre les grandes puissances et avec les principes de la plus parfaite égalité entre l'un et l'autre état, ne sera plus admise en France ; que rien ne pourra obliger le Gouvernement français à disposer des pays qui ne lui appartiennent point ; et qu'il ne reconnaîtra jamais à l'Angleterre le droit de violer, en quelque point que ce soit, les traités qu'elle aura faits avec lui. Enfin le soussigné réitère la proposition de mettre Malte entre les mains d'une des trois puissances garantes. Et pour tous les autres objets étrangers au traité d'Amiens il renouvelle la déclaration que le Gouvernement français est prêt à ouvrir une négociation à leur égard. Si le Gouvernement anglais donne le signal de guerre, il ne restera plus au Gouvernement de la République qu'à se confier en la justice de sa cause et au Dieu des armées. Le soussigné a l'honneur de renouveler à Son Excellence Lord Whitworth les assurances de sa haute considération.

Ch. Mau. Talleyrand.

Paris, le 23 Floréal, an XI de la Rép. franç.

My Lord,—Je remplis l'ordre du Premier Consul en vous adressant la note ci-jointe. J'aime à penser qu'elle est de nature à modifier les propositions de votre Gouvernement, et je saisis cette occasion de vous renouveler, avec l'expression du regret que m'a causé votre départ, l'assurance de ma haute considération.

CH. MAU. TALLEYRAND.

Paris, 23 Floréal, an XI.
To Lord Whitworth.

LORD HAWKESBURY TO LORD WHITWORTH.

Downing Street, May 16, 1803.

Your Excellency's despatch of the 14th instant by the messenger Sylvester has been received here this morning at two o'clock. The proposition which it contains, being entirely repugnant to the principles by which his Majesty has been uniformly actuated in the late discussions with France, and incompatible with that security which it has been the great object of his solicitude to obtain, must have been considered by the French Government as wholly inadmissible, and can only have been dictated by their desire to procrastinate the negotiation, the protraction of which has already been so injurious to the interests of this country. I have it, therefore, in command from his Majesty to signify to your Excellency his pleasure that immediately on receipt of this despatch you embark for Dover with as little delay as the circumstances of wind and tide will allow.

LORD WHITWORTH TO LORD HAWKESBURY.

Boulogne, May 16, 1803.

We arrived here last night from Abbeville, and shall be at Calais early this evening. I found Mr. Mengaud waiting for me at this place to be informed of the precise time when

I proposed to embark, in order that he might acquaint General Andréossy with it, who, he supposes, will set out from Dover at the same time. I propose embarking in the evening rather than with the morning's tide, having some reason to believe that I shall in the morning of to-morrow receive a messenger from Paris. Although they have suffered me to come so far, I should not be surprised yet to receive a proposal on our own terms. This expectation is, however, too vague to induce me to delay my departure farther than from the morning to the evening tide of to-morrow. From Paris to this place I have witnessed but one general appearance of gloomy discontent and despondency at being thus dragged into a war by the obstinacy of one man, and for a cause totally foreign to France. I enclose a letter from Mr. Talbot, and some newspapers which I have received this morning, by Basilico. The journey of Mr. Mandeville and Mr. Huber was on occasion of the papers which I transmitted to your Lordship by Sylvester. We expect to be at Dover to-morrow in the night, and in town on Wednesday.

Mr. Talbot to Lord Whitworth.

Paris, May 14, 1803.

My dear Lord,—I avail myself of the opportunity afforded me by Basilico's return from Madrid to communicate to you the very little which has come to my knowledge since the departure of Mr. Huber. There are rumours in circulation of various sorts, but all tending to calm and satisfy the hopes of the public. Mr. Mandeville's journey is pretty generally known, from which people are much inclined to argue favourably. I have seen nobody to-day who could give me the smallest information worth transmitting to your Lordship. There are, however, two articles which have appeared in the 'Moniteur' and 'Journal des Débats' of to-day which deserve some notice. Bonaparte came to Paris this morning, probably in consequence of what has appeared in the 'Moniteur.' I understand that he and Madame Bonaparte intend going to the Opera Buffa to-night. Count Marcoff called on me this morning and was extremely inquisitive, but mentioned nothing worth alluding to. I remain most perfectly quiet, and have not appeared in society since your departure. I beg your Lordship to present my best respects to the Duchess. I hope her Grace and the children are well, and that you have had a comfortable journey.

P.S.—I have written very much in haste, as I have not had a moment to myself, from the number of persons who have come to demand passports, etc.

Lord Whitworth to Lord Hawkesbury.

Calais, Monday, Six o'clock.

As Basilico is not yet gone from hence, I add a few words to my letter of this morning to acquaint your Lordship that we arrived here about an hour ago. I mentioned to your Lordship that I meant to embark to-morrow with the evening tide, so that unless something very extraordinary happens we shall be at Dover to-morrow night. My chief motive for troubling your Lordship with this is to say that I was received here to-day with the same honours as when I first arrived from England: thirteen guns were fired from the ramparts, and I was visited by the generals and the officers of the garrison, and the Mayor at the head of the municipality. I mention this to your Lordship, as you may perhaps think it right that General Andréossy should, if it is not too late, be received in the same manner at Dover. I have the pleasure to acquaint your Lordship that the Duchess is quite well; the children are rather fatigued, but we hope a good night's rest will restore them.

M. Huber to Lord Whitworth.

Paris, May 17, 1803.

Yesterday Mr. Talbot and I despatched one of the grooms to your Lordship at Calais with letters informing you of the particulars of my conference with Joseph Bonaparte and with Talleyrand on my return from Abbeville. I was strictly exact in the statement of all that had passed, and I rendered the latter's own words when I said that his injunction to me was 'de donner ma parole d'honneur que dans la nuit du Mardi au Mercredi il seroit expédié à Lord Whitworth un courrier qui lui porteroit une proposition analogue à l'esprit de l'ultimatum d'Angleterre.' We knew that our courier *alone* would not have the power of detaining your Lordship an hour longer than you had intended staying at Calais, unless fresh and discretionary instructions had reached you from London on the Tuesday morning; and this we looked upon as a possible consequence of the despatches sent last Friday to General Andréossy. The First Consul had not relied so much, it seems, on the success of those despatches as to prevent his listening to new suggestions from his brother and from Talleyrand more likely to decide the assent of England; so that when they both went to St. Cloud in the evening they hardly doubted of success. We were, however, again foiled in our expectations. A courier from Russia arrived that very evening, which, it seems, brought from the Court of Petersburg offers more consonant than the first with Bonaparte's wishes, and which, he thought, England would find it more difficult to refuse. On this new ground they found him deaf to their arguments, and I received a note at twelve o'clock at night informing me 'que tout étoit encore manqué,' and (as usual) Joseph went off to Morfontaine. I will not attempt to describe here my extreme mortification and disappointment. Your Lordship will, I know, form a just idea of both; and you will find the expression of my feelings in the copy of the letter which I wrote and sent to Talleyrand at Meudon at one o'clock in the morning. The answer was an appointment *aux Affaires Etrangères* at twelve o'clock. I will endeavour to render his conversation with precision. 'Vous me trouvez, ainsi que Joseph Bonaparte, extrêmement chagrin de ce nouveau mécompte, auquel certainement nous n'avions pas lieu de nous attendre, et qui reporte de nouveau nos espérances sur la proposition qu'Andréossi a dû faire au Lord Hawkesbury. Nous devrons apprendre demain que si cette proposition n'a pas été acceptée, au moins elle produira de la part de votre Gouvernement un aperçu des modifications sous lesquelles elle lui conviendroit mieux. Je vous répète que nous voulons la paix —que nous la voulons plus que jamais—que si elle nous échappe, ce sera par le simple effet du peu de ménagement que vous avez pour l'amour propre du Consul. Vous autres au dehors ne savez pas ce que c'est que cet amour-propre, mais nous le connoissons, nous qui avons à le manier. Si le cabinet britannique avoit voulu adopter des formes moins sévères vis-à-vis de lui, il auroit déjà réussi. Il ne peut pas souffrir de se voir dicter sur *tout*, et il répète sans cesse que l'Angleterre le traite comme une garnison qui demanderoit à capituler. Il se plaint de vos ultimatum qui sont des ultimatissimum et qui ne laissent pas à l'ambassadeur qui les présente la moindre latitude. Nous nous entendons pour le fond, nous nous entendons pour la forme de ce que l'ambassadeur voudra discuter. Nous changerons les mots qui ne vous conviendront pas ; vous adoucirez ceux qui peuvent nous blesser. Nous admettrons l'île de Lampedusa et l'article de Malte tels que vous les avez proposés. Nous rédigerons d'après votre propre rédaction (même d'une manière encore plus adoucie si vous voulez) l'article qui regarde Otrante et Tarente. Nous stipulerons dix ans de possession ou nous ne le stipulerons pas, tout comme vous voudrez. Que l'ambassadeur revienne et je lui demande seulement de ne pas tenir sa montre à la main vis-à-vis le Consul, ni de lui prescrire un nombre d'heures positif. Ce sera l'amour-propre blessé qui décidera la guerre. Car pour le fond il est impossible de ne pas s'entendre, et nous nous entendons. Dites à Lord Whitworth (dont le départ m'afflige sincèrement et blesse le

Premier Consul) que je vais faire porter dans sa cave à Paris mon meilleur vin d'Hautbrion en retour de l'excellent vin de Madeira qu'il m'a envoyé. Nous ne voulons pas qu'il s'en aille; il nous faut un homme aussi loyal et aussi excellent, quoique trop positif, et nous nous resterons amis.' Your Lordship knows my answer to all this, without my telling it —a repetition of all I had said before. 'Que signifie ce langage à présent que vous avez laissé partir milord W——? Qu'est-ce que c'est que cet enfantillage du Consul qui demande des bonbons pour ne pas mettre l'Europe en feu? Pourquoi ces regrets tardifs sur le départ de l'ambassadeur, quand il n'a tenu qu'à vous de le retenir en écoutant ses raisons présentées sous des formes si convenables et nullement mortifiantes? Voulez-vous que l'Angleterre caresse le Consul comme le font les cours du continent? Pourquoi parler sans cesse du petit nombre d'heures qu'il vous laisse pour la décision, lorsque sur les sept premiers jours vous en passez six et trois quarts dans le silence? Pourquoi parler des douze dernières heures de son séjour, quand vous en avez laissé écouler vingt-quatre sans rien dire? S'il passe la mer, vous l'aurez bien voulu, et le message d'Andréossi, tel qu'il a été présenté, aura certainement été refusé par Lord Hawkesbury. L'ambassadeur s'est expliqué d'avance là-dessus. Je vous l'ai dit en son nom de la manière la plus positive. Ainsi attendez-vous à un refus. Avez-vous donné à Andréossi des instructions péremptoires là-dessus?' 'Non, nous n'en donnons jamais, parce qu'en fait de négociations tout est susceptible de modifications.' Talleyrand asked me: 'Dans quel esprit avez-vous laissé milord Whitworth?' 'Convaincu que, si le Premier Consul avoit sincèrement voulu la paix, les propositions de l'ultimatum eussent été acceptées —dégoûté, jusques à satiété, de procédés si peu analogues aux siens et qui annoncent simplement le désir de gagner du tems.' 'Gagner du tems! et pour quel objet? Dans quel but?' (said he to me). 'Mais—je ne les comprends pas trop, je l'avoue—à moins que vous ne vous flattiez que l'Angleterre vous donneroit le tems de voir rentrer votre escadre de St. Domingue, à laquelle vous avez certainement envoyé l'ordre d'évacuer et de revenir (et par parenthèse, le Consul a-t-il bien pesé les difficultés de cette évacuation de St. Domingue, qui suppose un embarquement de trente ou quarante mille individus? Où sont vos vaisseaux pour les emmener, et vos vivres pour les nourrir? Il y a impossibilité, et vous pouvez vous attendre au massacre de tous ces individus par les noirs après le départ de votre escadre. Jugez de la réaction qui en résultera ici contre le Consul).' Talleyrand said: 'Quant à notre escadre, nous la regardons comme perdue. Peut-être cependant échappera-t-elle, mais sous aucun rapport nous ne pouvons penser que les délais s'étendissent jusqu'au moment nécessaire pour sa rentrée dans nos ports ou dans ceux d'Espagne.' This, my Lord, is a true and correct statement of what passed between T. and me. I thought it right and necessary to lay the whole before you; and now, for the acquittal of my conscience, I must say what followed. In an intricate case they might attempt, and most likely wish, to deceive; but here the known situation of affairs is the standard of their sincerity. They *do* wish for peace—they wish for it most ardently; but all their wishes avail nothing against the dreaded will and power of Bonaparte as to deciding the question. *He himself*, wishing for it from a just sense of his interests, will, nevertheless, rush to perdition rather than let it be said that he has shrunk before the power and threats of England. This imputation is what he is so anxious to do away, and he thinks it would be done away if England was less peremptory. All this is pitiful (as your Lordship has justly observed more than once); but when that is said, and the truth of it acknowledged, I must recur to the main point. What is the object in view for England? *Malta and Peace on honourable terms.* Who is the man you have to contend with? Bonaparte. Was he anything but Bonaparte, the present difficulty would not exist; but as he cannot be changed, and as he at present rules the Continent, if the horrors of war can be avoided by condescending to treat with him in a manner somewhat suitable to his temper, and with more apparent forbearance than you would with any old cabinet, is it not advisable to do it? Talleyrand expresses my meaning when he tells me confidentially, 'Je crois qu'il vous auroit fait présent de Malte si votre cabinet l'avoit traité avec plus d'égards.' I hope, my Lord, that you will receive with indulgence these free sentiments and expressions of a mind sincerely devoted to his Majesty's Government. I really think it my duty to lay them before you. The present respective situation of France and England is surely unparalleled in the annals of the two countries, the fate of Europe itself probably depending on the events of the next three months. Peace in view—peace wished for by the two Powers, the Ministers for Foreign Affairs, the Consul's brother, and the most marking men in France uniting their means to bring about that desirable blessing; the ground of a compromise seemingly agreed upon on both sides; and the pride and variable mind of the new Tamerlan the only obstacle to conclusion! Under such circumstances, how is it possible not to hope for peace yet, even if a first gun had already been fired? What would, however, render it more difficult would be a renewal of personal abuse of Bonaparte and scurrilous paragraphs against him in the English prints. What a serious misfortune that it should really be more or less in the power of the editor of a paper to mar the endeavours of two nations! I had this day a long conference with Fouché. I never knew a sounder understanding united to such strong nerves; he remains the same in his wish and expression for peace. He refuses at present to resume the Ministère de la Police *singly*, but that department may possibly be shortly united to the Ministère de l'Intérieur, in which case he would accept.

Friday morning.

Mr. Mandeville returned yesterday evening, and brought the intelligence of your Lordship's sailing from Calais. May Providence avert the impending calamities! I most sincerely thank you for the few lines you favoured me with. Such an approbation must at all times be an acceptable and flattering reward and encouragement for any services I may be able to render. If at your Lordship's recommendation they are thought worth the acceptance of the Government, I beg they may not be spared. I intend to remain here a few weeks longer, if possible, to see the last decided course things will take; and when I can be of no longer use here I shall proceed to some convenient place in Switzerland, from whence I shall have the honour of corresponding with your Lordship.

Sunday morning.

I shall join to this packet the 'Moniteur' of this day, by which you will see the proceedings of yesterday in the different constituted bodies. France will now be waiting for an act of aggression from England, and will of course make the most of it with the nation. Fouché gave me yesterday his opinion as to the kind of manifesto the English Government must and would produce, and of the course of conduct it would probably steer, just as an enlightened and liberal English character could have done. He is possibly mistaken in supposing that the English Cabinet may still make offers to this country, and I will not presume to hazard an opinion upon it. If I did, it would be to say that the articles of Lampedusa and Malta, such as they were presented in your ultimatum, or at least in that spirit, and the article relative to Otrante and Tarente, in the words of the redaction contained in my last letter, would meet with the concurrence of the Consul and decide immediate peace. It would be presumption, perhaps, to suppose that the Cabinet would in the presumed case honour me with any powers; and yet, unless provisional powers at least were sent me, so as to secure the Consul's assent and signature at once, we should remain *exactly where we are*: without powers, all I could do, all the able assistance I command here, would be of no avail on this point. After the message of yesterday, and considering the passive attitude France has taken, it appears to me impossible that overtures should now be made to England by this Government. Mr. Talbot intends setting out to-morrow (I mean Sunday). I shall take every opportunity of writing to your Lordship as long as any is left. I should presume that France will not be the first to cut the communication. Mr. Mandeville, who intends going on Monday or Tuesday, will be bearer of my next letter. I think I might receive a few from England under Perregaux's cover; he has no objection to it—I have asked him. Accept my apology for any incorrectness in this. I have not time to make a copy of it.

Lord Whitworth to Lord Hawkesbury.

London, May 20, 1803.

My Lord,—I have the honour to enclose to your Lordship an official note which I received from Monsieur de Talleyrand on the day of my departure from Paris, and my answer.

Note.

Le soussigné est chargé de faire connoître à Son Excellence Lord Whitworth, ambassadeur de Sa Majesté Britannique, que le Premier Consul ayant fait proposer dans la note du 14 de ce mois que l'île de Malte fût remise dans les mains d'une des trois puissances garantes, soit la Russie, l'Autriche ou la Prusse, il ne suffiroit pas, pour écarter cette proposition, d'arguer du refus que feroit Sa Majesté l'Empereur de Russie de ce dépôt, puisqu'il resterait à connoître les intentions de Leurs Majestés l'empereur d'Allemagne et le roi de Prusse. Que d'ailleurs l'assertion contenue dans la note de S. E. en date du 20 de ce mois, et qui est exprimée en ces termes : *par le refus de Sa Majesté l'Empereur de Russie de s'y prêter*, est entièrement contraire à la garantie que Sa Majesté impériale a formellement offerte sous la condition de quelques légers changements que le Premier Consul n'a fait aucune difficulté d'adopter et auxquels il est à sa connoissance que le ministère anglais s'est refusé, méditant sans doute alors l'étrange prétention de garder Malte. Que de plus cette assertion se trouve encore en opposition absolue avec les assurances que le Premier Consul a reçues de Pétersbourg depuis que le message de Sa Majesté Britannique y a été connu, et qui viennent de lui être renouvelées par une communication authentique que Monsieur le comte de Marcoff a donnée hier des intentions de sa cour. D'où il résulte qu'il est impossible de concilier la dernière transmission faite par Son Excellence Lord Whitworth avec la nouvelle confirmation qui vient d'être acquise des dispositions de Sa Majesté l'empereur de Russie, et qu'on ne peut se refuser à croire que Sa Majesté Britannique, mieux informée, sera elle-même empressée à faire donner à Son Excellence des instructions différentes de celles qu'elle a reçues et communiquées au nom de son Gouvernement.

Le soussigné saisit cette occasion de renouveler à Son Excellence Lord Whitworth l'assurance de sa haute considération.

(Signé)   CH. MAU. TALLEYRAND.

Paris, 22 Floréal, l'an XI.

Le soussigné a l'honneur d'accuser la réception de la note que le ministre des Relations Extérieures lui a envoyée en date d'aujourd'hui, et il ne manquera pas de la faire passer à sa cour. En attendant il prie le ministre des Relations Extérieures de vouloir bien lui envoyer les passeports qu'il lui a demandés.

Il saisit cette occasion de renouveler à Son Excellence l'assurance de sa haute considération.

(Signé)   WHITWORTH.

A Monsieur Talleyrand, Paris, ce 12 Mai 1803.

Mr. Talbot to M. de Talleyrand.

Paris, le 24 Mai 1803.

Le soussigné, secrétaire d'ambassade, etc., etc., rappelé par sa cour, doit avant son départ s'acquitter d'un devoir important et solennel—c'est celui d'exprimer à Son Excellence le ministre des Relations Extérieures l'étonnement et la douleur dont il a été saisi en apprenant l'ordre émané du Gouvernement de France pour la détention de tous les Anglois qui se trouvent aujourd'hui sur l'étendue de son territoire. Si c'est comme représaille que cette mesure doit être considérée, est-elle d'une nature reconnue parmi les nations de l'Europe? Elle offre un contraste si effrayant avec l'hospitalité protectrice que les Anglois voyageant en France y ont constamment éprouvée, qu'il est impossible de ne pas s'en promettre la révocation immédiate, et de ne pas l'attendre du sentiment de grandeur qui doit appartenir au Gouvernement de France. C'est ce sentiment que le soussigné invoque aujourd'hui auprès du ministre des Relations Extérieures—c'est le vœu de l'humanité—c'est le vœu profond du soussigné, qui, au moment de son départ et au nom de son Gouvernement, réclame avec confiance le rappel d'un ordre aussi alarmant.

M. de Talleyrand to Mr. Talbot.

Paris, May 24, 1803.

I duly received the letters you have done me the honour of writing of this day's date; but you will not conceive it extraordinary that, as it is not in my power to acknowledge that you any longer hold any public character or mission at Paris, I can return no answer to the representations they contain.

Mr. Mandeville to Lord Whitworth.

Calais, May 26, 1803.

My Lord,—When I had taken leave of your Lordship the Tuesday evening on the pier, I returned to the hotel with the intention of setting out directly for Paris; but I found that the groom who had been despatched by Mr. Talbot to your Lordship on Monday was too much fatigued to accompany me the same night, so that I was under the necessity of deferring my departure till the next day. Upon my arrival in Paris I lost no time in putting together the different papers belonging to the mission and in arranging my own private concerns, that I might be able to leave Paris with as little delay as possible. On the Monday I was ready to set out; but I waited till the evening through my wish to accompany Mr. Talbot, who had intended quitting Paris at that time. On that day the enclosed *arrêté* (which I procured at Boulogne) was submitted to the Senate and immediately adopted; but it has been executed with this difference, that instead of considering as prisoners of war those who are actually inrolled in the Militia it has included all the English between the age of eighteen and sixty (women excepted) who are now in France. Those who were in Paris received an order early in the same morning to present themselves at General Junot's, the Commandant de la Place, when each person received a number, and according to that number they were to be provided the next day with a pass to proceed to Fontainebleau, where they are to remain upon parole. Mr. Huber, who was included amongst the English, waited immediately upon M. de Talleyrand, where he received some faint hopes of being permitted to leave France; but he was informed at the same time that none other could hope for the like indulgence, and that even Lord Elgin would be considered as much a prisoner as any other individual of his nation who might happen to be now within the territory of the Republic. Mr. Talbot wrote to M. de Talleyrand with the view of obtaining some alleviation of the decree in his Lordship's favour. I left Paris that night and met with no interruption on the road. I arrived here yesterday; and your Lordship, I think, will not be less surprised than I was when Mr. Mengaud informed me that unless my passport was of a date posterior to that of the *arrêté* he could not allow me to leave Calais; that all the indulgence he should have it in his power to show me was that he would not exact of me to appear before the Commandant, but that he would himself receive my parole not to quit the walls of Calais; that if I chose I might send a courier to Paris, and that I might make use of one of his own. I this morning, however, wrote a note to him requesting a passport to return myself to Paris, upon my parole to go straight and immediately there without leaving the road, in order to acquaint Mr. Talbot, whom I shall most probably meet on his way here, with these circumstances, and then to adopt whatever measures he may think proper to take: mine would be to wait personally upon M. de Talleyrand to represent to him the stigma this extreme violation of the right of nations would throw upon the French Government in thus vexing three or four individuals without any possible benefit to themselves; to demand a free permission for those attached to the Embassy and in your Lordship's service to return to England; as also the liberation of the two packets which have been seized—the men imprisoned and the masters put upon parole—to convey the remainder of the mission to Dover. I have obtained the promise of my passport, and I shall set out on my return to Paris the moment I have it in my possession. I request your Lordship to offer my respects to the Duchess of Dorset, and to believe me to be, my Lord, your Lordship's most obedient and most faithful servant,

J. H. MANDEVILLE.

P.S.—I should add, my Lord, that Sir James Craufurd is at Calais and upon parole. Captain Hammond asked him on the Monday last, just before he sailed, if he would take his passage on board his vessel; he said that he would wait two or three days longer. One would very naturally be much at a loss to imagine what could prevent Sir James Craufurd, under the present circumstances, to refuse such an opportunity of returning to England. The arrival of a lady from Paris the next day explains the motive of his refusal, and brings consolation, I trust, to the love-sick prisoner. Quentin Craufurd is the only Englishman at Paris who has permission to remain there. Lord Yarmouth has just landed, and is now upon parole within the walls of Calais. The ship that brought him is seized and the crew made prisoners.

Mr. Talbot to Lord Hawkesbury.

Calais, May 27, 1803.

As I expect some difficulty in transmitting this letter to your Lordship I shall confine myself to a very few words. I quitted Paris on Tuesday night last. On the preceding day all Englishmen between the ages of eighteen and sixty were constituted prisoners of war. I was induced (which step I trust your Lordship will not disapprove) to address a note on the subject to M. de Talleyrand, a copy of which I have the honour to send enclosed, together with his answer, on the receipt of which I immediately ordered my post-horses and proceeded on my journey, and after some considerable interruptions reached Calais to-day. Mr. Mengaud refuses to suffer me to embark until he shall have received the orders of his Government, and has despatched a courier to Paris for that purpose. The two packet-boats which were first sent from Dover after the arrival of Lord Whitworth for the remainder of his Majesty's mission have been seized and the crews imprisoned, with the exception of the captains and mates. The last which arrived, under the command of Captain Hammond with a flag of truce, has been respected, and I hope to be able, with the permission of Mr. Mengaud, to forward this letter to your Lordship by his means. I have likewise the honour of enclosing to your Lordship a copy of the orders received by Mr. Mengaud with respect to the detention of his Majesty's subjects, and have the honour to be, with the highest respect, my Lord, your Lordship's most obedient and very humble servant,

J. TALBOT.

P.S.—Lord Elgin and Mr. Cockburn, H.M.'s Consul at Hamburgh, have not been able to obtain any exception in their favour with regard to this measure. The former is in a very precarious state of health, and if his detention be protracted to any length of time it may be attended with very dangerous consequences to his Lordship.

Le Grand-Juge, Ministre de la Justice, au Commissaire Général de Police à Calais.

Paris, le 2 Prairial, an XI de la Rép. franç.

Je vous transmets, citoyen commissaire, l'arrêté du Gouvernement relatif aux Anglais qui se trouvent actuellement en France. A l'instant de sa réception vous en donnerez connaissance à ceux qui sont dans votre arrondissement. Je vous observe que la mesure enveloppe sans distinction tout Anglais âgé de plus de dix-huit ans et de moins de soixante; et que nul prétexte, nulle exception ne peut l'y soustraire, attendu que, d'après les loix britanniques, il n'en est aucun qui soit excepté du service de la milice. Tous seront tenus, dans les vingt-quatre heures de la notification qui leur sera faite de votre ordre, de venir se constituer prisonniers de guerre près du commandant de la place dans les villes où il y en a, et près de l'officier de la gendarmerie dans les autres villes. Et s'il n'y a ni commandant de place ni officier de gendarmerie dans le lieu où l'Anglais réside, il se constituera prisonnier près du commandant de place ou de l'officier de gendarmerie de la ville la plus voisine. A défaut d'avoir rempli ces obligations, ils ne pourront être admis à donner leur parole. Les Anglais qui, quoiqu'ils se fussent constitués prisonniers dans les vingt-quatre heures, seront jugés n'être point admissibles à être retenus sur leur parole, ainsi que ceux qui ne seraient pas venus dans le délai fixé pour se constituer prisonniers, seront conduits dans un point central de la division qui sera désigné par le ministre de la guerre. A l'égard de ceux qui seront admis à demeurer prisonniers sur leur parole, s'ils habitent une ville, ils y resteront; s'ils habitent une commune rurale, ils viendront habiter la petite ville la plus voisine. Quant à Paris et à Versailles, les Anglais qui pourront être admis à donner leur parole seront envoyés par le commandant de la division à Fontainebleau. Je vous charge, citoyen commissaire, de me rendre compte, dans le plus bref délai, de l'exécution de ces mesures et de m'en faire connaître le résultat. Je vous salue, (Signé) REGNIER.

EXTRAIT DES REGISTRES DE DÉLIBÉRATIONS DU GOUVERNEMENT DE LA RÉPUBLIQUE.

St. Cloud, le 2 Prairial, an XI de la République.

LE GOUVERNEMENT DE LA RÉPUBLIQUE.

Arrêté.

Tous les Anglais enrôlés dans la milice et âgés de dix-huit ans au moins et de soixante au plus, ou tenant commission de S. M. Britannique, qui sont actuellement en France, seront immédiatement constitués prisonniers de guerre, pour répondre des citoyens de la République qui auraient été arrêtés et faits prisonniers par des bâtimens ou sujets de Sa Majesté Britannique avant la déclaration de guerre. Les ministres sont chargés, chacun en ce qui le concerne, de l'exécution du présent arrêté.

Le Premier Consul. Signé BONAPARTE. Par le Premier Consul.

Le Secrétaire d'Etat. Signé HUGUES B. MARET. Pour Copie Conforme.

Le Grand-Juge, Ministre de la Justice. Signé REGNIER.

LORD WHITWORTH TO LORD HAWKESBURY.

London, May 29, 1803.

I have the honour to enclose your Lordship a correct copy of the note which I presented to the French Government on the eleventh instant, and by which your Lordship will perceive that the following words, '*Et cette proposition ayant été jugée impraticable par le refus de Sa Majesté l'empereur de Russie de s'y prêter et en même tems au-dessous des justes prétentions de Sa Majesté*, have been omitted in the copy which was transmitted the same day to your Lordship's office. This clerical error must be attributed to the multiplicity of business which my secretary had upon his hands at the moment of my departure from Paris.

LORD HAWKESBURY TO M. DE TALLEYRAND.

Downing Street, May 29, 1803.

Sir,— His Majesty's Government have just received the information that all British subjects who are between eighteen and sixty years of age and who happened to be upon the territory of the French Republic have been made prisoners of war by order of the French Government, and that even the Secretary of his Majesty's Embassy has been comprehended in the order and is now detained at Calais. His Majesty cannot refrain from expressing his surprise and astonishment at this extraordinary and unexampled proceeding, it being wholly unusual in the practice of the nations of Europe, though in a state of actual hostility, to treat the persons of individuals in civil situations as if they were amenable to the laws of war. If, however, there could be any doubt upon this subject, the claim advanced by General Andréossy on May 6 (a copy of which and of my answer I enclose), that all French citizens might be permitted to embark for France without molestation, and the acquiescence in that claim by his Majesty's Government, give his Majesty the right to demand an entire reciprocity with regard to his own subjects who may happen to be in France in the present conjuncture. His Majesty expects that the French Government will give immediate orders for the liberation of all British subjects now detained in France, and that, conformably to the example which his Majesty has afforded, they may be allowed to quit the territories without molestation. If his Majesty's expectations in this respect should unfortunately be disappointed, he would feel himself justified in retaliating upon the persons and property of all the French citizens who may be within his power. It would be with the greatest reluctance that his Majesty would have recourse to such measures of severity against individuals; but he entertains no doubt that his motives in this respect would be justly appreciated throughout Europe, and that these harsh and unusual proceedings would be ascribed exclusively to the system and conduct of the Government of France.

Note.

Paris, le 11 Mai 1803.

Le soussigné, ambassadeur extraordinaire et plénipotentiaire de S.M. Britannique près la République française, ayant transmis à sa cour la proposition qui lui a été faite par le ministre des Relations Extérieures le 4 du courant, et cette proposition ayant été jugée impraticable par le refus de S.M. l'empereur de Russie de s'y prêter et en même tems au-dessous des justes prétentions de Sa Majesté, vient de recevoir l'ordre de remettre à Son Excellence le projet de convention ci-joint, fondé sur la seule base que S.M. croit, dans les circonstances actuelles, susceptible d'un arrangement définitif et amical. Le ministre des Relations Extérieures ne manquera pas d'observer jusqu'à quel point Sa Majesté a cherché de concilier la sécurité de ses intérêts avec la dignité du Premier Consul. Le soussigné se flatte que le Premier Consul, rendant justice à ces sentimens, adoptera, d'accord avec Sa Majesté, un moyen aussi propre à rendre une tranquillité permanente aux deux nations et à l'Europe.

Le soussigné saisit cette occasion de renouveler à S.E. l'assurance de sa très-haute considération.

Mr. Talbot to Lord Whitworth.

Calais, Monday, May 30, 1803.

My dear Lord,—I avail myself of the opportunity which is afforded me by a French flag of truce of writing a few lines to your Lordship, and of thanking you for the letter which you had the goodness to write to me from Dover. On my arrival here I had the honour to address a few lines to Lord Hawkesbury, but from the nature of my situation I was under the necessity of doing it in great haste, and of confining myself to a very few lines. On my road from Paris I was twice arrested by the gendarmerie (who are stationed on all the roads to a considerable distance)—first at St. Denis, where I was detained from one o'clock in the morning till seven, whilst a soldier was despatched to the Grand Juge with a copy of my passports. The same soldier conducted Mr. Charles Sturt as a prisoner, whom, he informed me on his return, he had deposited in the Temple. At two posts further I was again detained six hours. As I was quitting Boulogne I met Mr. Mandeville, who was returning to Paris, having been refused permission to embark here. I have heard nothing of him since further than that he was met on the way by Doctor Maclaurin and Mr. Hodgson, who arrived here yesterday evening. A similar refusal has been notified to me by Mr. Mengaud, and I am now waiting the answer to a despatch which he has written to Paris on the subject. The captain of a packet-boat which arrived here this morning from Dover under a flag of truce was merely suffered to land and deliver to Mr. Mengaud the letters with which he was charged. The only satisfactory article of news that I have to communicate is, that the parcel containing the Duchess's dress for the King's birthday is embarked, and will leave Calais this evening. Cole informed me on leaving Paris that it would require ten days from that time (Tuesday last) for the furniture, etc., to be packed up.

I beg your Lordship will present my best respects to the Duchess.

Mr. Mandeville to Lord Whitworth.

Calais, June 4, 1803.

The last letter that I had the honour to address to your Lordship from this place ended, I believe, by my saying that I had succeeded in obtaining permission to return to Paris for the purpose stated in that letter. I did not, however, receive my passport that evening till after the gates of the town were shut, and my departure was thus deferred till morning. I set out early, and reached Paris the next day (Saturday) in the evening; and that no time might be lost—for I was well aware that I should not have an opportunity of seeing M. de Talleyrand on the Sunday, as he would be the greater part of the day at St. Cloud—I took a cabriolet and went directly to Meudon to acquaint him with the circumstance of the remainder of the Embassy being comprised in the *arrêté* that had lately come out, and that I had been myself arrested at Calais. It was late when I got there—past twelve; but he was at home, and received me. After many inquiries had been made about your Lordship—where I had left you, and what was the object of my journey to Paris—I put into his hand the enclosed letter (I.), which I had prepared in the event of my not seeing him, mentioning the object and motive of my journey, and the unseasonable visit I was then making him. When M. de Talleyrand had read it he turned to me and said that what had been done in regard to my arrestation was throughout the whole an error; that it was an affair of the police and the marine; that he should see the First Consul the next day at St. Cloud, when he would report to him the substance of my letter, and that he was sure he would be very sorry for what had happened; and that he did not doubt but orders would be immediately given for the free return into their native country of every person attached to the Embassy. I took that opportunity of pressing him on the subject of the two packet-boats that were seized at Calais, and which were waiting there for the purpose of taking the rest of the mission to England, and that he would allow me to hope I should be the bearer of an order for their release, as well as for that of the masters and crews, who had been made prisoners of war, for they in this instance belonged wholly and entirely to the Embassy. His answer was, 'Certainly they do, and all that belongs to the Embassy is sacred.' After some little conversation, in which he seemed very desirous to learn if I had or if I was likely to have any communication to make from your Lordship, I retired thanking him for the reception he had given me. Very late on the Sunday night I received the enclosed note (No. II.) from M. de Talleyrand, which, as I expected would be, was of the same tenor as his language to me of the preceding evening; but I certainly had no reason to expect the extraordinary *empressement* of sending it, or rather, perhaps, dating it, from St. Cloud. I conceived the hope now that there was nothing left for me to do but to call for my passport the next day, and return the next day to Calais; and for this purpose I went to the Bureau des Relations Extérieures on the Monday morning, and was directed to send at five in the afternoon of the same day, and that it would be ready for me. It was delivered at that time, and with it one for Mr. Talbot (which I had not asked for, supposing it in no shape necessary after the letter I had received the day before), accompanied by the note (III.) which I have the honour to enclose to your Lordship. I think, my Lord, you will imagine the surprise I felt at reading this note. I was greatly embarrassed—not in what I had to do: there was but one thing: to stay till all conditions were taken off, which I could not, and of which M. de Talleyrand was perfectly aware I had no authority to subscribe to—but in the reply I was called upon to make to so extraordinary a proposition. I immediately took the letter to Lord Elgin, whom from my arrival I had always consulted, begging his assistance and advice, which I now so much stood in need of that I should not be justified in acting without it. The following day the note (IV.) was sent on my part to M. de Talleyrand, who making wait the servant who carried it, returned me the answer (V.), which I likewise enclose to your Lordship. Lord Elgin being of opinion that I ought not to go without taking with me the passports for Mr. Hodgson and Dr. Maclaurin, who had directed me to mention them in my note to the Minister, I remained in Paris until they were delivered to me, and in the night of Wednesday I set out for this place, where I arrived in time to see that these precautions had been unnecessary, for the vessel which Mr. Talbot and those gentlemen were on board was half-way between Dover and Calais as I entered the walls of the latter place. I made application directly to Mr. Mengaud and the Commissaire de Marine for any sort of vessel they might choose to give me, and to be allowed to sail immediately, but without success; the former proffering me all the means in his power to that effect, which insured to me every difficulty and prevention on the part of the latter. I am very happy to see, however, by his letter to me of this morning (VI.) that I may still hope that my application to M. de Talleyrand on the subject of the detention of the two packet-boats at this place is likely to be attended with success. I trust, my Lord, that the line of conduct which I have adopted and pursued from the moment of my arrestation here may meet with your Lordship's approbation, and that the zeal which actuates me always may make up for whatever deficiency I may show in the means I employ to obtain it.

No. I.

M. Mandeville, secrétaire attaché à l'ambassade d'Angleterre, parti de Paris en cette qualité lundi dernier, a été arrêté à Calais par ordre du Gouvernement de France et placé dans la classe de l'arrestation générale des Anglais qui se trouvent en France. Convaincu que cette arrestation ne peut être que l'effet d'une méprise du commissaire général à Calais, il en a obtenu la permission de venir sur sa parole en rendre compte à Son Excellence Monsieur de Talleyrand.

Il doit l'informer aussi que les deux vaisseaux destinés à l'embarquement de la légation ont été saisis et leurs équipages mis en prison, à l'exception des capitaines qui sont prisonniers sur parole. M. Mandeville prie Son Excellence de l'instruire de ce qu'il a à faire en conséquence de cet événement.

Paris, ce 28 Mai 1803.

No. II.

A St. Cloud, le 9 Prairial, an XI.
29 Mai 1803.

C'est par erreur, Monsieur, que vous vous êtes trouvé compris dans la mesure de représailles que le Gouvernement françois a cru devoir prendre relativement à vos compatriotes. Le Premier Consul a donné des ordres pour que vous, Monsieur, Monsieur Talbot et les personnes qui appartiennent à la légation anglaise puissent retourner librement dans leur pays. Je suis personnellement fâché des retards et des contrariétés que vous avez éprouvés à cet égard.

(Signé)   CH. M. TALLEYRAND.

A M. Mandeville.

No. III.

Le ministre des Relations Extérieures remet à Monsieur Mandeville les passeports qu'il lui a demandés pour Monsieur Talbot et pour lui, sous la condition expresse que le citoyen

Lemoyne, secrétaire de la commission pour l'échange des prisonniers, ainsi que de tout autre François attaché à la commission ou à la légation, seront libres de repasser en France et recevront du Gouvernement anglois les passeports nécessaires à cet effet.

      (Signé)   Ch. M. Talleyrand.

 A M. Mandeville.
Paris, ce 10 Prairial, an XI. 30 Mai 1803.

No. IV.

 Monsieur Mandeville a l'honneur d'accuser la réception de la lettre que Son Excellence le ministre des Relations Extérieures lui a fait l'honneur de lui écrire en date d'hier, avec les deux passeports qui l'accompagnent. Monsieur Mandeville voit avec une peine extrême la condition que Monsieur le ministre attache à l'emploi de ces passeports. Il n'a aucune connoissance de la détention d'individus françois quelconques en Angleterre à l'occasion de la rupture entre les deux pays, mais il ne feroit qu'induire en erreur s'il hésitoit à déclarer qu'il n'est point autorisé par sa situation de secrétaire ni de traiter ni de contracter aucun engagement au nom de son Gouvernement. Il ose donc espérer, d'après l'assurance que Son Excellence a bien voulu lui adresser dimanche de St. Cloud, que Monsieur Talbot, secrétaire d'ambassade, et les personnes qui appartiennent à la légation anglaise, pourront retourner librement dans leur pays. Il doit remarquer en même tems à Son Excellence qu'outre Monsieur Talbot il y a encore en France Monsieur Hodgson, aumônier, et Monsieur Maclaurin, médecin, tous les deux membres de l'ambassade.

 A Monsieur de Talleyrand.
  Paris, ce 31 Mai 1803.

No. V.

Paris, ce 11 Prairial, an XI.
31 Mai 1803.

La condition, Monsieur, sous laquelle des passeports vous ont été donnés ne peut importer de votre part aucun engagement. C'est à votre Gouvernement, qui, informé par vous, à votre arrivée à Londres, de la condition que le Gouvernement de la République a attachée à vos passeports, de remplir la condition imposée par le droit des gens, et d'autoriser le retour du citoyen Lemoyne et autres François qui pourroient être attachés à la légation de la République française. J'ai l'honneur de vous saluer.

(Signé) C. M. TALLEYRAND.

A M. Mandeville.

No. VI.

Le Commissaire de Marine à Monsieur Mandeville.

Calais, le 15 Prairial, an XI.
4 Juin 1803.

Monsieur Pigaud vient de me remettre, Monsieur, la lettre que vous m'avez fait l'honneur de m'écrire. Je regrette beaucoup de ne pouvoir adhérer à la demande que vous me faites d'un bâtiment exprès pour vous transporter en Angleterre, le ministre de la Marine ne m'ayant autorisé par le courrier de ce jour qu'à l'expédition des paquebots de malle françois, et c'est d'après une nouvelle décision du Premier Consul. Je ne peux que vous engager à profiter du premier qui s'expédiera, peut-être demain ou au plus tard après-demain, peut-être même pourrez-vous profiter d'un des bâtimens anglois qui sont en ce port, car je pense que je recevrai très-incessamment l'ordre de les rendre. Je suis, Monsieur, avec une haute considération, votre serviteur.

(Signé) FRANCY.

M. DE TALLEYRAND TO LORD HAWKESBURY.

Paris, le 20 Prairial, an XI.

Je me suis empressé de mettre sous les yeux du Premier Consul la lettre en date du 19 Prairial que vous m'avez fait l'honneur de m'écrire. Le Gouvernement français a constitué prisonniers de guerre tous les individus anglais voyageant sur le continent pour des affaires de commerce ou tous autres objets, parce que Sa Majesté fait constituer prisonniers tous les individus français qui sont trouvés sur mer voyageant pour leur commerce ou pour d'autres objets. Ni les uns ni les autres n'ont les armes à la main, et le Premier Consul reconnaît la justice de ce qui est pratiqué entre les puissances du continent, qui ne considèrent comme prisonniers de guerre que les hommes pris les armes à la main ; mais l'Angleterre, en suivant d'autres principes, met la France dans la nécessité d'agir comme elle, et de suivre sur le continent les mêmes règles qu'elle veut établir sur la mer. Si le Gouvernement britannique veut ne plus considérer comme prisonniers tous les individus arrêtés sur des bâtiments de commerce non armés, le Premier Consul est prêt à ne regarder pareillement comme prisonniers et à ne retenir pour tels que les individus qui auraient été saisis les armes à la main.

Recevez, milord, l'assurance de ma plus haute considération.

CH. MAU. TALLEYRAND.

M. DE TALLEYRAND TO LORD HAWKESBURY.

Paris, le 21 Prairial, an XI.

Milord,—Après un léger engagement avec les troupes de Sa Majesté Britannique, l'armée française occupe le pays d'Hanovre. Le Premier Consul, n'ayant eu en vue que d'obtenir des gages pour l'évacuation de Malte et de travailler à accomplir l'exécution du traité d'Amiens, n'a point voulu faire éprouver toutes les rigueurs de la guerre aux sujets de Sa Majesté Britannique. Cependant le Premier Consul ne peut ratifier la convention conclue entre l'armée française et celle de Sa Majesté, dont j'ai l'honneur de joindre ici copie, qu'autant qu'elle sera pareillement ratifiée par Sa Majesté Britannique, et dans ce cas le Premier Consul me charge expressément de déclarer qu'il est dans son intention que l'armée du roi d'Angleterre en Hanovre soit d'abord échangée contre tous les matelots ou soldats que les vaisseaux de Sa Majesté ont fait ou sont dans le cas de faire prisonniers. Le Premier Consul verrait avec peine que Sa Majesté Britannique, en refusant de ratifier ladite convention, obligeât le Gouvernement français à traiter le pays d'Hanovre avec toute la rigueur de la guerre et comme un pays qui, livré à lui-même, abandonné par son souverain, se serait trouvé conquis sans capitulation et laissé à la discrétion de la puissance occupante.

J'attendrai avec empressement, milord, que vous me fassiez connaître, à cet égard, les intentions de Sa Majesté Britannique.

Recevez, milord, l'assurance de ma plus haute considération.

Ch. Mau. Talleyrand.

Lord Hawkesbury to M. de Talleyrand.

Downing Street, June 13, 1803.

Sir,—I have the honour to acknowledge the receipt of your letters of the 9th and 10th inst. by the messenger Cormon. I shall lose no time in laying them before the King; and I will transmit to you such answers as his Majesty may be pleased to direct me to return to them, by one of his Majesty's messengers, whom I will despatch to Paris with as little delay as may be possible. I desire you to accept the assurances of the high consideration with which I have the honour, etc.

Lord Hawkesbury to M. de Talleyrand.

Downing Street, June 15, 1803.

Sir,—I have laid before the King your letter of the 10th inst. I am commanded by his Majesty to inform you that, as he has always considered his character of Elector of Hanover as distinct from his character of King of the United Kingdom of Great Britain and Ireland, he never can consent to acquiesce in any proceeding by which he shall sanction the idea that he is liable in justice to be attacked in the one capacity for the line of conduct which he may have felt it to be his duty to adopt in the other. This principle is not now advanced for the first time. It has been recognised by most of the Powers of Europe, and by none more particularly than by the French Government, who in the year 1795, in consequence of his Majesty having acceded to the Treaty of Basle, acknowledged the neutrality of his Majesty in his capacity of Elector of Hanover, at a time when they were engaged in a war with him as King of Great Britain. It has been further confirmed by the conduct of his Majesty on the occasion of the Treaty of Lunéville, and by the arrangements which have lately taken place relative to the German Indemnities, and to the constitution of the Empire—arrangements which must have been intended to provide for the independence of the Empire; which have been solemnly guaranteed by some of the principal Powers of Europe, but to which his Majesty, as King of Great Britain, was no party. Under these circumstances his Majesty has determined, in his character of Elector of Hanover, to appeal to the Empire and those Powers of Europe who have guaranteed the Germanic Constitution, and thereby his rights and possessions as a prince of that Empire. Until his Majesty shall be informed of their sentiments, he has commanded me to say that, in his character of Elector of Hanover, he will scrupulously abstain from doing any act which can be considered as being in contravention to the stipulations contained in the convention that was concluded on June 3 between the deputies appointed by the Regency of Hanover and the French Government.

Lord Hawkesbury to M. de Talleyrand.

Downing Street, June 15, 1803.

Sir,—I have laid before the King your letter of the 19th inst., and he has commanded me to return to it the following answer. His Majesty cannot sufficiently express his surprise at the new and extraordinary demands advanced by the French Government; demands which are in direct contravention of all the known and admitted law of nations—of that law upon which France, in common with every other Power in Europe, has consented to act down to the present period. Notwithstanding that by the strict rule of the law of nations, considered independently of such modifications as it has received from convention or usage, all the subjects of the hostile state, whether in arms or not, are just objects of the rights of war, yet the practice of states has agreed in showing an indulgence to each other's subjects who were resident in the territories of the other party before it became belligerent, under the expectation and faith of that forbearance which general usage has bound their Governments mutually to allow. But the same general usage has invariably admitted the exercise of the right of belligerents to detain and make prisoners the subjects of each other *who are employed upon the seas, and who are not merely passing thereon;* no faith of any Government being pledged to them, and it being perfectly understood in consequence of universal usage that they were exposed to the casualties of an intervening war. The maritime hostilities of all European states have been carried on in conformity to this principle; the hostilities of France just as much as those of any other country. His Majesty is therefore acting upon the common law of Europe when he detains the subjects of the enemy so taken.

He is equally acting upon the same common law when he re-claims his own subjects who were resident in France at the time when the two countries were at peace; and to demand that he should give up his prisoners, whom he lawfully detains, in order to purchase the restitution of his own subjects, who are detained contrary to the practice of all civilised nations and to the faith of the French Government itself, is to demand a surrender of those rights which the law of nations has hitherto held inviolate, and a submission to an unexampled outrage upon the universal principles and practice of that law.

Lord Whitworth to Lord Hawkesbury.

Knole, Aug. 14, 1803.

Mr. Huber has expressed to me his regret at not having succeeded in rendering his services acceptable to your Lordship. Your Lordship will permit me to repeat that they were highly useful to me, although not successfully exerted; and indeed so much so, that had I remained longer at Paris I should have undoubtedly recommended him to your Lordship for some remuneration on that account. Since my return he has been exposed to much personal inconvenience, and incurred much expense on account of those services; and I must confess to your Lordship that if no indemnification is to be made to him by Government, either in money or in employment, I shall conceive myself bound at least to reimburse him, if he will accept it from me, not only such expenses, but also that which he has been put to by his forced journey from Paris hither. The Duchess desires her kind remembrance to your Lordship and Lady Hawkesbury, to whom I beg leave to add my respects.

Lady Elgin to Lord Hawkesbury.

Paris, Dec. 3, 1803.

It would be superfluous to trouble your Lordship with details on the subject of Lord Elgin's detention, or of the measures that have been in vain tried to obtain his release. But an event has now taken place which induces me to address your Lordship without losing a moment's time. In consequence of accounts having reached this Government that General Boyer had been arrested and sent into confinement in Scotland, the First Consul, by way of reprisal, gave orders that Lord Elgin, who had been allowed to pass the winter at Pau, should likewise be arrested and confined in the Château of Lourdes, a place in the most unhealthy situation, on the borders of the Pyrenean Mountains, a few leagues from Barèges. I had left him a month ago, and came here with the hopes of going home for a few weeks to see my parents and my children. Some delay in obtaining my passport made me renounce my journey, and I was just again setting out to join Lord Elgin when this cruel and unexpected event was announced to me. I immediately applied to M. de Talleyrand; and in consequence of his representations the First Consul has consented that Lord Elgin shall be released and allowed to return to England on condition that General Boyer shall be set at liberty and permitted to return to France. That is to say, that one shall be *exchanged* for the other. I cannot think it necessary, my Lord, to excite your interest for us on this occasion by talking to you of Lord Elgin's bad health, and consequently the risk he runs in his present confinement. The dreadful anxiety of my mind in my present situation would altogether overwhelm me did not the hopes of the result of my application to you bear me up. Lord Elgin's release now altogether depends on his Majesty's giving his consent to this exchange; there seems no hope of an end to his sufferings or to mine if it should be refused. But I am confident that our present situation will excite his Majesty's compassion, and I am sure that your Lordship's support will not be wanting to second my wishes. I send my courier by Rotterdam; he is to be allowed to return by Morlaix. I beg most sincerely that he may be sent off with an answer as soon as possible. May I indulge the hopes that you are to announce the speedy return of General Boyer to France with your authority to be exchanged for Lord Elgin? The sincerest sentiments of gratitude will ever accompany the lasting obligation you will thus confer on me.

I enclose a copy of Lord Elgin's *arrestation*.

LORD WHITWORTH TO LORD HAWKESBURY.

Friday morn.

My dear Lord,—I beg leave to enclose to your Lordship a letter which I have received from Mr. Huber. Although I place much greater confidence in the vigorous measures which are now carrying into effect than any diplomatic exertions, yet I cannot but think that such a correspondence as Mr. Huber might establish would be highly interesting.

Paris, le 13 Août 1803.

Il est vrai que la cour d'Espagne a refusé de fournir les secours que la France demandait; mais aussi celle-ci vient de faire demander à la cour de Madrid une réponse catégorique en quinze jours—savoir, si elle veut fournir les secours stipulés par le traité d'alliance, ou bien, comme un équivalent, payer à la France quatre-vingts millions de livres par an. De bonne part j'ai entendu que l'Espagne ne nie point l'obligation qui lui est imposée par le traité, mais qu'elle prétend que le traité lui donne le droit d'être informée au préalable des causes de la guerre et d'épuiser tous les moyens de conciliation. Il n'est point douteux que cet état de choses nous donne le tems qui nous manquoit; mais quand je me rappelle le passé, je ne compte pas plus sur la fermeté de l'Espagne que je n'attache de prix à son alliance. En attendant M. Talleyrand, *à peine arrivé, m'a tout de suite interpellé et demandé la réponse.* Je lui ai repondu *évasivement* et sans le désabuser. J'ai expédié un *courrier,* et vous pouvez *compter que je tâcherai de gagner le plus de tems qu'il me sera possible.* De votre côté tâchez d'obtenir des réponses bien claires. Je vous le répète, les secours de l'Angleterre me semblent trop conditionnels; et si l'on ne vous fournit pas ce qui est indispensable pour notre propre armée, ils sont insuffisans.

Lord Hawkesbury to Lady Elgin.

Downing Street, Dec. 23, 1803.

I have received the honour of your Ladyship's letter, which I lost no time in laying before his Majesty. It would have given his Majesty the most sincere satisfaction to have contributed to the release of Lord Elgin by allowing his exchange for General Boyer; but a sense of duty renders it impossible for him in any way to admit or sanction the principle of exchanging persons made prisoners according to the acknowledged law of war against any of his own subjects who have been detained in France, in violation of the law of nations, and of the pledged faith of the French Government. The account of the imprisonment of General Boyer was wholly without foundation: that officer has never been in confinement, but has been considered merely as a prisoner of war on parole, and is at present residing at Chesterfield in the enjoyment of as much liberty as is ever accorded to prisoners in similar situations. I can assure your Ladyship that it is with very deep regret that I find myself unable to render you the assistance you desire. I should have felt the greatest pleasure in contributing by any practicable means to Lord Elgin's release, and to the deliverance of your Ladyship and him from the very unpleasant situation in which you have been placed by the arbitrary proceedings of the French Government.

INDEX.

ABBEVILLE, a town in the north of France, 262, 265

Aboukir, the ancient Canopus. Nelson destroyed the French fleet there August 1, 1798. Bonaparte vanquished the Turks July 24, 1799. Abercromby fought the battle of Canopus and took Aboukir March 7, 1801. 79

Addington (Henry, Viscount Sidmouth), 1755–1844. Speaker 1789, prime minister 1801–1804. 87

Alexandria in Egypt, in the occupation of the French from 1798 to 1801. 16, 50, 61, 62, 72, 78, 79, 93

Algiers. No serious attempt was made to put down the piracy of these tribes till the French expedition of 1830. 55, 56, 57, 72, 81, 102, 144

Almeida, Chevalier d', minister of foreign affairs and of war in Portugal. A quarrel having arisen between him and Lannes, minister of France at Lisbon, Napoleon recalled Lannes and ordered the court of Lisbon to dismiss Almeida, August 18, 1802. Lannes was, however, sent back again, January 12, 1803. 56

Alsop, Mr, 110

America, President of (Thomas Jefferson), 1743–1826. President, 1801–1809. 87

Amiens, Treaty of, between England on one side, and France, Holland, and Spain on the other, signed March 27, 1802. 10, 54, 61, 62, 65, 72, 73, 81, 82, 84, 93, 94, 97, 107, 113, 115, 121, 123, 124, 127, 128, 146, 149, 154, 159, 162, 164, 165, 166, 168, 170, 185, 187, 189, 196, 222, 243, 250, 251, 252, 253, 258, 261, 289

Ancona, a port on the east coast of Italy, 17

Andréossy (Antoine François, comte), 1761–1828. Under the Empire ambassador in London, Vienna, and Constantinople. 10, 14, 16, 62, 64, 83, 93, 95, 99, 101, 120, 121, 125, 129, 130, 135, 140, 141, 144, 148, 151, 152, 153, 175, 195, 196, 201, 230, 241, 242, 250, 263, 264, 265, 266, 267, 279

Anduaga, Chevalier, Portuguese minister in London, 174

Antwerp on the Scheldt. The French took it in 1792 and 1794. Napoleon wished to make it a great war-port opposite the Thames. 138

Arbuthnot (Mr. Charles), English minister at Stockholm, 77

Arras, Bishop of, 79

Artois, Comte d', born at Versailles October 9, 1757; died at Goritz November 6, 1836. Married Maria Theresa of Savoy 1773; emigrated 1789; lived in England after 1795; succeeded to the throne of France as Charles X. 1824; abdicated August 2, 1830. 38, 39

Azzara (Don Joseph Nicolas, chevalier de), 1731–1804. Ambassador at Rome, and afterwards at Paris; distinguished in letters and arts. 25, 41, 104, 116, 174

BADEN, Margrave of (Karl Ludwig), 1755–1801. The daughter here mentioned was Wilhelmine Louise, born September 10,

BAD

1788, who married on June 19, 1804, Ludwig II., the Grand-Duke of Hesse Darmstadt. Her two sisters had married Alexander I. of Russia and Gustavus IV. of Sweden. 31

Badini, conductor of the 'Argus' newspaper, 96

Bâle, Treaty of, signed 1795 between Prussia and France. .290

Barbasaude, General, commanding the garrison at Calais, 11

Barèges, in the district of Bigorre, 293

Barthélemy (François, marquis de) 1747–1830. Diplomatist; nephew of Abbé Barthélemy; negotiated the treaties of Bâle in 1792; transported, but returned to France after 18 Brumaire; senator in 1800; attached to the Emperor, but left him in 1814 and supported the Restoration. 23

Basilico, Foreign Office messenger, 79, 263, 264

Batavian Republic, the name given to the United Provinces from the flight of the Stadtholder William IV. in May 1795 to the accession of Louis Bonaparte in June 5, 1806, 7, 8, 226

Bavaria, Elector of (Maximilian I. Joseph), 1756–1825. Succeeded as Elector February 16, 1799; became King of Bavaria December 26, 1805. 45, 75

Bayonne, a town in France on the Adour, near the frontier of Spain, 144

Beauvais, episcopal city in the north of France, 11

Bedford, John, 6th duke of, 1766–1839. Lord-Lieutenant of Ireland 1806–1807. 223

Berlin, the capital of Prussia, 41

Bernadotte (Jean Baptiste Jules), 1764–1844. King of Sweden under the title of Charles John XIV.; married Mdlle. Clang, sister-in-law of Joseph Bonaparte. He left Napoleon in 1812; became king in 1816, having been elected as Crown Prince in 1810. 41, 174

Berthier (Alexandre), 1753–1815. Prince of Wagram and of Neufchatel; duc de Valengin; served in America with La-

BOY

fayette; chief of Bonaparte's staff in Italy; minister of war after Brumaire 18; deserted Napoleon at last; thrown out of a window at Bamberg. 133

Beurnonville (Pierre de Ruel marquis de), 1752–1821. Fought at Valmy and Jemappes. He was now ambassador at Madrid. He became marshal of France in 1816. 41, 104

Bickerton, Sir Richard, English admiral, 72

Bidon, Rear-Admiral, 72

Blanchot, M., 154, 155

Bonaparte (Joseph), 1768–1844. Elder brother of Napoleon; King of Naples 1806; of Spain 1808; lived in America, and in England, 1832–1837; died at Florence. 22, 34, 100, 107, 132, 157, 166, 169, 173, 176, 178, 180, 184, 190, 194, 200, 201, 210, 211, 214, 228, 229, 230, 233, 236, 237, 238, 241, 242, 244, 246, 263, 265, 266

Bonaparte (Lucien, Prince of Canino, younger brother of Napoleon), 1775–1840. Disgraced after 1801 on account of his marriage; assisted his brother in 1815; died at Viterbo. 22, 77, 100

Bonaparte (Louis), 1778–1846. Married Hortense Beauharnais in 1802. King of Holland, May 24, 1806, abdicated July 1, 1810; separated from his wife 1815 (father of Napoleon III.). 22, 71

Bordeaux, capital of Guienne; became French in 1453. 49

Boulogne, French port in the English Channel, 12, 136, 179, 274

Bourmont (Louis Auguste Victor, Comte de Ghaisne de) 1773–1846. One of the heads of insurrection in La Vendée in 1799. Napoleon offered him terms, but he refused, and was imprisoned in the Temple and in Besançon. He became a marshal in 1830. 64

Boyer, General (Pierre François Xavier, baron), 1772–1851. Aide-de-camp to Kellerman; served Napoleon throughout his career; after 1815 retired to Egypt. 293, 294, 295

BRA

Bradano or Brandano, a river of South Italy flowing into the Gulf of Tarentum, 243
Breda, a town in North Brabant, 144
Brest, a seaport on the west coast of France, 34, 44, 55, 61, 137, 138, 144
Breteuil, on the Noye, a town on the road between Paris and Calais, 248
Brindisium (Brindisi), a seaport in the Terra d'Otranto, 124
Brussels, 72
Bussy, Commander de, 20

CADOUDAL, Georges, 1771-1804. Supported the Royalist cause in Brittany and La Vendeé. He was son of a peasant farmer near Auray. He twice took refuge in England. 64, 65, 79, 81
Calais (36 hours from Paris), 15, 114, 179, 208, 238, 240.
Cambacérès (Jean Jacques Régis de), 1753-1824. Member of the Convention; a trusted counsellor of Napoleon; second Consul; took great part in the Code Civil; became Duke of Parma. 21, 26
Candia, or Crete, Venetian from 1204 to 1669. Then taken by the Turks. It belonged to the Pacha of Egypt from 1833 to 1841. 166, 169
Cape of Good Hope discovered by Vasco de Gama in 1497. Colonised by the Dutch in 1652; taken by the English in 1795 and 1806; secured to England by the Treaty of Vienna. 146, 152
Caprara, Cardinal (Jean Baptiste), 1733-1810. Cardinal in 1792. Legate in France in 1801; assisted much in the Concordat; crowned Napoleon King of Italy at Milan in 1805. 20, 105
Chanteloup, a village four miles from Amboise, famous for the château of the Duc de Choiseul, which passed into the hands of Chaptal, and was destroyed in 1823, 49
Chantilly was the country seat of the Montmorency and the Condé

COR

family. Joseph Bonaparte's house, called Mortefontaine or Morfontaine, belonged to President le Pelletier. 194
Chapelle, Marquis de la, 64, 65
Chaptal (Jean Antoine, comte de Chanteloup), 1756-1832. A distinguished chemist; minister of the interior 1801-1804; peer of France in 1819. 49
Cherbourg, a military port of France opposite Portsmouth, 136, 191
Chesterfield, in Derbyshire, 295
Choiseul (Claude Antoine Gabriel, duc de), 1760-1838. Duc et pair in 1787; colonel of Royal Dragoons in 1789; concerned in the flight to Varennes 1791; imprisoned, exiled, and recalled by Bonaparte; was made a peer of France at the Restoration; was aide-de-camp to Louis Philippe. 47, 49
Chouans (*chat houant* owl), a name given to the peasants who supported the Royalist cause in Anjou, Maine, Brittany, and a part of Normandy. Their name is derived from the nickname of Jean Cottereau of Laval. They are often confounded with the Vendeans, but rather carried on a guerilla warfare. 64
Clément de Ris (Dominique, comte), 1750-1827. He was seized by a number of Chouans in Touraine and kept 19 days prisoner under guard; made peer of France in 1814. 64
Cobenzl (John Philip, count), 1741-1810. Negotiated the Treaty of Teschen 1779; Austrian ambassador at Paris 1801-1805. 28, 34, 52, 57, 58
Cockburn, Mr., 277
Colbert (Auguste Marie François, comte de), 1777-1809. Aide-de-camp to Napoleon; killed in Spain. 117, 118, 119
Cole (a servant), 282
Constantinople, 99
Corfu, the capital of the Ionian Islands; French from 1797 to 1799 and from 1807 to 1814; then under British protection; passed to Greece in 1866. 166, 169
Cormon, Foreign Office messenger, 289

COR

Corsica. Finally joined to France in 1768; but it resisted, and was only finally subdued just before the birth of Napoleon in 1769. 61, 71, 212

Courvoisier, Foreign Office messenger, 114

Craufurd (Mr. Quentin). Resided much in Paris; a friend of Count Fersen and Marie Antoinette. 276

Craufurd (Sir James, second baronet, 1761–1839), 275, 276

Croker (Rt. Hon. John Wilson), 1780–1857. Secretary to the Admiralty. 109

Czartorinski (Adam Georges Czartoryski), 1770–1861. Was sent to Petersburg as a hostage in 1792. Paul I. made him ambassador at Turin, and Alexander I. minister of foreign affairs. He was president of the Provisional Government of Poland in 1831; was banished, and lived an exile in France. 36, 118

Decaen (Charles Matthieu Isidore, comte), 1769–1832. General in 1800; was made captain-general of the French East Indian establishments, 1803–1811. 45, 137

Desmunier (Jean Nicholas, comte de). One of the four commissioners appointed to treat with the representatives of Switzerland. 23

Despard, Colonel, 136

Devereaux, Mr. An Irishman recommended by Lord Moira to Lord Whitworth. 139

Dorset, Duchess of (Arabella Diana), daughter of Sir Charles Cope, Bart.; married the Duke of Dorset in 1790. He died in 1799. Her first husband had been ambassador in France, 1783–1789. 26, 41, 275, 282, 292

Dorset, Duke of (George John Frederick), 1793–1815. Son of Lord Whitworth's wife; friend of Lord Byron at Harrow. 139

Drake, Mr. Francis, English minister at Munich; summarily expelled by Napoleon on the rupture of the Peace of Amiens. 34

Drummond, Mr., 42

ELG

Dunkirk, after suffering various fortunes, was purchased from the English by Louis XIV. in 1662. From 1713 to 1783 the port was closed by the Treaty of Utrecht. 136, 142, 144, 254

Durand, M., chef de cabinet to M. de Talleyrand, 233, 234, 240

Duroc (Geraud Christophe Michel), 1772–1813. Aide-de-camp to Napoleon in Italy and Egypt; sent on missions to Berlin and Petersburg; Napoleon was much attached to him. 117, 153, 156

Duteille, M., 79

Edgeworth de Firmont (Henri Allen, abbe de). An Irish priest educated in France; confessor to Princess Elizabeth; accompanied Louis XVI. to the scaffold; followed the Comte de Provence to Mittau. 51

— (Richard Lovell) 1744–1817. A man of music and letters; lived a great deal in France; was father of Miss Edgeworth the novelist. 51

Edim¹ ourgh. Charles X. was living at Holyrood Palace. 65

Egypt, French designs on, 16, 18, 19, 29, 54–56, 58; Sebastiani's report on, 67, 74, 79, 81, 84, 86, 87, 89, 93, 98, 99, 101, 102, 104, 107–109, 113, 122, 129, 159, 160

Eichstadt, a town in Bavaria; formerly capital of an ecclesiastical principality given to Bavaria in 1805, and to Prince Eugène Beauharnais in 1817. 34, 46, 76

Elba, an island of the Tuscan archipelago. It belonged first to Pisa, then to Piombino. Napoleon got possession of it in 1802, and joined it to Tuscany. He became Emperor of it in 1814. It was given by the Congress of Vienna to Tuscany. 46, 51, 59, 151

Elgin, Lord (Thomas, seventh Earl of Elgin), 1766–1841. Ambassador at Constantinople, having previously been at Brussels and Berlin. Brought the 'Elgin Marbles' to England.

INDEX. 301

ELS

58, 196, 274, 277, 284, 293, 294, 295
Elsworth, Foreign Office messenger, 97
Ernouf (Jean Auguste, baron), 1753-1827. Sent to Guadeloupe in 1803; in 1810 surrendered to Lord Cochrane, and was disgraced by the Emperor. 138
Etruria, kingdom of. An ephemeral state given to the Bourbons of Parma by the Treaty of Madrid, 1801. The King dying in 1803, his widow, Marie Louise, accepted for her son by the French treaty of Fontainebleau the kingdom of Lusitania, while Etruria was divided into three French departments. 28, 151, 198, 226, 232, 252

FLORIDAS, North and South, forming a province of North America. Discovered in 1512 on Palm Sunday. Pasqua Florida, from which it derives its name, ceded to the English by Spain in 1763, and restored in 1783; surrendered to America in 1821. 28, 29, 37, 41, 60, 87, 128, 154
Flushing, a port at the mouth of the Scheldt, 49, 98, 179
Fouché (Joseph, Duc of Otranto) 1763-1820. Guilty of massacres at Lyons; minister of police, 1799-1802, 1804-1810, during the Hundred Days, and for a short time under the Restoration; died very rich. 23, 133, 210, 211, 269, 270
Fox, General, 28
Francy, Commissaire de Marine at Calais, 287
Frankfurt, Imperial town in Germany, 23
Fraser, Colonel, Governor of Goree, 154-156
Frere (John Hookham), English representative in Spain from 1802-1809, 41

GALLO, Marquis de, Sicilian minister to the Italian Republic, 24
Genoa, 54, 55, 61, 71, 72
Georges. See Cadoudal

HUN

Gibraltar, taken by the English in 1704; besieged in 1705, 1708, and from 1779 to 1782. 168
Goldsmidt, editor of the 'Argus' newspaper, 96
Goree, an island two miles south of Cape Verde; port of the coast of Senegambia; colonised by the Dutch in 1617; taken by Admiral d'Estrier in 1677; ceded to Louis XIV. by the Treaty of Nimeguen 1678. 154

HAGUE, Treaty of the (1795), 8
Hamburgh, one of the Hanse Towns, 172, 173, 212
Hammond, Mr. George, undersecretary for Foreign affairs, 15, 60, 139, 202
Hammond, Captain, 275, 276
Hanover, occupied by Prussia in 1801; seized by Napoleon in 1803, and ceded by him to Prussia in 1806; taken again in 1807, and joined to the Kingdom of Westphalia; independent in 1813; made into a kingdom by the Congress of Vienna 1815. 114, 117, 288, 289
Havre, Le, important French port on the Channel, founded by Francis I. in 1557 and first called Ville Françoise, then Havre de Grâce, 228
Helvetian Republic, the name given to the Swiss Confederation from 1798 to 1803, 7
Helvoetsluys, a military port in Holland. It was taken by the French in 1795. 114, 161, 169, 176
Hittorf, Major-General. Sent by Emperor Alexander to Napoleon with letter about the affairs of Switzerland and Germany, with a mission to examine into military matters. 71
Hodgson, Rev. Mr., chaplain to the Legation, 207, 281, 284, 286
Holland, affairs of, 49, 50, 55, 66
Huber, M. A Swiss, a friend of Lord Auckland when at Paris, and of the English generally; one of the Commissaires de la Trésorerie. 214, 242, 246, 263, 274, 292, 294
Hunter, Foreign Office messenger, 139

ITA

ITALIAN REPUBLIC. The Cisalpine republic founded in 1797 was reorganised by Austria at the treaty of Campo-Formio; it was dissolved in 1799; re-established after Marengo in 1802; Novara being added, it was called the Italian Republic. It consisted of 13 departments with Milan for capital. In 1805 it became the kingdom of Italy. 32, 151, 198, 226, 232

JAMAICA, an island in the West Indies taken by England from the Spaniards in 1655, 24
Jenkinson, Lieutenant George, 140
Jersey, Island of, 65.
Josephine (Marie Josephine Rose Tascher de la Pagerie), 1763-1814. Born at Martinique; married the Vicomte de Beauharnais in 1779; Napoleon, March 9, 1796; crowned December 2, 1804; divorced, December 16, 1809; died May 29, 1814. 22, 26, 32, 116, 117
Junot (Andoche), duc d'Abrantes, 1771-1813. Secretary to Napoleon at the siege of Toulon, and attached to him from that time until 1812, when he was rebuked by him. He killed himself in a fit of madness. In 1802 he was military commandant of Paris. 274

KING, Mr., 60, 174

LA COCARDE, French frigate, 24
Lampedusa, a small island about thirty miles in circumference half way between Malta and the coast of Tunis; occupied by Neapolitan government as a prison in 1843. 171, 177, 178, 184, 185, 193, 198, 216, 225, 226, 230, 232, 237, 255, 257, 266, 270
Lannes (Jean, duc de Montebello), 1769-1804. Son of a groom; much distinguished in the campaigns of Italy, Egypt, and Marengo; died of wounds received at Essling. 56, 58, 77, 104, 174

LOU

Lauderdale, Lord (James, eighth Earl), 1759-1839, 139
Lauriston (Jacques Alexandre Bernard Law, marquis de), 1768-1821. Of Scotch extraction, the same family as Law the financier; was with Bonaparte at the military school; brought the ratification of the Treaty of Amiens to London 1802; commanded the rear-guard in the retreat from Moscow; served under the Government of the Restoration. 195, 196, 200, 201
Laval (Anne Pierre Adrien de Montmorency-Laval, duc de). Born 1769; served in the army of Condé in 1792; returned to France in 1801; remained all his life a devoted Royalist. 49
Lebrun (Charles Francis, duke of Plasentra), 1739-1824. Took part in the 18 Brumaire. Third Consul; Lieutenant-General of Holland. 21, 26
Leclerc (Victor Emmanuel), 1772-1802. Served in Italy under Napoleon; married Pauline Bonaparte at Milan in 1797; commanded the expedition against St. Domingo in 1801; carried off Toussaint-l'Ouverture; died of yellow fever in Tortola. His widow married Prince Borghèse. 43, 50
Leghorn, 72, 212
Lemoyne, M., 287
Ligurian Republic. Formed out of the old Republic of Genoa in 1297; incorporated with France in 1805; under the three departments of Genoa, Montesotte, and the Apennines; re-established in 1814; incorporated by the Congress of Vienna with France in 1815. 32, 151, 198, 226, 232
Lille, capital of French Flanders, 23, 72
Lima, M. de, Portuguese ambassader at Paris, 55
Lisbon, 56, 58
Livingston, Mr., American minister in Paris, 37, 60
Loftus, Lord (John, viscount Loftus, afterwards second marquis of Ely), 1770-1845. 139
Louisiana. Originally comprised nearly the whole basin of the Mississippi. The part east of

this river was ceded by Louis XV. to England in 1763; the part west in 1764 to Spain, to compensate her for the loss of Florida. In 1801 Spain ceded Eastern Louisiana back to France, and in 1803 Napoleon sold it to the United States for eighty millions of francs. 25, 29, 46, 60, 87, 128, 137, 147

Lourdes, formerly capital of the Lavedan en Bigorre; now a place of pilgrimage. 293

Luchesini, (Jerome, marquis de), 1752-1125. Diplomatist, librarian, and reader of Frederick the Great, 1778-1786. Prussian minister at Warsaw, 1778; at Paris after the Peace of Lunéville; retired to France in 1807. 25, 191

Lunéville, Treaty of, between France and Austria, 1801, 8, 252, 290

MACLAURIN, M., physician to the Legation, 207, 281, 284, 286

Malouet (Pierre Victor, baron), 1740-1814. As deputy to the Constituante favoured constitutional monarchy; fled to London in September 1792, and returned 1801; died as minister of marine under the first Restoration. 210, 211, 214

Malta, Island of. Given to Knights of St. John 1530; taken by Bonaparte 1798; and by the English 1800, who kept it. 9, 10, 17, 19, 23, 28, 30, 40, 41, 50, 54, 61, 65, 67, 72, 74, 78, 79 82, 84, 85-87, 93, 94, 97, 98, 102 -104, 107, 108, 110, 112, 113, 118-120, 123, 124, 125, 127, 129, 130, 131, 133, 134, 137, 145, 149, 150, 151, 157, 160, 164, 165, 167, 168-170, 172-174, 176-178, 180, 182-184, 185, 187, 193, 197, 216, 217-219, 221, 224, 225, 232-237, 245, 246, 251-255, 257-261, 266, 270, 271, 288

Malta, Order of, founded in the eleventh century. It came to an end when Bonaparte took the island in 1798. 76, 123, 125, 151, 157, 168, 171, 193, 198, 219, 257

Mamelukes (= slaves), a body of soldiers who dominated Egypt from the time of St. Louis to the expedition of Napoleon. They were massacred by Mehemet Ali in 1811. 55

Mandeville, Mr., secretary of Legation, 207, 233, 234, 237, 239, 242, 247, 248, 263, 269, 271, 274, 281, 282, 285, 286

Marcoff, Count, Russian ambassador in Paris, 12, 23, 28, 30, 31, 35, 36, 42, 46, 51, 59, 70, 71, 85, 88, 101, 108, 110, 116, 117, 118, 143, 157, 201, 204, 206, 214, 223, 238, 264, 272

Maret (Hugues Bernard, duc de Bassano), 1763-1839. Diplomat in 1792; prisoner 1793-1795; served Napoleon faithfully; peer of France in 1831. 278

Mason, foreign office messenger, 110, 115

Masséna (André), 1758-1817. Served in Italy under Bonaparte, fought at Zurich 1799, at Genoa 1800; marshal 1804; duc de Rivoli 1807; prince of Essling 1809; fought in Spain 1810-11. 87, 133, 212

Mengaud, General, commissary at Calais, 11, 262, 275, 276, 281, 282

Merry, Mr., chargé d'affaires at Paris; Lord Whitworth's predecessor. 9, 11, 12, 13, 15, 20, 23, 32, 34, 48, 49, 53, 92, 97

Meudon, a few miles from Versailles, with a château built by the Dauphin in 1695. 234, 265, 282

Middleton, Mr., 98

Minorca, taken by the English in 1708; retaken by the French in 1756; restored to the English in 1763, and taken by the French in 1782. The English occupied it from 1798 to 1802. 124

Moira, Lord, 1754-1827. First marquis of Hastings; was a general commanding in Scotland; governor-general of Bengal 1812-23. 139

'Moniteur,' official French journal, founded by Pancoucke, November 24, 1789; called 'Moniteur Universel,' after January 1, 1811. 9

Monroe (Mr. James), 1759-1831. Minister in Paris 1794; negotiated the transfer of Louisiana

1803; president 1817-1824; author of the 'Monroe doctrine' that foreign powers have no right to intervene in America, 174

Monsieur, Comte de Provence, afterwards Louis XVIII., 38

Montchoisi (Louis Antoine, baron de). General of division; served under Dumouriez 1792-93; disgraced in 1801; restored in 1803. 138

Morea, the Peloponnesus. It was conquered by the Turks 1463-1479; retaken by the Venetians 1687-1715; fell again into the hands of the Turks 1718; became Greece after the War of Independence, 1821-1828. 104

Moreau (Jean Victor), 1763-1813. Fought the battle of Hohenlinden in 1800; compromised in the plot of Cadoudal 1804. He lived eight years in America, returned to Europe 1813, and was mortally wounded at the battle of Dresden, 77, 191

Morfontaine, 265. See Chantilly

Morlaix in Brittany, 294

Murat, General (Joachim), 1771-1815. Married Caroline Bonaparte 1800; marshal 1800; Grand Duke of Cleves and Berg 1806; King of Naples 1808; shot at Pizzo October 13, 1815. 107

NAPLES, King of (Ferdinand IV.), 1751-1825. King of Naples and Sicily 1759-1825. 107, 124, 243, 246, 247

Nepean, Sir Evan. Under-Secretary at the Foreign Office; Lord-Lieutenant of Ireland 1804. 109

Nimeguen, a town on the Rhine, 212

OFANTO, the ancient Aufidus, in South Italy, 243

Ostend, seaport in Belgium, 142

Otranto. Otranto, in the south of Italy, gave the title of duke to Fouché. 237, 243, 245, 246, 247, 266, 270

Otto (Louis Guillaume, comte de Mosloy), 1754-1817. A German by birth; in the French diplomatic service under Louis XVI.

and Napoleon, in America, at Berlin, London, Munich, and Vienna. He negotiated the marriage with Marie Louise. 41

PAGET, Mr. (Sir Arthur), English ambassador at Vienna, 58

Parma, Duchy of, from 1545 to 1802 and from 1815 to 1860; ceded to France in 1802; it became the department of the Taro. 7, 28

Passau, on the Danube, at the junction of the Inn and the Ilz; formerly capital of a bishopric, which was given (except the town, which went to Bavaria) to the Grand Duke of Tuscany, but surrendered by him to Bavaria in 1805. 34, 57

Passy, a village to the west of Paris; now a suburb. 51

Pau, formerly capital of Béarn, 293

Paul, 1st Emperor of Russia (1796-1801), son of Peter III.; assassinated. 14, 36

Peace, Prince of the (Don Manuel Godoy), 1767-1851. Became Premier Minister after Oranda in 1792. At the Treaty of Bâle received the title of Prince of the Peace. During his later career he was a mere tool of Bonaparte. He followed the Napoleons into exile, and had a pension from Louis Philippe. 41

Pelham, Lord (Thomas), afterwards Earl of Chichester, 1756-1826. Home Secretary 1801 to October 1803. 79

Peltier (Jean Gabriel), journalist, as a refugee in London, published 'L'Ambigu' 1800-1819, attacking Bonaparte. He was only slightly punished (defended by Mackintosh). Returned to France in 1815, and died 1825. 92, 95

Perregaux, M., banker at Paris, 199 271

Petersburg, V., 70

Picardy, a province in the north of France, 12

Piedmont, occupied by Joubert 1798; divided into French departments 1802; restored to House of Savoy 1804. 82, 252

SET

born at Ampugnano, near Bastia, in Corsica, 1772-1851. Fought in the campaign of Italy; assisted Napoleon on 18 Brumaire; fought at Marengo; sent on a mission to the East in 1802; made general on his return; afterwards ambassador to Constantinople; held office under the Restoration, and under Louis Philippe. 15, 16, 42, 46, 54, 57, 59, 62, 67, 74, 81, 84, 93, 118, 122, 150, 159, 180, 215

Set Suzanne (Gilbert Joseph Martin Bruneteau, comte de), 1760-1830. Served in the army, but retired early; senator 1804; comte 1809; peer of France 1814. 137

Shaw, Foreign Office messenger, 18, 208, 241

Siennese, The, the territory of Sienna; part of the Grand Duchy of Tuscany joined to France in 1808 as the department of the Ombrone. 35, 59, 134

Sierra Leone, on the coast of Guinea, between Senegambia and Liberia; colonised by the English in 1792. 155

Souza (Couttinho, chevalier de), Portuguese ambassador at Paris, 55, 104

Spain, King of, Charles IV. (1748-1819). Reigned from 1788 to 1808. 93, 124, 216

Spezzia, a seaport between Genoa and Pisa, 38

Stahremberg, Count, Austrian ambassador to England. Expelled from Paris. 17

Stockholm, capital of Sweden, 77

St. Quentin, M., 202

Stuart, General, 15, 59

Sturt, Mr. Charles, 281

Suchet (Louis Gabriel, duc d'Albuféra), 1770-1826. Served in the army of Italy; fought at Marengo; served under Louis in 1805; was especially distinguished in Spain, 1809-1812. 191

Sweden, King of (Gustavus IV. Adolphus, 1778-1837). Abdicated March 29, 1804. 31

Switzerland, affairs of, 36, 42, 66, 73, 82, 114

Sylvester, Foreign Office messenger, 19, 223, 224, 230, 262, 263

TUS

TALBOT, W., secretary of Legation, 14, 16, 21, 22, 132, 207, 234, 240, 242, 248, 263, 265, 270, 273-276, 281, 283, 284, 285, 286

Talleyrand, Périgord (Charles Maurice de, Prince of Beneventum), 1754-1838. Minister of Foreign Affairs. 12, 13, 15, 19, 21, 23, 24, 26, 28, 30, 31, 37, 38, 39, 40, 43, 52, 57, 58, 68, 69, 73-75, 78, 81, 84, 86, 95-102, 111, 113, 121, 125, 126, 129, 130, 132, 134, 135, 138, 140-143, 145, 152, 153, 156, 157, 159-162, 164, 166, 167, 169-172, 178-180, 184, 186, 187, 190, 192, 193, 195-197, 199-204, 206, 207, 209, 211, 213, 215-219, 221-223, 225, 226, 229-231, 233-236, 238, 239, 241, 242, 244, 261, 262, 265, 268, 271, 273-276, 279, 282-291, 293, 295

Tamerlan, another name for Timur the Tartar (1336-1405). Timur leng = Timur the Lame. 269

Tarentum, a port in the south of Italy. It gave a title, Duc de Tarente, to the French Marshal Macdonald. 101, 115, 124, 243, 247, 266, 270

Teutonic Order, founded by Frederic of Swabia in 1190. Its property was secularised in 1525. It was suppressed by Napoleon in 1809. 76

Thornton, English banker at Paris, 138

Tommasi, Bailli of Cortona. Nominated Grand Master of Malta by the Pope. 105, 106

Toulon, the principal war-port of France on the Mediterranean, 17, 44, 55, 166

Toussaint-l'Ouverture (François Dominique), 1743-1803. Leader of the insurrection in St. Domingo; was taken prisoner by the French; died a prisoner at the Fort de Joux. 50

Turkey, partitions of, 71, 80, 86, 90, 94, 99, 101, 104, 105, 108, 118, 123

Turks, defeat of, 54

Tuscany, Grand Duke of (Ferdinand III., 1769-1824). Received at the Peace of Lunéville Salzburg and Wurzburg in exchange for Tuscany; was restored in 1814 and reigned till his death. 28, 34, 46

VAL

VALAIS. Became an independent republic in 1801; from 1810 to 1814 formed part of France in the department of the Simplon; since that time has been a canton of Switzerland 84

Van der Goes, secretary of state in Holland, 26

Verona, a town in N. Italy, on the Adige, 144, 243

Vick, Foreign Office messenger, 30

Vienna, 57

Vos van Steenvich, Batavian ambassador at Paris, 25

WAGSTAFF, Foreign Office messenger, 156, 160

Warren (Admiral Sir John Borlase), 1754–1822. English minister at St. Petersburg, 1802–1804. 117

YAR

Warsaw, capital of Poland, 38

Wilson, Major, 160

Winter (Jean Guillaume de), Dutch Admiral, 1750–1812. Beaten by Admiral Duncan at Camperdown, 1797. As an officer of the Batavian Republic he was now under the orders of France. 61

Woronzow, Count, Russian ambassador at Paris, 23, 24, 28, 31, 33, 35, 88, 103, 110, 118, 140, 143

Wright, Captain. Had been prisoner in France, but escaped. 131

YARMOUTH, (Lord Francis Charles). Afterwards became third Marquis of Hertford. Died 1842. 276

PRINTED BY
SPOTTISWOODE AND CO., NEW-STREET SQUARE
LONDON

www.ingramcontent.com/pod-product-compliance
Lightning Source LLC
Chambersburg PA
CBHW030017240426
43672CB00007B/985